It's Time for a Change

School Reform for the Next Decade

Matthew Lynch

ROWMAN & LITTLEFIELD EDUCATION
A division of
ROWMAN & LITTLEFIELD PUBLISHERS, INC.
Lanham • Boulder • New York • Toronto • Plymouth, UK

Published by Rowman & Littlefield Education
A division of Rowman & Littlefield Publishers, Inc.
A wholly owned subsidiary of The Rowman & Littlefield Publishing Group, Inc.
4501 Forbes Boulevard, Suite 200, Lanham, Maryland 20706
http://www.rowmaneducation.com

Estover Road, Plymouth PL6 7PY, United Kingdom

British Library Cataloguing in Publication Information Available

Library of Congress Cataloging-in-Publication Data

Lynch, Matthew, 1978–
It's time for a change : school reform for the next decade / Matthew Lynch.
p. cm.
Includes bibliographical references and index.
ISBN 978-1-61048-062-8 (cloth : alk. paper)—ISBN 978-1-61048-063-5 (pbk. : alk. paper)—ISBN 978-1-61048-064-2 (electronic)
1. School improvement programs—United States. 2. Educational change—United States. I. Title.
LB2822.82.L96 2012
371.2'070973—dc23
2011033716

Printed in the United States of America

This book is dedicated to the teachers, administrators, parents, citizens, and politicians who have been fighting for genuine school reform in the U.S. for decades. Thank you for caring about our children. Also this book is dedicated to countless scores of children who were not properly educated by the U.S. education system. These children are the collateral damage that should spur us to create lasting change. I have dedicated my life to ensuring that every child in America receives a quality education, and I will not rest until it becomes a reality.

Contents

Preface

Dear America:

The U.S. public education system is in a state of emergency. When compared to educational systems in other developed countries, the process for educating children and youth of the world's preeminent nation is lacking. The culprit is a public education system that simply does not prepare enough of our children for academic or real-world success. Even with the tremendous changes taking place since enactment of NCLB, serious problems persist. The cost per pupil in the United States soared to five times the 1950s level, after adjusting for inflation. With this kind of money being pumped into the system, why are our school systems in their current state? Statistics, and common sense born of observation, tell us that the biggest crisis in our schools is finding ways to educate students who live in low-income areas throughout the nation. However, our educational problems are not limited to poverty-stricken areas alone. As Lesley Chilcott, producer of the *Waiting for Superman* documentary, puts it, "The dirty little secret . . . is that middle- and upper-class communities are suffering as well.

When we talk about U.S. students ranking twenty-fifth in math, we're not just talking about underserved communities, we're talking overall (as cited in Weber, 2010), including more affluent communities as well. Yet, despite decades of knowing that these problems exist, little improvement has been made. Of course, everyone wants to improve our system; they just do not seem to know how to do it.

The American public must believe that educational reform is a top priority issue in these times of severe economic troubles. Today, people are concerned about their jobs and putting food on the table. Upgrading education, although theoretically important, can hold a low priority to the more pressing problem of keeping a roof over one's head. The paradox here is that this is precisely the time to make an investment in education.

When times are tough, workers need to improve their skills to compete effectively in the marketplace. Education can provide needed skills. Furthermore, enhanced skills and improved technological capabilities are going to be desperately needed in the future. Skills needed for the workplace of the future are different from those possessed by many workers who cannot find jobs today. Planning to turn out workers for the factories of today is crucial, however those same workers also need to be able to adapt to technologies that are just now being developed. Workers taught in a subpar educational system will cripple America's competitiveness.

Educational reform will occur once we decide that enough is enough and make the commitment to make change happen—no matter what it takes. When America realizes all children deserve a stellar education regardless of where they are from, who their parents are, or what their socioeconomic status happens to be, we will be able to reform our educational system. Americans have to stop treating minority students in underperforming urban environments like collateral damage.

The disheartening reality is that America has billions of dollars to fight a two-front war, but cannot or will not properly educate its children. If a hostile country attacked America today, it would take less than twenty-four hours for American troops to be mobilized into battle. However, we seem unable to mobilize a sea of educated teachers and administrators to wage war against academic mediocrity, which is a bigger threat to our national security than Iran or North Korea. The American educational system has reached a turning point, and yet some simply sit idly by "waiting for Superman."

Rather than waiting, educators, educational leaders, government officials, parents, and citizens need to educate themselves about problems inherent in our educational system. We need to stop placing blame. Rather, we must come together with an understanding that Superman is not coming to save our children, and that we must work together to find innovative ways to rise to the challenge of fixing our educational system. If we simply work together, we can restore the U.S. educational system to its former preeminence, and give our children the bright futures they deserve. We must become the Supermen and Superwomen that we have been waiting on.

Sincerely,

Matthew Lynch, Ed. D.

Acknowledgments

First, I would like to thank God for being my strength and my refuge. I would also like to acknowledge the collective unconscious of my ancestors. You paved the way for my ascendancy into the upper echelons of academia and served as a catalyst for my intellectual development.

Of course, I have to acknowledge my parents, Jessie and Patsy Lynch, for giving me their love and support. Also, I want to thank my sisters, Tammy Kemp and Angelina Lynch, for having my back. To their children, Adicuz, Kayla, Kerri, and Kelton: I hope my accomplishments will motivate each of you to live up to your limitless potential. No matter what, remember that your uncle loves you. You are the reason I am so passionate about reforming America's schools.

I would like to also acknowledge my mentor, Dr. Rodney Washington, for his invaluable support, guidance, knowledge, and inspiration. Thanks for being the big brother that I never had! I also have to thank the scholars and academics who agreed to critique the manuscript and gave invaluable feedback. Your assistance has ensured that my book is of the highest quality and will make a solid contribution to the field of education.

I would like to acknowledge the teachers, administrators, parents, citizens, and politicians who have been fighting for genuine school reform in the United States for decades. Thank you for caring about our children. I would like to acknowledge and apologize to countless scores of children who were not properly educated by the U.S. education system. These children are the collateral damage that should spur us to create lasting change. I have dedicated my life to ensuring that every child in America receives a quality education, and I will not rest until it becomes a reality.

Introduction

The United States entered the twenty-first century as the world's sole superpower. Our diplomatic strength, military might, financial resources, and technological innovation were, and continue to be, the envy of the world. However, in the crucial area of education, the United States lags behind many other developed countries. Although the United States spends more per student than almost any other country in the world, international exams have demonstrated that we consistently perform well behind countries such as South Korea, China, Japan, and Finland in the areas of reading and math.

There are even more disconcerting elements at play, however. Paramount among these is that the U.S. educational system is becoming ever more stratified. Despite efforts such as the George W. Bush administration's No Child Left Behind Act (NCLB), the disparity between students from middle and low socioeconomic backgrounds continues to grow. The ramifications of this trend are considerable. China, Japan, and South Korea understand that well-educated workers are crucial for survival in the competitive global economy. Thus, they are placing enormous emphasis on education, ensuring that their students are given not only foundational reading and math skills, but also that they are able to think creatively and solve problems. Their youth are poised to take on and conquer the world.

The United States, on the other hand, is losing the battle. School systems are using more money but have less to show for it. Test results, especially among the children from low socioeconomic backgrounds are dismal. America has extraordinary natural resources, a solid, functioning democracy, and an excellent infrastructure, but unless we can reform our educational system to produce students who are able to take advantage of new technologies and compete in the global economy, we will cede our position as world leader.

A number of recent books and films have brought this situation to the attention of the American public. Foremost among these is *Waiting for Superman*, the 2010 film that exposed some of the faults inherent in the system. What is needed now, though, is a plan to solve those problems: we need to learn to *become* Superman.

It's Time for a Change: School Reform for the Next Decade is the first book to take an in-depth look at reforming the U.S. educational system in the second decade of the twenty-first century. It dissects the issues, paying special attention to students from low-income and high-immigration areas, who will form the core of our labor force in the coming decades. And it looks at some of the challenges facing school administrations and districts, offering solutions based on successful case studies around the country. The educational system involves seven major players: the federal government, district authorities, the community, parents and family, the school administration, teachers, and the students themselves. *It's Time for a Change: School Reform for the Next Decade* looks at each of these players, investigating the interactions among them, and offering suggestions for bolstering involvement and efficacy.

The No Child Left Behind Act (NCLB), while admirable, has also proven fundamentally flawed. It is not producing the anticipated results, and has had the effect of forcing schools to teach to the exam, rather than fostering a love of learning among students. *It's Time for a Change: School Reform for the Next Decade* looks at the mounting evidence that NCLB is failing our students, and offers suggestions for reform. Appropriate engagement and direction by district authorities is crucial to creating a quality learning environment. Too often, cronyism, corruption, and misuse of resources diminish the influence of the district-level administration. Using case studies, the book outlines some of the major problems associated with school districts, especially when trying to implement reforms.

In areas where schools are successful, community involvement has proven to be a critical element. In low socioeconomic communities, there is often a sense that schools are separate entities, run by elite elements that have little connection to the community. The chapter on community engagement outlines some of the ways in which a school can reach out to a community, fostering greater integration and involvement. Perhaps the starkest difference between students from low socioeconomic environments and those from wealthier environments is the amount of parental involvement in students' education.

It's Time for a Change: School Reform for the Next Decade demonstrates how critical parental involvement is in the educational process. It looks at ways to bring teachers and parents together, and to make those encounters comfortable for all parties. No single factor is more important in education than teachers. Educating, hiring, and retaining high-quality teachers are key to lasting reform. The teaching profession in America is undervalued, certainly in comparison with countries like Finland and South Korea. The book looks at the reasons for this, and at reasons for the dearth of male teachers in our schools. It offers suggestions for retaining quality teachers, particularly in areas where most of the students are from low socioeconomic backgrounds.

It's Time for a Change: School Reform for the Next Decade also looks at several of the hot topics of the moment in the sphere of education. The concept of year-round education has been gaining acceptance in certain circles. The book devotes a chapter to this structure of schooling, and its potential for improving educational outcomes. A second topic of national interest is charter schools. The book looks at how charter schools have performed nationally, and what elements have been critical in their success or lack of it.

It's Time for a Change: School Reform for the Next Decade arrives at a point when the U.S. educational system rests on a knife-edge. NCLB mandates expire in 2014. European and Asian countries are eroding our economic advantage. Minorities, who are typically underserved by the education system, will soon become the majority in the United States. Meanwhile, technological advances are making for a society and workplace where immeasurable amounts of information are available for use by those educated to take advantage of it.

If we fail to deliver accomplished students into the workforce, we risk falling behind in innovation. Will we choose to continue with the status quo, pushing through reforms that have been proven to fail? Or will our great country learn from its mistakes, create meaningful reform, and retain our superpower status? *It's Time for a Change: School Reform for the Next Decade* offers a blueprint for educational success, not only for the present, but for the decades to come.

Chapter 1

The Current State of the U.S. Educational System

The American educational system is in a seriously chaotic state. The problems are numerous and complex. Among the challenges the system faces is the long-standing inability to assist specific groups of students who continuously fail to reach levels of proficiency expected by educators and society at large, along with the uncertainty as to whether the system, as currently organized, is able to educate most students for the needs of the twenty-first century.

Alternative avenues to education, such as charter schools, home schooling, and the use of vouchers for parents to apply toward the cost of educational settings of their choosing, have alternately been proposed as complements to, and replacements for, traditional public education. While the incorporation of technology as a tool to improve education is routinely put forward, the capability of educators to take advantage of various technologies has been called into question, along with issues of equity when it comes to the availability of cutting-edge technologies for all of the nation's children.

Quality teaching has been proven to have the most profound impact on children's learning, yet the nation's schools continue to struggle with motivating the most caring and talented individuals to enter into and remain in the teaching profession. Added to these challenges is the process of assessment the nation has chosen to measure the effectiveness of schools, a process that has been the target of much criticism over the past several years.

Educational funding juxtaposed to educational effectiveness is an additional area that contributes to the perplexing state of education today. Maine, for example, spends $9300 per student while Utah spends $4800 per student. Yet, reading and math scores for Utah fourth graders have improved over the past decade while reading scores in Maine actually declined among fourth graders, and math gains were not comparable to those made by fourth graders in Utah (Peterson, 2006).

Let's consider National Assessment of Educational Progress (NAEP) results, which are based on assessments administered nationally to fourth-, eighth-, and twelfth-grade students. There was no change in the average reading scores for fourth graders between 2009 and 2007, although 2007 scores were higher than the scores during the 1992–2007 assessment years. Even so, for 2009, two-thirds of fourth graders performed at or above the NAEP's Basic level, which means that they have partial knowledge and skills needed for proficient work at the fourth-grade level.

Only one-third of these students performed at or above the Proficient level, which means they have demonstrated competency over challenging subject matter (National Center for Education Statistics, 2009b). The story was even worse in mathematics, with 82 percent of fourth graders performing at or above the Basic level in 2009, which was not significantly different from average fourth-grade performance in 2007.

Differences in performance among white, black, and Hispanic students are also disturbing. There was a twenty-six-point gap between the performance of white and black students and twenty-one-point gap between white and Hispanic students—gaps that did not change significantly between 2007 and 2009 (National Center for Education Statistics, 2009a). With such appalling levels of performance, it is no wonder that a number of students decide not to enter college, and many who do lack the type of preparation needed to complete a college degree (Bound, Lovenheim, & Turner, 2009).

Many students, in fact, do not graduate at all, but choose to drop out of school before they complete high school. As long as the nation's school systems are allowed to continue to churn out students ill-prepared to enter college or the workforce, or to have drop rates of up to one-third of the student population, we will remain trapped in a cycle of hopelessness. Solutions are available for these and other problematic educational issues, but we must first carefully explore the current state of affairs in our educational system in order to better understand the issues that need to be addressed.

NO CHILD LEFT BEHIND

In concept, the notion that no child be left behind as the nation seeks to educate its youth was and continues to be commonsensical. If the nation were to move forward in ensuring that all children were educated, then school systems would need to be accountable for improved performance among children from all backgrounds. The No Child Left Behind Act requires states to develop standards-based assessments as a means for gauging student performance.

The act tied accountability to federal education funds—school districts were required to reach 100 percent proficiency in both math and reading by the 2013–2014 school year in order to maintain federal funding. On their way to achieving this level, schools were required to show "adequate yearly progress" (AYP). This tracking system required schools to demonstrate higher levels of proficiency each year.

Consequences were put in place for schools not demonstrating AYP in any given year—ranging initially from extra support based on an improvement plan to more punitive consequences such as school restructuring. In the latter case, schools could be closed and reopened as charter schools, staff could be replaced, or school operations could be taken over by the state or a private company.

Much attention was directed toward Texas as the NCLB Act was being formed. In fact, the accountability system in Texas provided the model for NCLB accountability requirements. Texas has the second-largest state population in the United States and a very diverse student population. While the Texas accountability system was touted as a success, sadly this success was accomplished at the expense of large numbers of children, the majority of whom were poor, of color, and for whom English was a second language (McNeil, 2005).

Still, the NCLB Act, which received bipartisan support in Congress, was enacted during the first year of George W. Bush's administration. In April 2006, the Department of Education declared NCLB a success, claiming it had resulted in great improvements in performance among all students in the areas of math and reading, and had closed the performance gap between white, and Hispanic and black students. This conclusion was based on the results of the NAEP scores.

Even so, many pundits questioned the effectiveness of the act, and whether the benchmarks cited were even quantifiable. A review was conducted on those assessments, as well as a number of other available studies pertinent to the NCLB Act, and the results were mixed. Critics unequivocally state that NCLB places too much emphasis on standardized testing and too little on the education of individual students.

In an effort to meet NCLB dictates, schools become driven solely by the need to ensure that students show only minimal improvement on standardized tests year after year. Rather than aspire for excellence, the bar is set low, thereby assuring mediocrity. For many constituents concerned about the ever-reaching tentacles extending from Washington, D.C., to the smallest political subdivision across America, the NCLB Act, with its tremendous bureaucracy, embodies that phenomenon.

A number of problematic patterns emerge when severe consequences result from failure of students to perform at required levels on assessments. When a new test mechanism is introduced, teachers and students are not familiar with the content or the format of the test. Scores in this environment tend to drop. As time passes, and the teachers and students become acquainted with the test and the subjects involved, the scores climb until they reach a plateau. After that point, additional improvements in the scores become less achievable.

A survey of teachers conducted by the Center of Education Policy discovered that, because of the stress and the potential ramifications of poor scores, teachers began teaching to the test. More time was spent with academically challenged students, sometimes even causing them to miss other classes, and the amount of time spent exclusively on material covered by the test was greatly increased.

Teachers sometimes changed their teaching styles to concentrate more on content, as opposed to theory. Their students could demonstrate rote knowledge, but could not apply it or appreciate it in context. Test-score improvement could be attributed to the alteration of the teaching parameters, but this would not improve students' problem-solving abilities or critical thinking skills (Laitsch, 2006).

Another issue concerns ethical pedagogical methods. In some schools, limited resources are allocated to students who are likely to make the largest impact on the school's annual yearly progress. Teaching time is reduced with students who will obviously complete assessments successfully, as well as with students who appear to have a very slim chance of reaching proficiency. Instead, teachers focus their attention and efforts on the students who are close to the "cutoff line." Clearly, these students could have the greatest short-term impact on the school's standing—however, do the practices represent a moral approach to education?

The NCLB Act thrives on bureaucracy. To ensure consistent and impartial results, the rules for implementation are set in stone. While analysts have the smug satisfaction that they are comparing apples to apples and oranges to oranges, the real-life situation of many schools is rendered unimportant. The only factor considered in the assessment process is the test performance of students in the specific grades and in the specific subjects flagged by the act. At issue here is that not only are critical areas of learning being ignored, but also resources for teachers of subject areas not being assessed are restricted.

The pressure to achieve the necessary test scores permeates all facets of the school system. Superintendents and principals have a lot riding on these results. Their positions may depend on the success of their students on required assessments. If test scores begin to drop, out go the administrators, regardless of the true cause. This pressure to achieve on standardized assessments trickles down to teachers, and subsequently to the students.

If a third-grade student in Texas does not pass the third-grade reading test, he or she will not be allowed to proceed to fourth grade, and will be forced to repeat the third year. Likewise, a high school senior in Texas with A's in every class will not be allowed to receive his or her high school diploma without passing the exit-level exam required of all students. In this educational environment, innovative ideas, individual programs important to the community, or instructional methods tailored to the needs of individual students are of no concern—only test results matter.

The danger here is that we are relying on standardized-test scores to prove to ourselves that we are improving the educational system, when in fact this approach to education has yet to be validated by any broad measure. Studies need to be designed to show a correlation between test scores and an educational system that is turning out better students. Credible longitudinal studies have to be developed and administered to demonstrate the effectiveness of the numbers-orientated system in which we are now so heavily invested (McNeil, 2005).

EDUCATION UNDER THE OBAMA ADMINISTRATION

The Obama administration has decided to maintain the premise of NCLB. As a result, standardized testing as an indication that students are progressing toward established goals will continue to an important component of the president's agenda. The lack of consistency between states on state-generated standards, which served as the basis for assessments, and the levels of student performance that representational proficiency on those assessments were problematic. Massachusetts may be venerated for its stringent policies and implementation of the Massachusetts Comprehensive Assessment System (MCAS) of standardized testing, but that level of stringency was not replicated in other states. In fact, many states preferred to do only what was required to ensure that they received federal education funds, and nothing more. The level of inconsistency on standards and assessment existing among states was also problematic for students. Students relocating from one state to another might find themselves under pressure to perform better than what was required in their previous school.

This was one of the driving forces behind a national curriculum. Proponents of this movement advocated for a curriculum that would be the same whether the student lived in Boston or San Antonio. If the requirements for what students should know were standardized, there would be no obstruction to learning among children moving from one state to another. President Obama advocated for equality as a foundation of his education agenda.

Obama stated that he wanted results, and wanted to see expectations rise so that the United States would be on equal footing with other nations (Mathis, 2010). The core of his plans for education was to provide all students with the same opportunity to reach high levels of proficiency. In the past, disadvantaged students were not provided the same educational pathways as other students. They were not held to the same high standards as their classmates; their lower achievement outcomes were readily accepted.

President Obama's goals were advanced by the Common Core State Standards (CCSS) initiated by the National Governors Association Center for Best Practices (NGA Center) and the Council of Chief State School Officers (CCSSO). These two groups gathered teachers, school administrators, and other experts together to develop standards that would be consistent across states in mathematics and language arts. The goal is to increase educational proficiency among high school graduates, regardless of where they live, so that they will be able to enter a career of their choice or continue to higher education once they complete high school.

Efforts are also underway to develop assessments aligned with CCSS. Two state consortia, Partnership for the Assessment of Readiness for College and Careers (PARCC) and the SMARTER Balanced Assessment Consortium (SBAC) were awarded funding from the U.S. Department of Education in support of this effort. The essence of the principles undergirding CCSS and linked assessments is evident in the *Blueprint for Reform*, which is the Obama administration's request for reauthorization of the Elementary and Secondary Education Act.

The CCSS may turn into required national standards (Office of the Press Secretary, 2010). States have been encouraged to adopt the standards. For example, states competing for Race to the Top grant funds were required to adopt CCSS standards, and be a member of the consortia generating linked assessments. To date, forty-eight states, as well as the District of Columbia, have preliminarily signed on to adopt the standards. As a result, America is now on the cusp of adopting a set of national standards for mathematics and language arts.

The agenda being pushed by the Obama administration may have some legal obstacles to surmount. Whether or not the federal government has the authority to mandate, through funding, such sweeping, multistate requirements, is being questioned. The U.S. Constitution does not explicitly give such power to the national government, and it could be construed that this agenda represents an encroachment by the federal authority in the jurisdiction of local and state governments. This trend is not new, but in fact has been occurring for decades, facilitated by the rulings of the U.S. Supreme Court.

EDUCATING IN A CHALLENGED ECONOMY

The Obama administration's educational agenda is being pursued in the midst of one of the worst economic downturns since the Great Depression. Many districts are forced to curtail hiring of new teachers, and are developing incentives for older teachers to retire, as the districts face huge budget cuts. Teacher-to-student ratios expand as class sizes increase, which means less face time per student.

Studies have been conducted (and replicated several times) that show the influence of high-quality teachers on students is significantly more important than any other factors that have been identified. In other words, the teacher's ability to make a genuine connection with each student is vital—however, this important act is being severely undermined in today's educational environments (Gelberg, 2007).

Clearly the economic situation affects the task of balancing budgets by school systems and governmental bodies. More money, however,does not necessarily mean more improvement. Adjusting for inflation, financing for public school systems jumped 24 percent per pupil between 1991 and 2002. The bulk of this money was generated from the state coffers (47 percent), with local governments contributing approximately 44 percent. The federal government chipped in about 9 percent (Gropman, 2008). With the lion's share of the funding coming from local and state governments, the risk of a backlash against new, more stringent federal standards is a very real possibility.

School budgets are not the only entities affected by the economic crisis. Financial difficulties within students' families also play a huge role in educational problems existing in the United States. Most American homes are dual income, with both parents working one or more jobs to try to meet their financial obligations. With more parents scrambling to make ends meet, less time is available for parental involvement in the education of their children—either at home or with the school.

Parents have less time to teach their children basic fundamentals that were often taught at home when only one parent needed to work. With less time for parents to connect with schools, students may become unmotivated and put less effort into their schoolwork. They also may exhibit behavioral problems at school and require more time and effort from school administrators, which in turn detracts from administrators' efforts to improve schools.

There also exists today a larger segment of the student population who arrive to school from homes where English is not the primary language spoken. With many immigrants swelling the schools' attendance rolls, school systems have added pressure to provide quality instruction for these students. This is especially true of southwestern-border states and many high-population-density urban areas.

Expansion of special-needs education adds additional pressure to school districts even as budgets cuts threaten to dismantle hoped-for increases to better serve this population of students. In some instances, local and state budget cuts have resulted in elimination of services. As an example, Massachusetts eliminated early intervention services for special-needs students and cut compensation for disabled-student services. These are areas of critical needs, especially since special-needs students are required to be assessed under NCLB. By reducing aid provided to assist special-needs students, assessment results will suffer, further damaging NCLB goals.

DRIVEN BY SANCTIONS

Another problem facing the nation's school systems is that our children are overtested, sometimes to an extreme. Still, the nation relies heavily on standardized testing as an indication that students are progressing toward established goals. Nationwide testing creates the risk of losing a broad variety of learning experiences and critical-thinking instruction so valuable in high-quality education. Concentrating on the topics of upcoming tests, far from expanding critical thinking, actually stifles students.

Testing often tends to focus on a narrow spectrum of items that can be easily assessed. However, higher-order skills such as analysis and reasoning are more critical in the real world and at the college level. Progressive teachers nowadays are engaged in cooperative learning with students. The emphasis is on producing students who can think at a critical level. This is a reflection of society's influence.

The technology-driven nature of our economy demands that our schools produce students able to think independently and critically. There is a contradiction in the fact that we test students as a group on knowledge and not on valued skills. Society's needs should be reflected in our schools. Nonetheless, our nation's schools are required to administer tests measuring the limited levels of thinking and problem solving, and risk sanctions when students do not perform well.

There is some argument regarding whether or not sanctions from the NCLB Act really work. With so much pressure being mounted on schools, administrators, teachers, and students, it is important to understand whether the sanctions in place really facilitate improved performance. State tests that place teachers or administrators in some type of jeopardy, such as job retention, prestige, and income, have been compared to assessments such as the NAEP, where such potential penalties are not an issue. Results seem to indicate that state assessments generally showed an upward trend, but when compared to the NAEP the results did not correlate well. Curiously, at the elementary level, there was a strong positive correlation between NAEP and state assessments. When an examination of large studies concerning this issue was completed using a meta-analysis, there was no significant improvement in closing the performance gap between white and minority students and different socioeconomic subgroups. If the sanctions were actually functioning as expected, many of the substandard schools should be moving out of their troubled status, however the Center for Education Policy found that this was not the case.

As mentioned earlier, adequate yearly progress (AYP) is a term used by the federal government to chart the progress of school systems across the country toward NCLB's goal of 100 percent proficiency. AYP is compared to an annual set target, tracking the average number of students who meet the performance levels of given schools. It does not show that below-average students may be making significant progress while the school is still not improving with the AYP. Because of this, schools in the "need improvement" category and schools that have met AYP can show similar gains in student performance.

Incorrectly identifying passing and failing schools in all but the most lenient states produces an unmanageable list. If this master list is deemed unreliable and is too large, the sanction system will ultimately be a failure, because the sanctions will be applied to undeserving schools. As pointed out in the U.S. Department of Education's *Blueprint for Reform,* this process for measuring progress may result in some schools having administrators and teachers fired, or consigning a school to a restructuring process.

Upon examination of the sanctions issue from various sides, it becomes apparent that attempting to improve schools through punitive means does not prove a convincing path for increasing overall performance of schools throughout the nation. In fact, if there were even a reasonable correlation between the schools under sanctions and the performances of students at those schools, there would be a strong case for continuing with the sanction-based system and trying to improve it. There is too much ambiguity, however, in the data to create confidence in the sanctions that are being used.

Even states that have modest rigor in their expectations of their school system are found to be failing under the NCLB Act. Simple, cookie-cutter assessment requirements and mandatory sanctions do not allow enough flexibility in achieving improvement. It is telling to observe that, in a relatively short amount of time, most state educational systems have turned away from high pressure and serious sanction methods such as those required by NCLB. These systems now propose a method whereby moderate pressure is used to extract desired changes. This appears to have much better results (Mintrop & Sunderman, 2009).

FEDERAL AUTHORITY IN SCHOOLS

While most of us imagine that the federal government is not necessarily in a position to dictate what states do in their own schools, the fact is that the federal government can largely impose its will on state and local governments. The impetus is monetary. The imposition of NCLB upon states is unparalleled in scope. Traditionally, local and state governments were responsible for the details concerning the operation of their schools. Some of this local control has eroded under NCLB. The federal government has a firm hand in the local school systems because of strict and unrealistic performance outcomes mandated by NLCB.

The annual testing is just part of the overreaching of federal authority. The requirements also involve the standards concerning the credentials of the teachers. With these requirements, local systems may not even be allowed to hire the best instructors for their locale and circumstances. Penalties are in place to punish those states and localities that do not conform. Consider this: the United States Constitution contains approximately seventy-five hundred words; the NCLB Act contains an astronomical three hundred thousand. And, as with any federal law involving schools, the local schools are responsible for following all the details to the letter (Boaz, 2007).

RACE TO THE TOP

The Race to the Top (U.S. Department of Education, 2010a) competition instituted by the federal government provides an example of how the federal government can use the promise of federal funds to insert itself into state and local school operations. During the first round of awards, the only states that were provided with federal money under that competition were those who agreed to base teachers' salaries on how well their students performed.

States also had to have a plan for dismissing teachers whose students consistently performed poorly. They agreed to provide professional development for these teachers, but had to eventually terminate them if improvements were not made within a certain period. Of course, this instigated an outcry from teacher unions across the country, however even unions needed to sign on to some aspects of the Race to the Top criteria, in order for the state to fare well in the competition.

The competition also addressed the performance of administrators, and required that districts in the states have plans to turn around the lowest-performing schools. To be clear, Race to the Top articulated detailed criteria meant to effect comprehensive school reform—and included both supportive and punitive elements. Still, the competition clearly represented an example of how the federal government is able to get states and local education agencies to implement its visions and goals for public education.

ALTERNATIVE ROUTES TO EDUCATION

Charter schools are receiving a great deal of attention as an alternative to traditional public schools. While many have lauded charter schools as emblematic of reform and possibility (and, indeed, many are truly impressive), there are several important factors to consider when discussing them. One of those points is accountability. Even though charter schools receive public funds, they are not accountable in the traditional manner.

While they must meet specified standards of performance, there is no agreed-upon level of performance across state lines, so the levels of evaluating and monitoring these types of schools vary widely across the country (this will change with the implementation of CCSS, especially for states that receive Race to the Top funds). Many local, state, and federal standards must still be met, but some are waived.

The free market also enters into this equation, because parents exercise their choice whether to "purchase" the services that a charter school is providing (Garn & Cobb, 2008). Charter schools do not have to educate every student who walks through their door. Indeed, most charter schools have very low numbers of students who need second-language instruction or special-education services. If a student at a charter school becomes a discipline problem, the charter school is free to ask that student to leave. Public schools, on the other hand, are required to educate every eligible student.

The numbers of English as a Second Language students, special-education students, and even students with discipline problems are much higher in traditional public schools than in charter schools. Having more students requiring additional resources further stresses a system that is already under pressure. These groups of students could cause problems with adequate yearly progress reports of a school, simply because of the number of problem students and their inability to keep up (Laitsch, 2006). For example, English as Second Language students cannot be expected to compete on equal footing with native English speakers.

Another learning environment that is taking hold in the twenty-first century is the online format. Standards for judging the effectiveness of this type of teaching and learning environment have not been established, primarily because this form of education is so new, even though it is being used across the United States. Charter schools have embraced online learning and often use this method (in part or as a total mode) of education delivery. Because this mode of education is growing in popularity, a method of tracking performance is being developed, however it has yet to be completed.

Yet another educational option is homeschooling, where a parent stays home and provides instruction to their children. According to the National Center for Education Statistics, an estimated 1.1 million children are being homeschooled (Garn & Cobb, 2008). State-by-state standards for homeschooling need to be addressed. As it stands, very few states choose to exercise control over homeschooling. Those states that do show some control may require that homeschooled children be able to pass state appropriate-grade-level assessments.

Lastly, the voucher program has been toyed with since the 1950s. Many agree with the use of vouchers in theory, however practical problems make it difficult to implement the use of vouchers in practice. It is difficult, for example, to come up with an equal system when private schools and public schools may have widely varying costs per pupil. Also, no one has agreed on requirements for eligibility for particular categories of students. Currently, students can fall into widely divergent categories, depending on the school system involved. Categories could range from autistic students to disabled students to students grouped by age, income, or residence.

The use of private vouchers, as it turns out, are less popular than the vouchers associated with public systems. In the private voucher systems, monies are typically collected from individual donors, such as religious organizations or corporations. The funds are then awarded through grants to low-income families. A very similar program to the voucher system involves tax-credit programs.

Expenses for schooling are credited through the tax system with reimbursements (Garn & Cobb, 2008). While the voucher and tax-credit programs may appear to be controlled by market forces, that is not the case in practice. Issues have arisen during the administration of these types of programs, including limits on particular students allowed to participate, the entanglement of bureaucracy, and monetary limits.

CHALLENGES FACING THE OBAMA ADMINISTRATION

President Barack Obama has his work cut out for him. During the presidential campaign, education was not a hot-button issue and was not addressed in much detail. Nonetheless, the Obama administration has floated a couple of plans to assist with the problems in our educational system. Several challenges concerning education face the Obama administration, all of which are solvable with popular consensus.

Obama's plans include increasing the number of public education teachers from kindergarten through grade twelve, and helping low-income families with the rising costs of a college education by giving tax advantages to those that fall in this category. An initiative labeled the Zero to Five Program is challenged with improving education for the early years (Ladson-Billings, 2009). While these proposals are noteworthy, the plans are insufficient to address the true needs of our current educational system.

Obama's plans will likely be compromised by different agendas among various constituencies. The middle class will have to agree with the wealthy, and both will have to side with the underprivileged. This may seem insurmountable, given the current political climate, but that is not necessarily the case. It requires that each of us realize that our best interest is the same as everyone else's.

Everyone could win if this was accomplished. Consensus will not only benefit the people involved; it will benefit the entire country for decades to come. Imagine an entire army of newly educated graduates entering the workforce and providing the necessary skilled labor to raise the productivity of the country to levels never seen before. Gone will be the cries that the United States is falling further and further behind countries such as Japan, China, and South Korea.

The Program for International Student Assessment (PISA) evaluates fifteen-year-old students from countries that belong to the Organization for Economic Cooperation and Development. The skills assessed include reading, science, and mathematics. Test results from the 2003 tests highlighted American students' lackluster placement, in the lowest third (Gropman, 2008). Some observers believe that a more active role of the federal government in the nation's educational system will result in an improved system of education, and subsequently improved academic performance of U.S. students.

This view is certainly not universal, and the U.S. Department of Education concedes that the educational system of the United States has historically been centered on local control (U.S. Department of Education, 2010). Consequently, the federal influence on education was nearly nonexistent. The Office of Education, formed in 1867, handled any involvement with education in the states, but it did not have the authority to intervene in state and local school operations. Its duties were to primarily collect information on the best schools across the country and disseminate that information to the states and localities.

Federal help to the states and local governments steadily increased in the form of grants, benefits, loans, and other payments. More actual control began creeping in with the passage of Title VI of the Civil Rights Act, Title IX of the Educational Amendments of 1972, and Section 504 of the Rehabilitation Act of 1973. These laws dealt with discrimination, which continues to be a problem today.

In 1980, the Department of Education was formed as a cabinet-level position, and has since been upgraded to an even more important role. The ever-increasing expansion of federal power over schooling systems presents an opportune time to flex federal muscle and inject a dose of powerful motivation. This could infuse the educational system with a boost of energy to raise achievable standards in the years to come.

The American public must feel that education of the nation's children is a top priority, even during severe economic difficulties. Today, people are concerned about their jobs and putting food on the table. Upgrading education, although theoretically important, is a low priority when compared to the more pressing problem of keeping a roof over one's head. The paradox here is that this is precisely the time to make an investment in education.

When times are tough, workers need to improve their skills to compete effectively in the marketplace. Education can provide those skills. Furthermore, those enhanced skills and improved technological talents are going to be desperately needed in the future as America continues to struggle in the twenty-first-century labor force. Production is not getting easier and simpler. In fact, the opposite is true.

The skills needed in the world marketplace require a better education and more advanced abilities. Education is the fountain from which those abilities emerge. Planning to turn out workers for the factories of today is a crucial element, but those same workers also need to be able to adapt to technologies that are now in development. A subpar educational system will cripple America's competitiveness.

National defense, too, is an area that would benefit from improved education. With our students falling behind in science, math, and reading, critical action must be taken. The Obama administration uses these conditions as one of the rationales for national standards, in the administration's *Blueprint for Reform.* The future must be planned for now. It certainly will not be an overnight process; however, by taking steps one at a time, an enormous amount of ground can be covered in the coming years.

Americans need to be convinced that the public education system in the United States is worth saving. This is especially true of public school systems across the country that appear to be on a downward spiral. If the voting public in suburban America is dissatisfied with their school systems, it will be even more difficult to obtain their support, since they may well believe that the troubled systems are not actually worth funding.

A common perception among taxpayers is that the U.S. educational system is beyond redemption. If citizens do not believe the system is worthy of intervention with public funds, what is going to happen to it? It is not America's way to ignore problems—even when the problem is improving educational experiences for children living in poverty or students who speak English as a second language. Our current educational challenges cry out for attention. The future of our country lies in a quality educational system. Without one, jobs, our standard of living, and America's place in the world's economy may well fall to unrecoverable levels.

THE STATUS OF TEACHING

Our teaching force across the country is in crisis. Teachers often contend with the loss of professional status. It is difficult enough to retain and motivate the best teachers without them feeling that they are not treated as professional. For example, teachers are forced to teach using the current popular instructional method. This can be like trying to hit a moving target. Just when a teacher becomes familiar with a new technique, a new flavor of the month appears, and additional time and energy must be expended to master that scheme. Respect and stature must come from the top down.

While administrators have their own difficulties, every member of a school system must be a part of the solution. Respect must cross occupational titles, whether they are administrative in nature or the faculty. If excitement returns to the teaching profession, motivation will follow. Shockingly, many believe it takes no real skill to teach— that anyone can teach. This line of thought is disparaging to teachers who have developed their talents over years. If any person can perform this simple task, then a teacher is merely part of a production line, repeating the same thoughtless task. This type of thinking devalues our educational system.

The methods being used today in many challenged school systems to retain teachers are ineffective at best and destructive at worst. A number of the quick teacher-certification programs, such as weekend and online programs, have good intentions but are turning out teachers who are unprepared to the meet the challenges that they soon will face in troubled classrooms.

Although these teachers are inexpensive, since they are brand-new and have not worked their way up to better pay scales and benefits, they are more likely to jump ship instead of staying on to nurture their profession. Of course, the next group of teachers to replace them will be new and inexperienced, too—and so the cycle repeats itself. This is good for the budget, but not so good for long-term performance, morale, and achievement.

Schools must consider the value of "institutional memory," before they rush to replace teachers. Institutional memory occurs with teacher longevity in a particular school system. It provides a sense of continuity that can be appreciated by all—students, siblings, parents, other faculty, and administrators. Students experience a sense of belonging and commitment to a school when an older sibling, or even a parent, was taught by their teacher. This intergenerational experience fosters a sense of belonging and dedication throughout a community. A greater stake in ensuring a high level of quality educational institution often materializes.

FINAL THOUGHTS

While Washington, D.C., is expanding its authority and requirements concerning the NCLB Act, most of the remainder of the world is moving in the opposite direction—away from central control. The cost per pupil in the United States has soared to five times the level in the 1950s, after adjusting for inflation. With this kind of money being pumped into the system, why are our school systems in the condition that they are?

These are not the only problems facing our nation's educational system, but they are among the biggest. Moreover, far from being easily separated and handled individually, the systemic problems facing our schools are inherently interwoven and are therefore even more challenging. However, with all the problems that are present, it is possible for real change to take place. The need, then, is for a system of reform that radically shifts our perceptions of what encompasses adequate education, transforming us all into a nation of educators.

President John F. Kennedy evoked this when speaking about another challenge: putting an American on the moon. "We do this not because it is easy," he said, "but because it is hard." America's educational system deserves no less of an effort: not because it is easy, but because it is hard . . . and well worth it.

Chapter 2

Those Who Cannot Learn from History Are Condemned to Repeat It

Reform is a deeply embedded tradition in the history of education in the United States. This practice continues today as we find ourselves deeply entrenched in reform. In order to make sense of actions meant to facilitate educational change today, we must have a clear understanding of the reforms of the past.

LET'S START FROM THE TOP

We look initially at reform efforts of the late 1880s, and continue with present-day efforts. We will also examine the nature of modern-day education reform and the changes these reforms seek to implement. Three prominent themes in education reform will be presented: achieving equity in the distribution of education funding; reform at the local school level; reform of teacher education. Reform is currently underway in all three areas, as efforts are taking place to improve the quality of education and achieve the goal of excellence in schools.

Of fundamental importance to any discussion of educational reform is the role played by major stakeholders in the U.S. educational enterprise. We address the roles played by school districts, the states, and the federal government, and their impact on education reform. The current educational system in the United States is the product of many historical reforms. Despite changes in the purpose of schooling and the nature of students over time, the effects of earlier reforms remain.

The Late 1800s: The Committee of Ten

In the latter part of the nineteenth century, significant reform took place within the U.S. education system. This was not surprising, as the nation itself was in the midst of unprecedented transformation. The United States was in the process of receiving the largest number of immigrants ever to arrive at the nation's shores. The country was also experiencing social and economic changes brought about by urbanization and industrialization. The late 1800s was a time of great change for multiple aspects of society, not just education.

Within this social context, the National Education Association (NEA) established the Committee of Ten in 1892. The committee was charged with the responsibility of policy development for high schools across the United States. There was a growing sense that a uniform curriculum in high schools was long overdue. The committee, headed by Charles Eliot, president of Harvard University, primarily consisted of a number of college presidents and professors.

Not surprisingly, the committee believed high schools should offer traditional academic courses that would train the intellect. They also recommended that courses be taught in sequence and that a smaller number of electives be offered. High school, the committee believed, should be a fast track to college. The creation of the one-year Carnegie Unit to evaluate competency was another outcome of the committee's deliberations (Ornstein & Levine, 2008).

High schools of the late nineteenth century were seen as incubators for gifted students preparing for college, and not for the masses. Still, aspects of the committee's recommendations continue to impact the modern educational system.

Twentieth-Century Educational Reform

It is not uncommon for reforms of one historical period to stimulate the need for reforms in another. The NEA established a new committee in 1915 to address issues of the high school not addressed by the Committee of Ten. While the Committee of Ten focused on high school as a place to prepare students for college, the Commission on the Reorganization of Secondary Education directed their attention to the needs of students for whom college was not a goal.

Rather than a committee comprising college presidents and professors, the membership of the commission included a cross section of individuals, including high school principals, professors, and the U.S. Commissioner of Education. The commission's 1918 report, the *Seven Cardinal Principles of Secondary Education*, was clearly influenced by the Progressive Movement.

In addition to an academic component, the commission also recommended that high schools address health, home membership, vocation, citizenship, use of leisure time, and ethical character.

Recommendations to reform and improve the high school also surfaced in the 1930s, 1940s, and 1950s. In the 1930s, the Progressive Education Association (PEA) recommended that high schools incorporate curriculum components to develop social qualities and personal development. Recommendations in the 1940s and 1950s resulted in further changes to high schools, to include suggestions for an increase in the number of electives offered, the introduction of guidance counselors into the school system, and the broadening of the vocational-education programs of study.

By the late 1950s, there were strong recommendations that all schools needed to focus more on science, mathematics, and foreign language. These suggestions were due primarily to the nation's embarrassment that the Soviet Union was winning the race to space, when the country launched Sputnik ahead of the United States space exploration efforts.

Efforts to improve the high school provide an excellent study of the nature of educational reform. The public high school has been influenced by different points of view regarding the purpose and goals at the secondary education. As discussed above, reform at one point focused on the high school as a place to develop the intellect—only to be followed by reform of the high school as a place for preparation for life in the real world.

It becomes clear that reform of public education is grounded in a set of beliefs held by stakeholders able to advance change. As it turns out, both perspectives are evident in high schools today, albeit likely not in the total form proposed by earlier reform documents. High schools are able to accommodate college-bound students, while at the same time accommodate non-college-bound students, and include as well curriculum that include leans toward personal development of the student.

A Nation at Risk

Another significant milestone in education reform in the 1900s came about in 1983, when the National Commission on Excellence in Education produced a gloomy report on the American educational system. The document, titled *A Nation at Risk: The Imperative for Educational Reform,* suggested that the nation's education system was not reaching the heights of excellence and rigor becoming a nation of the stature of the United States. The "risk" in the title referred to the consequences of a failing educational system to the economy, and the ability of the nation to compete with other nations. The *Nation at Risk* report stated that the nation "in effect [had been] committing an act of unthinking, unilateral educational disarmament" (National Commission on Excellence in Education, 1983). The commission attributed the declining state of education to problematic situations in four areas: the high school curriculum, expectations of students, the use of time, and the quality of teachers. According to the commission, the high school curriculum had become diffuse and diluted, and lacked a central purpose. With respect to expectations, the commission proposed that a decline in expectations of students was caused by a reduction in assigned homework, weakened college admissions requirements, and a decline in the expectation that students would enroll in courses in math, science, and a foreign language.

When the commission compared how American students used education-related time to how peers in other industrialized nations used time, they found that American students spent less time on schoolwork, and that time spent was used ineffectively. According to the commission, the quality of teaching was in jeopardy because more academically capable students were not entering the profession. Teacher-education programs needed to be overhauled. The commission also mentioned that there were serious teacher shortages in key subject areas (e.g., math and science).

A Nation at Risk was published in an era of mass discontent with public education, and its impact was considerable. As a result, the nation set about introducing reforms based on the recommendations in the report. Changes included extension of school hours, and in some instances, the school year; careful monitoring of graduation requirements; and the seeds for standards-based teaching and testing were planted (Gouwens, 2009; Spring, 2009). Additionally, many states revised teacher qualifications and overhauled teacher-education programs.

Standards-based Teaching and Testing

A Nation at Risk precipitated a number of reforms in the 1980s, and well into the 1990s. Academic content standards were adopted by many states, along with standardized assessments to evaluate students' comprehension of the standards. The 1990s reforms were characterized by the use of high-stakes tests, along with impassioned arguments for and against their increased use. High-stakes tests have specific consequences for test takers. For example, a state may deny a high school diploma to students unable to pass a required test.

Content or curriculum standards and standardized tests were instituted with the ultimate goal of increasing student performance. However, this reform effort was criticized by teachers who viewed standards-based instruction as an effort to micromanage what took place in the classroom. Other critics of standardized high-stakes tests believed such a reliance on tests would adversely affect minorities. They maintained that standardized tests would be a detriment to students who did not perform well on standardized tests for any number of reasons (Hewitt, 2008).

Influences: The Main Phases of Educational Reform in the 1980s and 1990s

Education reform of the 1980s and 1990s can be viewed as distinct phases of educational reform which represented different conceptions of schools and schooling, and produced different proposals for education reform. The first phase of reforms centered on recommendations designed to maintain America's defense capabilities and competitive position in the international economic marketplace. As a result, students needed a more rigorous education, which provided them with skills and abilities to interact with industries' increasing reliance on advances in technology.

Another phase of educational reform focused on teacher practice rather than solely on the need to maintain economic and technical competitiveness. This phase is best represented by teachers' reactions to the standards-based education discussed above. Teachers felt powerless to use their creativity, and the teaching skills and abilities they believed to be at the center of being a teaching professional.

Many felt that teacher practice was being dictated to them, as they were required to address the content embedded in specific standards—content that would later appear on standardized state tests. Even so, standards-based instruction became an integral component of teacher practice, as well as a central component of teacher education responsible for teaching preservice teachers how to teach.

A subsequent phase of education reform took place at the end of the 1980s and the beginning of the 1990s. This reform was unlike the other two phases, and was founded upon the principle that not all students could afford a first-rate education. Instead of the school system being just about education, reform was based on the provision of a range of services, including health, counseling, and even parent education. Instead of school policy, the focus turned to children's policy. The school models that resulted were referred to as "full-service schools" (Spring, 2009).

REFORM DISCONTENT, SCHOOL CHOICE, AND DIVERSE EDUCATIONAL MODELS

Despite efforts to reform public education by addressing a number of problematic areas in the system, many with an interest in education have been frustrated with the direction reforms have taken, and the time it takes to make any progress. As a result, alternative school models have been proposed and many have been initiated (Spring, 2009). Disillusionment with the school system and its lack of flexibility can be traced to the 1950s.

Milton Friedman, a renowned economist, maintained that schools would work much better if they operated in a free-market environment. Friedman believed requiring students to attend the nearest local school was a problem. In this environment, there was no competition among schools and therefore no motivation for one school to do any better than the next. The only alternative was private school, which many students could not afford. Friedman advocated that school choice should not be limited to only those who could afford it.

The push for greater school choice surfaced again in the 1970s. If schools were going to be desegregated, as required by law, students would need to choose schools outside their local areas. The call for more educational choice got another boost from research conducted by James Coleman in 1981. According to Coleman's findings, private school students were outperforming their public school counterparts academically and socially.

While Coleman's study was heavily criticized by the educational community, another point that appeared to resonate with certain sectors of society was the notion that choice (by students and teachers) in educational attendance and teaching sites appeared to have a positive impact on students' performance. A number of school models had begun to emerge in the 1970s that offered families a choice of attendance sites for their children beyond the traditional neighborhood school. Coleman's study seemed to support this trend.

Magnet Schools

Magnet schools were established to attract students to attend a school other than their assigned neighborhood school. Not only did these schools offer a distinctive curriculum, but many also offered a first-rate education based on innovative approaches to teaching. Given these educational opportunities, many parents were persuaded to choose a magnet school for their children (Wright & Alenuma, 2007). There are currently thousands of magnet schools across the United States. They tend to be more expensive to run than their traditional public school counterparts; however, research indicates that they also tend to be more effective. Magnet schools have attracted over two million students since their inception. They have had a positive influence on desegregation in some school districts, which was an additional goal for the initiation of magnet schools. On the other hand, in places of deep racial segregation, they have not helped with desegregation (Kridel, 2010).

Open Enrollment

Open enrollment also promotes the concept of school choice. Here, students are able to attend any public school that has vacancies. Minnesota was the first state to introduce the concept of open enrollment in 1988 (National

Center for Education Statistics, 2008). Today, the majority of American states have legislation allowing open enrollment. If school choice is allowed to proceed along its current trajectory, the neighborhood school could very well become a school-attendance model of the past, or at least be radically altered.

Virtual Schools

Instruction is delivered without the need for a physical space or infrastructure in virtual schools, as learning takes place primarily via technology. Virtual schools also offer everything available to students in physical schools, such as rules that must be followed, a teaching staff, organized field trips, and teacher-parent conferences. Even though they did not surface until the 1990s, the popularity of virtual schools is evidenced by the fact that half of all states in America now offer some type of online learning program.

Almost three-quarters of a million students incorporate online learning into their education. In fact, due to the need of this generation to possess online literacy, Michigan recently made it compulsory for students to include online learning as part of their education (Inoue, 2009). One of the most significant characteristics of virtual schools is the ability of these schools to offer specialized programs that are not offered at conventional high schools.

Another unique feature of virtual schools is the 24/7 accessibility—a feature that has proven very attractive to students. There are no set times for class. As a consequence, the virtual classroom not only tailors classes to students' individual learning interests by offering specialized courses, but they also make it easier for students from anywhere in the world to participate in offered classes and programs.

The initial rationale behind establishing virtual high schools was to supplement conventional high school programs. However, the convenience and unique qualities possible with virtual learning formats resulted in the development of fully functioning high schools. From a personnel perspective, the virtual school is touted as a solution to teacher shortages (Klein, 2006).

Perhaps the greatest benefit of the virtual high school model is that it has opened up new possibilities for serving the learning needs of certain student groups, such as those with disabilities, homeschooled students, and even students who attend schools that lack the funding to provide specialized courses. Even so, virtual high schools are not without their skeptics. Opponents suggest the virtual schools are unable to teach social as well as academic skills, as they believe social skills cannot be taught online.

For-Profit Schools

For-profit model schools surfaced amid discontent by parents and other educational stakeholders with the seeming inability of traditional schools to address achievement and other educational needs of students. This school model is based on the notion that a different approach to school management would lead to better educational outcomes. Educational management organizations (EMOs) are for-profit companies that manage schools from a corporate model.

In order to stay in business, EMOs believe that they must deliver the "product" (i.e., student achievement) to clients (i.e., parents, students, and school boards). Since they receive the same per-pupil funding as traditional schools, they must be able to use funds more efficiently if they are going to make a profit. Unlike schools that have been unable to raise achievement levels, EMOs believe they must do so in order to remain viable. EMOs primarily manage charter schools; however they also work in collaboration with school districts to manage traditional schools.

Edison Schools, Inc., is currently the largest educational-management organization in the nation. EMOs like Edison contend that privatization of schooling serves as motivation for improved schools and, subsequently, improved achievement among students. Given the choice, parents would send students to successful schools, thus causing unsuccessful schools to go out of business. This is not the case with government-run schools, EMOs would suggest, since some state- and district-run schools are allowed to operate year after year without improving student achievement.

Edison Schools, Inc., manages 150 schools with eight-five thousand students across the United States. Their schools rely heavily on technology, and they often supply both teachers and students with computers. Edison Schools also have longer school days than traditional schools, with students normally attending school for eight hours a day. Teachers have more preparation time than is normally granted in public school settings.

Researchers at Columbia University found that teachers at Edison Schools had higher morale and were passionate about teaching in Edison-run schools (Spring, 2009). Nonetheless, EMOs like Edison Schools, Inc., are not without critics. Some education advocates believe that if schools were privatized, companies might focus more on their profit than on the education and well-being of students.

Effective Schools

The foregoing discussion makes it clear that the desire to reform education in the United States has led to initiation of a number of schooling models. In some instances, the models emerged in reaction to perceptions of ineffectiveness and inadequacies of traditional schools, despite reform efforts. Although diverse school models exist, a fundamental question remains—how are we to know whether or not a school model is effective and how can effectiveness be judged?

A number of research studies focus on characteristics of effective schools. However, there is debate over which attributes should be considered when describing successful schools. According to some researchers, student performance should be the primary indicator of a successful school. A study conducted by the Office of the Superintendent for Public Instruction (OSPI) used performance on standardized tests as a measure of effectiveness, and was able to generate nine characteristics typical of schools with positive standardized-test performance.

Other researchers propose that students' social characteristics, such as personal growth, should be included when determining effective schools. Another issue with school-effectiveness research is that findings are predominantly based on research conducted at elementary schools or unique school settings in the inner city. Consequently, it is suggested that these findings cannot be generalized to all schools.

Attributes of Effective Schools

A number of attributes influence school effectiveness. As suggested above, the context of schooling will impact factors that contribute to effectiveness in specific schools. At the same time, there are attributes and factors that contribute to effectiveness across schooling contexts. By understanding an array of effectiveness attributes, we are able to observe which attributes exist at a particular school and which, if adopted, might facilitate effectiveness in a particular school context.

A 2008 study describes five common characteristics that make up an effective school. These characteristics, and the theory behind them, have been described as the five-factor theory (Sadker, Sadker & Zittleman, 2008). The first factor is *quality leadership.* In other words, students perform better in schools where the principal provides strong leadership. Effective leaders were visible, able to successfully convey the school's goals and visions, collaborated with teachers to enhance their skills, and were involved in the discovery of and solutions to problems (Sadker, Sadker & Zittleman, 2008).

The second factor is having *high expectations* of students and teachers (Bourne, 2008). Having high expectations of students has repeatedly been shown to have a positive impact on students' performance. More attention needs to be paid to the high expectations of teachers, however. Teachers who are expected to learn at high levels of effectiveness are generally able to reach that level of expectations, particularly when teacher evaluations and teacher professional development are geared toward improving instructional quality.

The third characteristic of a successful school is the *ongoing screening of student performance and development.* Schools should use assessment data to compare their students with others from across the country (Odden, 2009). Effective use of assessment data allows schools to identify problem areas of learning in the classroom and school levels, so that solutions can be generated that will best address the problems.

The fourth characteristic of a successful school is the existence of *goals and direction* (Odden, 2009). According to research, successful school principals actively construct goals for their schools. They understand the importance of effectively communicating those goals to appropriate individuals (i.e., students, teachers, and the community-at-large).

School principals must be open and willing to incorporate innovation into goals for school processes and practices. Hence, it is important to invite input from all stakeholders in the process of developing school goals. Student performance has been shown to improve in schools where all in the school community work toward goals that are communicated and shared in the learning environment.

The fifth and final factor of a successful school is the extent to which the school is *secure and organized.* For maximum learning to occur, students need to feel secure (Capper & Frattura, 2009). Respect is a quality that is promoted and is a fundamental aspect of a safe school. There should also be a number of trained staff, such as social workers, who work with problem students before situations get out of hand.

Apart from the five factors of a successful school already mentioned, the size of the school seems to be a key factor in school effectiveness (French, Atkinson & Rugen, 2007). Research has found that the smaller the school, the better students perform, especially in the case of older students. This is the rationale behind the concept of schools-within-schools. Students in smaller learning environments feel more connected to their peers and teachers, pass classes more often, and have a higher probability of going to college.

A number of school districts are looking at preschool education as a factor that will influence overall effectiveness across all schools in the district. Evidence suggests that children with preschool experiences fare better academically and socially as they enter kindergarten and beyond. Preschool experiences in literacy and numeracy prepare preschoolers for a kindergarten curriculum with heightened expectations. They also help identify early learners who will need additional support to ensure they are able to have positive learning experiences later on.

THE ROLE OF STATE GOVERNMENT IN EDUCATIONAL REFORM

First Phase: Results-Centered Reforms

The role of the state governments in school reform is located in two main areas—implementing results-centered policies and reducing the regulatory burdens on schools at the local level. States' initial educational-reform actions were focused on policies and practices that were straightforward and could be easily implemented and easily measured to determine effectiveness.

Policies for teacher qualifications and the introduction of testing models fit into what can be described as "results-centered" initiatives. Still, problems—either perceived or real—resulted from the first phase of reforms. Despite the desire of many groups to move away from homogeneity, the end result was a move toward standardization. Another setback of first-phase reforms was the negative teaching behaviors that came about, due to a reward system for higher test scores.

There were instances where teachers had given students questions on an upcoming test, in order to boost student scores. Other teachers were instructing students with test questions from past exams or giving students similar tests to complete as student activities. Instead of teachers teaching normally, teachers were engaging in activities designed to improve test scores. Students were not learning a broad range of subject matter. Rather, they were being exposed to limited areas of knowledge presented to them by teachers concerned about test performance.

Despite these problems, reform efforts continued, and many associated problems were largely ignored by the then governors of the states. Education reform was so important that governors during this period strived for the label of "education governor." This honor was so sought after and highly regarded that, following their tenure as governor, many ended up in top-tier political positions. Regardless of the motivation—reputation or interest—their achievements in school reform helped their careers.

The 1980s was also a time when states were taking regulatory power away from the federal government. Although conservatives suggested this shift would help reduce regulatory burden, in time states were perceived as being just as bad at placing demands and directives on local educational units as was the federal government. During this same period, federal funding was also more restricted. This was quite a paradox, because, at the time, states had more power over how funding would be spent—the problem was that there was a lot less funding to disperse.

Second Phase: Unburdening the Regulatory Burden

The second phase of states' school-reform involvement took place in the latter part of the 1980s. Their actions were in response to discontent that had arisen from first-phase involvement in the early to mid-1980s. The states' main goal was to liberate schools from an overabundance of regulation and control from higher authority. Discontent emerged however, and this approach to reform was short-lived, lasting only a decade and then losing all support.

The method used to reduce the regulatory burden was increased management at the school level. Administration and organization were now schools' responsibility. This approach promoted decentralization rather than the top-down, centralized school administration model. The power to make decisions passed predominantly to those on the ground (such as teachers and parents). As a working model, it gathered much support from education professionals and was seen as a model of inclusion, where power shifted from bureaucratic decision-makers to stakeholders on the ground.

This site-based model was certainly locally grounded. However, it was still centered on the school principal. As a result, the inclusive model that was purported to improve school administration did not exist. An additional flaw in the model surfaced. The actual stakeholders on the ground who were required to participate in the inclusive decision-making process were far too busy to be involved.

The new model was viewed negatively by teachers, who saw it as infringing on the time they needed to plan and teach. The end result, paradoxically, was that this reformed model of school management received as much criticism as did the previous model, where regulation was burdensome. Consequently, the site-based model was discontinued in most districts within a decade.

The 1990s and School Restructuring

The notion of restructuring became popular in the late 1980s and early 1990s, primarily in reaction to the failure of previous attempts to improve existing educational structures through reform. The goal of restructuring was to change the organizational structure of schools in ways that supported student learning. Three main areas were the focus of restructuring school-reform efforts during this period (Dynarksi, Gleason, Rangarajan & Wood, 1998).

First, teachers were to have a larger role in managing the school and have more flexibility in choosing instructional methods and materials. With more input into school management, teachers would also have more say about how the learning environment, school resources, and the use of time at school could support student learning.

Student learning and achievement was the second area of focus for restructuring efforts. With the changes in teachers' roles and responsibilities in the learning environment, proponents of restructuring believed students would have increased opportunities to learn, and that learning at higher, more rigorous levels could be accomplished. The final area of focus for restructuring was to make schools more inviting places where school faculty and staff would be more aware of and responsive to the needs of students and their families.

A number of reforms were implemented during the 1990s that were consistent with the notion of restructuring. Stricter requirements for graduation were implemented, which included increases in the number of high school credits as well as changes in course requirements. For example, all students were required to complete courses in math and science, even though levels of difficulty in courses existed. Reforms focused on increasing the amount of time available for students to learn were also pursued (National Center for Education Statistics, 2003).

Standards-based education also emerged during this period. Specific standards of what students should know and be able to do were identified. Students were then tested based on standards, using standardized tests. How students and schools performed indicated the success or effectiveness of that school, the staff, and the state. The most negative aspect of standards-based testing was that it represented a one-size-fits-all approach to measurement and did not account for differences among learners, schools, and districts (Marzano & Kendall, 2008).

Higher expectations of teachers were also an outgrowth of the reforms in the 1980s and 1990s. Requiring new teachers to pass tests at the end of training or prior to receiving a teaching license was one method of ensuring teacher knowledge (El-Khawas, 2010). How and what to test, however, has been at the center of the teacher-testing debate. Some complained that the testing standards were so low that they were not meaningful.

It is important to note that the meaning and the purpose of restructuring changed in the 2000s, as NCLB came into being. Restructuring now refers to an action taken by states for schools consistently unable to meet annual performance targets as required by NCLB. In this instance, restructuring refers to the process by which schools may be changed to charter schools; school administration and staff may be replaced; and an outside entity (e.g., EMO) may be contracted to operate the school.

While states are required to sanction poorly performing schools under NCLB regulations, some reward high-performing schools at the same time. These actions are likely based on the notion that rewarding schools will lead to improved performance among teachers. Other states, however, sanction poor-performing schools, even when they are not required to do so. In many ways, rewarding schools and providing assistance to poor-performing schools is more in keeping with the teacher-empowerment goals of the school- restructuring efforts implemented in the 1990s.

THE FEDERAL GOVERNMENT'S ROLE

Following the *Nation at Risk* report, the federal government became more focused on the achievement of all students in the nation's schools. The 1994 reauthorization of the Elementary and Secondary Education Act (ESEA), *Goals 2000: Educate America Act,* was passed with the goal of supporting efforts by states to develop curriculum standards that would outline what students should know and be able to do, as well as state and district efforts to improve student achievement within the standards.

The act did not stop at standards-based education, however. It included goals focused on safe schools, parental involvement, and teacher development, all of which ostensibly influence student achievement. Goals for education from early childhood to adulthood were addressed in the act as well. *Goals 2000* included the following:

- All children in America will start school ready to learn.
- The high school graduation rate will increase to at least 90 percent.
- All students will leave grades four, eight, and twelve having demonstrated competency over challenging subject matter, including English, mathematics, science, foreign languages, civics and government, economics, the arts, history, and geography. Furthermore, every school in America will ensure that all students learn to use their minds well, so they may be prepared for responsible citizenship, further learning, and productive employment in our nation's modern economy.
- United States students will be first in the world in mathematics and science achievement.
- Every adult American will be literate and will possess the knowledge and skills necessary to compete in a global economy and exercise the rights and responsibilities of citizenship.
- Every school in the United States will be free of drugs, violence, and the unauthorized presence of firearms and alcohol, and will offer a disciplined environment conducive to learning.
- The nation's teaching force will have access to programs for the continued improvement of their professional skills and the opportunity to acquire the knowledge and skills needed to instruct and prepare all American students for the next century.

- Every school will promote partnerships that will increase parental involvement and participation in promoting the social, emotional, and academic growth of children (North Central Regional Educational Laboratory, n.d.).

REFORMING NCLB

The *No Child Left Behind Act* (NCLB), which was the 2001 reauthorization of ESEA, has had many critics, and there have been many calls to reform the law. Suggested changes include removing the 2013–2014 target year for eliminating the achievement gap that exists among different groups of children, as educators and policymakers alike believe the target year is unrealistic.

Additionally, it has been suggested that student growth be a measure of the difference between students' performance level at the beginning of the school year and their performance level at the end of the school year, rather than an arbitrary expectation for annual performance. Moreover, there have been calls to expand the measures used to determine student performance, so that standardized tests are not the only measures used.

The focus on testing only mathematics and reading has also come under scrutiny, with suggestions that knowledge and skills in other subjects should be assessed as well. Reauthorization of NCLB is scheduled for 2011, and the Obama administration has reportedly considered some of the suggestions that have surfaced. The administration seems to want a focus on flexibility with NCLB, by setting goals for states to reach but allowing them the flexibility to determine how best to reach those goals.

NATIONAL REFORM EFFORTS

States' responsibility for setting curriculum standards, as well as the assessment of those standards, resulted in differences among states in terms of the nature of standards and the performance levels required to reach proficiency. Critics perceived this circumstance as having a negative impact on the quality of education in the nation.

It was suggested that some states reduced the rigor of their standards in order to increase the number of students able to reach proficiency as required by NCLB.

In 2009, governors and chief academic officers from the states (and the District of Columbia and territories), along with educators, came together to develop the Common Core State Standards that would outline the knowledge and skills all should have during their elementary and secondary education.

The knowledge and skills identified were designed to ensure that students would be able to pursue a career or enter college once they completed high school. Standards in English language arts and mathematics have been completed, and to date forty-six states, the District of Columbia, and the U.S. Virgin Islands have formally adopted the standards.

Proponents of national standards maintained that national standards would provide all students with the same high standard of education, no matter where they lived. Critics are concerned that national standards, which are viewed as a step toward a national educational system, would result in the federal government having too much say in decision-making.

Another notable nationwide reform effort is the American Diploma Project Network. In 2005, a group of highly reputable individuals began a crusade to reform high school. The group believed that high school education had become archaic and needed to step into the twenty-first century. Among other reforms, the group called for an increase in standards, a stricter curriculum, and improved examinations to gauge students' competence for the workforce or future study. To date, thirty-five states are part of the Network (Achieve, Inc., 2010).

SCHOOL-LEVEL REFORMS

In the late 1990s, federal funds were made available to schools willing to adopt comprehensive school reforms. Comprehensive School Reform (CSR) encourages schools to move away from adoption of isolated strategies designed to improve one or more problematic area within the school. Programs under the CSR umbrella are research based, and designed to facilitate total school reform. Currently, a plethora of CSR programs exist, challenging schools to select a program that best fits the school context and specific needs.

James Comer's *School Development* program, for example, is based on the notion that student performance will improve when schools attend to students' physical, social, emotional, and academic well-being. Theodore Sizer's *Coalition for Essential Schools* focuses on helping students to learn to use their minds well. E. D. Hirsch's *Core Knowledge* program is based on the notion that student achievement will improve when students have a strong foundation of core knowledge upon which to build higher levels of learning.

Margaret Wang's *Community for Learning* links schools with community institutions, in order to improve social and academic success. While CSR programs approach school-level reform from different perspectives, the fact that they are research based and designed to restructure and revitalize the total school is generally viewed as a positive direction for reform at the school level.

TEACHER-EDUCATION REFORMS

The need for teacher-education reforms was an important part of the *Nation at Risk* report. Apart from the low levels of student attainment that the report brought to light, there was also condemnation of teacher training across the United States. A major criticism was that teacher-education programs focused too much on teaching methods and not enough on the content teachers would eventually teach in classrooms.

In 1996, the National Commission on Teaching and America's Future published its first report, titled *What Matters Most: Teaching for America's Future*. This report challenged the nation to "embrace a set of turning points that will put us on the path to serious, successful, long-term improvements in teaching and learning for America" (National Commission on Teaching and America's Future, 1996, p. 63). They listed as turning points that:

- All children will be taught by teachers who have the knowledge, skills, and commitment to teach children well.
- All teacher-education programs will meet professional standards, or they will be closed.
- All teachers will have access to high-quality professional development and regular time for collegial work and planning.
- Both teachers and principals will be hired and retained based on their ability to meet professional standards of practice.
- Teachers' salaries will be based on their knowledge and skills.
- Quality teaching will be the central investment in schools. Most education dollars will be spent on classroom teaching (National Commission on Teaching and America's Future, 1996, p. 63).

The recommendations of the commission did much to stimulate reform in teacher education. Many of the goals identified in the commission's report were subsequently encouraged or required of teacher-education programs by state departments of education and national teacher-education accrediting bodies.

Alternative Teacher-Education Programs

Alternative teacher-education programs have emerged rapidly across the United States over the past decade. These programs were precipitated by calls for change in teacher education, as well as to relieve teacher shortages in certain subject areas and in certain regions. Alternative programs exist in many forms. All programs, however, must meet state teacher-education program standards and requirements. Generally, alternative programs require a strong subject matter content background, and attempt to accelerate candidates' access to classrooms. The professional core in many programs takes place while candidates are actually practicing teachers. Candidates are able to gain entry into some alternative programs as long as they have a four-year degree. Such programs require short, concentrated educational training, with internships and direction from experienced or mentor teachers. They occur under strict guidance from university and education experts.

A major criticism of fast-track alternative teacher-education programs is that these programs focus on quantity and addressing teacher shortages in certain licensure/subject matter areas, rather than production of quality teachers. Despite criticisms, the numbers of alternative teacher-education programs continue to grow.

The Holmes Group

The Holmes Group consisted of a consortium of ninety-six higher-education research institutions that offered teacher-education programs. The institutions were concerned about reform not only of schools but also of teacher education and the teaching profession. The consortium was initially concerned that some of the most highly regarded universities in the nation had gotten rid of their teacher-education programs. It appeared that teacher education was poorly regarded by these institutions, as their attention was given to more prestigious professional preparation programs. The Holmes Group believed that prominent institutions needed to be intimately involved in the preparation of the nation's teachers. In 1986, the group published a report titled *Tomorrow's Teachers*, which declared that quality teachers provided the best hope for the success of school reform.

The report included suggestions for changes that would strengthen the preparation of teachers. Among the areas addressed were the need to improve the intellectual soundness of teacher-preparation programs, the need to develop standards for entry into the teaching profession, and the need to create induction and internship programs for beginning teachers. Many of the goals and the principles proposed by this group continue to be a part of the teacher-preparation process today (Holmes Partnership, 2007).

The National Council for the Accreditation of Teacher Education

All teacher-education programs must be approved by the state where they are located. As an additional stamp of quality, some programs seek voluntary national accreditation through the National Council for the Accreditation of Teacher Education (NCATE). In some states, NCATE accreditation is required. NCATE's accreditation process has undergone a number of changes over the last twenty years, many of which align with changes called for by other commissions and committees on teacher education.

The organization established standards for accreditation more than a decade ago, and continues to revise these standards so that they more clearly reflect quality in the preparation of teachers and other school professionals. In order to be accredited, teacher-education departments, colleges, or schools of education must present evidence that they meet six broad NCATE standards, each of which have more detailed criterion that reflect program quality.

The standards are Candidate Knowledge Skills; Professional Dispositions; Assessment System and Unit Evaluation; Field Experiences and Clinical Practice; Diversity; Faculty Qualifications, Performance, and Development; and Unit Governance and Resources. Each program must also show that they meet discipline-based standards generated by their respective discipline-specific organizations.

Programs submit materials to organizations such as the National Council of Teachers of Mathematics (NCTM), National Council for the Social Studies (NCSS), and National Science Teachers Association (NSTA), or meet program-specific state standards in order to be accredited. Even though programs are formally evaluated every five to seven years, they must show evidence that they are engaged in continuous improvement of their programs. Evidence must focus on outcomes (rather than inputs) to show that the institution operates a high-quality teacher program.

Both NCATE and the Teacher Education Accreditation Council (TEAC) accredited teacher-education programs for a number of years. Concerned over the fact that there was no single entity to speak for the professional preparation of teachers, administrations, and other school personnel, the two organizations joined together in 2010 to form the Council for the Accreditation of Educator Preparation (CAEP). The new organization will continue to focus on the educational practitioners' performance, and has as a major goal to raise the stature of educators throughout the nation.

The National Board for Professional Teaching Standards and National Teacher Certification

The National Board for Professional Teaching Standards (NBPTS) was established as a means for elevating the stature of the teaching profession, since those within the profession developed the standards. Teachers are able to gain national certification by completing a rigorous certification process. The vast majority of states offer some type of incentive to encourage teachers to pursue national teacher certification.

Many states reward teachers who have attained this voluntary certification, which goes beyond state-required certification, with additional compensation. The teacher unions— AFT and NEA—have supported the implementation of national certification and see it as a way to increase teachers' salaries and enhance professionalism.

REFORM AND ISSUES OF EQUITY IN SCHOOL FINANCE

Educational reform in the 1980s did not, for the most part, resemble the changes in the 1960s and the 1970s, which centered on equity. However, one element of 1980s reform was linked to equity—that of school finance. Growing disparity existed in funding between districts with resources and those without. In terms of school funding, districts located in areas with low-priced property could not generate funding comparable to property-rich districts.

Student achievement and attainment in resource-rich districts were naturally much higher when compared to that of students in poorer districts. Trying to achieve impartiality in relation to school funding was a product of the 1960s; however, it was not until the 1970s that funding equity was achieved. A case was brought to court in California (*Serrano v. Priest*, 1971), and the ruling was that educational quality should be founded upon the wealth of the state, not the school district.

Although a precedent, the Californian case was stifled by a later, 1973, case (*San Antonio Independent School District v. Rodriguez*) that found funding differences were not a violation of the Texas constitution. Consequently, to discover if funding inequity was a violation in other states, each state court would have to hear the case and judge it against their state constitution.

As a result, by the early 1990s, over thirty states had challenged funding inequity. The court rulings differed among the states; however, for the most part, the inequity that existed was allowed to continue. Justification for perpetuation of funding inequity was based on the argument that even though the funding might be less, poorer districts were still provided with an acceptable level to be able to fund good schools.

In states where disparity in funding was not viewed as a breach of the constitution, the problem of funding inequities was nevertheless recognized, and the legislature was used to remedy the problem. For example, in the mid-1980s, school-reform legislation was passed in Georgia to improve this very situation. There is much evidence to suggest that inequalities continue to exist between rich and poor districts, and that there is a long way to go in terms school-finance reform that would result in funding equity.

Chapter 3

What Can We Do About It?
Reimagining School Reform

THE CRISIS IN SCHOOL REFORM

With the budget crisis, skyrocketing costs, inconsistent curricula, poor standardized- testing scores, and poor morale among teachers, administrators, and students, the need for sustainable and pervasive educational change is greater now than ever before. Questions related to the quality of the U.S. educational system are at an all-time high. Many American parents have seen reports that rank American student performance well below the performance of students in countries such as China and Japan.

Parents have also heard President Obama declare a "dropout crisis" in the United States. Too many young people for any number of reasons are failing to complete a high school education. An abundance of reports such as these, along with numerous discouraging case-in-point studies has created panic among American parents, who want to know why American school systems are failing.

Many Americans believe only a small percentage of leaders understand the complexities of the school systems, and those who do understand the intricacies of the system use their knowledge to justify the mediocre performance of our teachers and students. The American school system is the best-financed system in the world, but is one of the lowest performing (UNESCO Institute for Statistics, 2007).

Reversing the Disastrous State of American Schools

On the whole, American schools have an appalling record. For children living in urban environments, the story is particularly alarming. Students from low socioeconomic backgrounds are often educated in dilapidated schools where the vast majority of educators lack the credentials and skills necessary to perform their duties adequately. High student-to-teacher ratios are found in most urban schools, and schools often lack the resources to deal with the diverse challenges they face, including unruly student behavior.

Education has been called the great equalizer, but for students living in poverty-stricken urban areas it is little more than a babysitting service and a place to get a hot meal. Many question whether the No Child Left Behind Act has contributed to achieving academic success. For many, NCLB has not lived up to the hopes of the federal government or schools, and has actually further reduced the subpar academics existing before the law was put into practice. If American educators do not make a concerted effort to develop effective accountability measures for the education of all of our children, then the education crisis will continue.

Of course there are exceptions to every rule—some urban school systems are providing a quality education. Unfortunately, if NCLB requirements are used as a measure, there are far too many schools not meeting the expected progress. The Center on Education Policy (CEP) reported that 38 percent of public schools failed to meet adequate yearly progress (AYP) in 2010, which was actually five percentage points higher than the 2009 rate. Even more disconcerting was CEP's report of the failure rate of schools in some states, to include 91 percent of schools in the District of Columbia, 86 percent in Florida, and 61 percent in California (Crawford, 2011).

For the underperforming urban school systems, the problem usually lies with the inability to sustain existing reform efforts and initiatives. Mayors and school superintendents in these areas often concoct grandiose reform plans that are merely political devices meant to beguile voters into believing they genuinely care about educational reform. The idea that politicians create school reform to gain popularity and votes is sad and sobering. It is discouraging to realize that our children's futures might be used as a political device to win elections.

Politicians are not the only people at fault for the shoddy education American children are receiving, no one is willing to accept responsibility for the subpar educational environments where children are suppose to be learning. If administrators were asked who was at fault, they might point to a lack of parental involvement and too few quality teachers. If teachers were asked who was at fault, they might also cite a lack of parental involvement and ineffective administration. If parents were asked who was at fault, they might blame teachers and administrators. Society in general seems to infer that the lack of quality teachers, effective administration, and parental involvement are all factors contributing to educational failure. Whatever the reason, Americans have become the laughing stock of the free world when it comes to P–12 education. The solution, of course, is for the country to unite and work together to carry the responsibility for enriching and continuing America's future via educational excellence.

Envisioning Teachers as Professionals

There is a tendency for American teachers to be treated like factory workers. They receive little recognition, a meager salary, and their training after hire consists of professional development that rarely fosters much growth. Since mediocre teachers earn the same salary as high-quality teachers, there is little monetary incentive to become a better educator. In addition, No Child Left Behind holds teachers entirely responsible for their students' performance on state assessments, regardless of all the variables that determine student performance on these tests. It is extremely difficult, if not impossible, for example, to prepare a sixth-grade student reading at a second-grade level to perform well on a state achievement test (Ambrosio, 2004). NCLB has caused schools and teachers to panic. Many educational professionals feel their jobs are in jeopardy if their students fail to meet state performance requirements, causing many teachers and administrators to wrongly identify some students as special-needs students. This misrepresentation of students can be connected directly to the strict rules and regulations of NCLB and educators' fears (Sullivan, 2009).

Even with the advantage of an Individualized Education Program (IEP) or a translator, a child with learning difficulties is still more likely to score poorly on state achievement tests. Generally, teachers are held responsible, as students' scores are directly attributable to their teaching. Politicians and businesspeople responsible for developing NCLB refuse to take into account all of the extraneous variables that lead to achievement gaps.

Most teachers do not have their class roster at the beginning of the year. Some teachers may end up having mostly high achievers and well-behaved students, whereas other teachers may consistently have classrooms filled with low achievers, special-needs students, and students with behavioral problems. In this case, it seems unfair to expect teachers with such different circumstances to be accountable for similar performance outcomes.

Even the best teachers are not miracle workers. The sad reality of education is that some children do not have the ability to achieve the standards of NCLB. Teachers should be held accountable for poor performance as an educator, but rather than isolating student ability to meet an arbitrary performance level in a given year, a teacher's ability to improve test scores should be considered. For example, a student may not have reached the expected proficiency level for a given school year, but their scores may have increased significantly year after year. This kind of situation should be factored into the overall equation.

In addition to concerns about job security and low compensation, teachers must also worry about subpar principals who are overcompensated for the successes of the teachers. Administrators certainly deserve to be fairly compensated for their work—however, their pay does not seem to be equitable when compared to that of teachers. If administrators are to be compensated fairly for the job performed, then teachers, too, should be fairly compensated.

The Need for Focused Professional Preparation

Administrators are prepared for their leadership roles and selected to serve as principals with minimal regard for the leadership needs of different school environments. Serving as an educational leader in an urban school is very different from serving as a leader in a suburban or rural school. Professional development should be tailored to individuals working in urban schools.

Urban school leaders should be exposed to knowledge and skills directed toward addressing issues and situations that are often present in urban settings (e.g., developing skill in managing situations that might arise in schools attended by gang members; learning how to facilitate and maintain university-school partnerships; and developing skills as an instructional leader for teachers working with students from low socioeconomic backgrounds).

Universities also need to prepare preservice teachers for the complexities of the urban environment and the personal turmoil that might result when beginning a teaching career in an urban school. Jill Jeffery and Jody Polleck (2010) have researched the positive results when universities and elementary and secondary schools collaborate on the preparation of preservice teachers.

Polleck and Jeffery found that time spent addressing teacher candidates' desire to teach in an urban school can have a positive effect on the candidates' eventual teaching practice in an urban setting. Preservice teachers are taught techniques that are most effective in an urban environment, as well as general techniques that work best in a rural or suburban environment. As a result, graduates are better prepared for the specific challenges they face when entering urban schools.

Change Is Unavoidable

America's educational system has not changed dramatically over the last century, although America certainly has. An increasingly erratic world economy requires Americans to possess a vast array of new skills and aptitudes. The more degrees and certifications a person maintains, the more marketable they are to potential employers. It is disturbing that American schools have not changed to keep pace with the global market, particularly since education is the foundation upon which economic success is built.

This quandary exists in part because professionals who have worked in the education system for many years fear change. People react to change with fear as they fear being taken out of their comfort zone (Brooks, Hughes & Brooks, 2008). Many feel America should not fix what, in their judgment, has worked for so long. However, with the world changing dramatically and swiftly, coupled with the economic and fuel crisis, change must take place, and this change will need to start in American education systems.

Educational change will occur once educators decide enough is enough and make the change happen no matter what it takes. When America realizes all children deserve a stellar education regardless of where they are from, who their parents are, or what their socioeconomic status happens to be, we will be able to reform our education system. Americans have to stop treating minority students in underperforming urban environments like collateral damage.

The disheartening reality is that America has spent billions of dollars to fight a two-front war, but cannot or will not properly educate its children. If we were attacked by a hostile country today, it would take less than twenty-four hours for American troops to be mobilized into battle. However, we seem unable to mobilize a sea of educated teachers and administrators to wage war against academic mediocrity, which is a bigger threat to our national security than Iran or North Korea (Meier, Kohn, Darling-Hammon, Sizer & Wood, 2004).

Visionary School Reform

Over the last century, many reform movements have come and gone, but in the end, it seems there have been no substantial changes. Some might even believe the American educational system is now worse off than ever before. From Bush's NCLB to Obama's Race to the Top, presidents have shown an inability to tackle the real issues of education reform. Reform is primarily used as campaign rhetoric, and when it comes time to take real action, the politicians simply unveil a grandiose plan with all the bells and whistles, amounting to a dog and pony show.

One of the biggest impediments to school reform is the failure to create an environment that nurtures and sustains school improvement. Teachers and school administrators have to realize that in order for reform to pay dividends, it must be fully embraced by the local district and community. Districts must show fidelity to school reform as if it were a symbiotic relationship.

Effecting change in the behavior of teachers and administrators is inadequate. All stakeholders have to be fully committed to making school reform a community effort. Not all community members have to agree with the proposed or recently implemented reform, but they have to be reasonable and adult enough to agree that something has to be done. In the case of struggling districts, most detractors change their minds once they realize that conflict will not be beneficial to student learning. Ultimately, no one in the community wants to see American children fail.

Schools will change only if the vision of school reform and improvement is alluring enough to entice the majority of the faculty and staff to buy in. They have to recognize that success is possible. Schools needing effective change must have leaders who can motivate and inspire the faculty and staff to implement instructional school reforms with confidence and diligence.

The result will be a cadre of educators diligently working to reach their potential, in turn fostering the academic achievement of their students. Educators should not have to be bribed into working harder in order to facilitate student reform; rather, if educators are enticed by a provocative reform plan and a strong and knowledgeable reform leader, they should become passionate enough to successfully implement the reform.

In order for school reform to be more viable, our politicians and legislators must confront the fact that boosting teacher salaries is one of the most effective ways to improve the U.S. educational system. Offering more money to educators will attract the best and brightest to enter the profession. The increase in teacher salaries should also increase the prestige and respectability the teaching profession should command (Berryhill, Linney & Fromewick, 2009).

Whenever educational reform is attempted, the community should be educated concerning the problems facing the school district. When a community is kept in the loop and made an integral part of the reform process, it begins to take ownership. Community members can provide important input about the needs and wants of the community. All communities have needs, and whenever possible, schools should help students improve the community they live in. Most civic-minded citizens know they have the right to participate in the educational process, and they will do everything legally and politically to exercise their rights. Without a school-community partnership, it will be difficult or impossible for genuine school reform to take place. In some respects, community members are the investors and stockholders of schools. After all, the community's tax dollars pay the teachers, administrators, and staff.

School districts must be aware that what works for children in one school may not work for children in another. Vast amounts of public funds have been spent on interventions and educational programs that simply do not work for the target population. It is clear in these instances that the school personnel did not research whether or not the program would fit their district's needs. After millions of dollars were wasted on the latest trend, American educators and administrators have begun to realize that common sense, a commodity that is unfortunately in short supply in the school system, is the key ingredient in any school-reform formula.

Road Map to School Reform

School improvement requires systemic change that must begin with a clear framework and guiding road map. Many of us have started out on a road trip without a map and have inevitably gotten lost. The same problem will arise when a school starts out on a path to school reform without a plan. Sadly, most school reform has been proceeding without a plan for the last forty years.

Americans have instituted countless measures to completely reform and revolutionize our educational system. For instance, standard-based reform was centered on the belief that schools would rally around this concept as a means for improving educational outcomes for children and youth. When schools failed to live up to expectations, stakeholders became impatient and entreated lawmakers to take a firmer stance on school reform. The result has been the implementation of a vast array of school-reform initiatives that have failed to make a significant impact on the issues that plague our education system.

A Nation at Risk: The Imperative for Educational Reform (Gardner, 1983) encouraged the American public to focus on creating a better educational system, pointing out that failing schools would have a negative impact on the nation's economy. At the time the report was published, the unemployment rate was at 10.7 percent. The report however focused on a more long-term consequence of a poor educational system on the world of work. The National Commission on Excellence in Education warned that the United States would soon not have a workforce educated to compete in a global economy. The caution was likely prophetic.

In the current economic crisis, many workers began losing their jobs in 2008, and by October of 2009, the unemployment rate had reached 10.1 percent. Many of the jobs the unemployed once possessed will disappear or will require different knowledge and skill sets. Workers of the future will need to be educated to be flexible, lifelong learners who are able to adapt a labor market influenced by new and changing technologies, an explosion of information, and competition for work that stretches beyond American shores.

America's schools were originally intended to ensure that all citizens were literate. The initial purpose for establishing a system of universal public education has long been obsolete. Americans must have the courage to realize that in order to remain a world power, we must institute change. American schools were instituted primarily to serve middle-class children. Children of the poor attended public schools, but were disadvantaged, owing to the fact that schools primarily reflected middle-class values and sensibilities.

Upper-class families were able to educate their children through the use of homeschooling with tutors, or by sending their children to private schools. With the economic conditions of today, more and more middle-class families are living at income standards that in more prosperous times were characteristic of families living in poverty. American schools are flooded with more children from single-parent homes than at any other time in history. Even when there are two parents in the household, normally both parents need to work, resulting in teachers spending more time with children than their own parents.

Education reform is possible, but it depends on what the nation is willing to do to achieve the necessary goals. Will America develop and pass effective educational laws aimed at creating viable solutions to the problems at hand? Or will America continue to develop laws, such as No Child Left Behind, that operate under the fallacy that 100 percent of our students will be proficient in identified subjects at prescribed periods of time? The bar for education should be set higher, but there have to be exceptions and differentiated goals in order to effectively accommodate all the differences among teachers, students, administrators, and school cultures.

CONSOLIDATING COMPONENTS OF POSITIVE SCHOOL CHANGE

Effecting school change requires that multiple factors that potentially impact a school's desire to engage in reform be considered. A detailed study should be conducted of school processes, procedures, and even the school's culture, in order to determine how these seemingly isolated school components can be consolidated to form positive and lasting change. In some instances, adjustments or modifications will be necessary, and in other instances elimination of the "way things have always been done" will be required, in order to make room for change that supports a new vision of what the school can and should be.

Effective Leadership for Change

Administrators cannot lead school reform by simply talking about change; they must lead by example, not by words. Administrators need to exemplify the type of commitment and work ethic they would like to see in their faculty and staff. If an administrator is nonchalant and lackadaisical about the school-reform process, then the staff will follow suit. Administrators need to be excited about the possibility of increasing student achievement and ensuring no child is left behind in their school district.

When the school district wants to implement a school reform effort, they must take baby steps. Attempting to implement too many initiatives simultaneously can be a counterproductive endeavor. This is not to say that it cannot be done, but the viability of such actions must be considered. The availability of resources or a school's capacity for implementing school-reform initiatives should be assessed at the outset.

In a school-reform effort, every decision and action must have intent. Administrators must prioritize suggested changes to ensure success and sustainability. Administrators will implement change based on the needs of their individual schools, then collect and analyze data to ensure the changes are occurring, and determine if they are related directly or indirectly to the reform. Too many amendments for school reform can cause frustration among the faculty and staff. It is important to make as few changes as possible, and implement the changes gradually.

As unscientific and unreliable as it may seem sometimes, it may be beneficial to follow gut instincts when making decisions concerning the viability of educational change. When reflecting upon the efforts of the school, the best barometer is each individual's evaluation of their performance compared to their potential. If, when attempting to implement an educational change, all members of the staff have done all they can to ensure the actions have been carried out correctly, the resulting effect on academic performance must be accepted.

Intuition also comes into play during the hiring process. If an administrator is interviewing a potential administrative or instructional candidate who is well qualified for the position, and feels that the candidate is not a good fit for the organization, the administrator should trust their instincts. Administrators sometimes find themselves needing to hire someone quickly, and may hire a person in spite of instinctual objections. If those objections prove to be correct, it would be in the best interest of the school not to renew the contract for a second year. It is the administrator's responsibility to ensure that faculty and staff can work together.

There is no point in implementing changes that will not affect student learning positively. Parents, students, and community members should be able to trust and respect the team of teachers and staff assembled by the administrator. Without strong student-teacher relationships and school-community partnerships, little will come of planned reform (Cole, 2010). Administrators often underestimate the human need to be valued and respected for their efforts and sacrifices (National Center for Education Statistics, 2010).

A key job function of administrators is to serve as the instructional leader for their school or district. The bulk of an administrator's time should be spent visiting classrooms to better aid teachers in the way of reform, and to reduce stress teachers may feel about the reform plan. Administrators should be well versed in current trends in the areas of curriculum and instruction, and should keep themselves abreast of the latest research.

Managing the day-to-day operations of their school is simply not enough; nor can administrators totally delegate the job of instructional leader to their assistant principals. In the eyes of a central office and the school board, the lead administrator is accountable for the academic performance of students and the instructional effectiveness of their teachers, making the importance of classroom visitation paramount (Margolis & Nagel, 2006).

The Importance of Collegial Trust

Many educators and administrator are "type A" personalities, meaning they like to have control over every action in their classroom or school. Too much control can be detrimental, however. Sometimes educators and administrators have to learn to trust others when school reform is taking place. To work effectively as a team, all of the team members must trust the others to complete the tasks assigned to them correctly and efficiently. In order to learn to trust people, one must learn to listen, and in order be a good listener, one has to have patience. In any effective relationship or partnership, trust, patience, and communication are the keys to success.

Administrators or teachers who disagree with the educational changes should give the reform the benefit of the doubt. Subordinates not in a position to influence decisions should make every effort to support the reform. It is human to resist change, and fear of the unknown sometimes makes teachers and administrators apprehensive about the changes being implemented. Most school officials are targeting the same goal as educators: the success of all students through effective learning (Brooks, Hughes & Brooks, 2008).

Involving the Community

Another effective tool in implementing school reform is to build a grassroots approach to education. The grassroots approach can have the most permanent effect on school reform, because it mobilizes members of communities who would not otherwise have become involved in the educational process. The community can become a school's biggest support system. Many community members, given the appropriate encouragement and support, will volunteer and contribute to the education of the youth in their community (Bilby & Charles Stewart Mott Foundation, 2002).

The Cost of Change

A major mistake is to table educational-reform efforts because of lack of funds. Since children are America's most precious commodity and the focus of the nation's educational system, the lack of funding is no excuse to forgo reform efforts. Many school-reform efforts are cost-effective and can be implemented by resourceful educators. When there is a lack of money, reform is contingent upon the faith and commitment level of the faculty and staff. Money should not be wasted on model programs and unsubstantiated trends. Reform groups will have to work diligently and efficiently to implement the chosen reform efforts properly and effectively.

When school reform is needed and schools have limited resources, spending money on curriculum can be intimidating. The curriculum chosen will need to be a good fit for both teachers *and* students. Math and reading should be of first concern, because they are the building blocks for future success, and are observed closely by NCLB evaluators. If students can show success in these two areas, the positive results usually trickle down to other subject areas.

Teachers' professional development is a key factor for successful school reform. When looking at reform budgets, it is important to set aside money to hire teachers with the ability to create and teach in-service professional-development programs. The ability to train the staff and educators internally will save the school money, and will give the teacher/expert a feeling of usefulness.

A teacher with thirty years of experience and a demonstrated ability to obtain amazing results from her specific teaching strategies might create a professional-development seminar to share expertise. This saves the school an enormous amount of money, and saves the administrator the trouble of hiring a consultant. Another low-cost/no-cost option is to hire professors from neighboring colleges and universities to provide professional-development services to a district as a form of community service or to fulfill requirements to obtain or maintain tenure.

Another effective way to maximize a limited budget is to prioritize what the school needs most. In many cases, schools choose to purchase technology for the classroom. Not only is technology used to engage students in lessons every day, it is a critical skill students will need to develop in order to excel in today's society.

When schools decide to spend money on technology, they invest in students' and faculty's ability to keep up with the ever-changing world around them. Our children are digital natives who have been raised to embrace technology. Schools lacking in this area should research and consider purchasing technologies that demonstrate potential for fostering academic achievement (Marks, 2009).

Allowing Time for Change

When attempting to respond to problems, many school districts panic and try to deal with the problem immediately, instead of stopping to assess the situation. Sometimes, making a decision too quickly leaves room for errors and lapses in judgment. Many of the problems school districts face will work themselves out if they give themselves enough time to evaluate if there truly is a problem.

Unfortunately, not all problems will work themselves out, causing administrators to use their professional judgment to decide if action is needed. If, after some time, there is little to no change, administrators might first try noninvasive interventions and then move to more invasive interventions. After amendments are made, the administration should continue to monitor the progress of the students. If there is still little to no change, a more structured reform might be required. When implementing school reform, it is important to remember that change sometimes causes a situation to get worse before it gets better.

Educators sometimes feel stress when the word "change" is bandied about. They must promote the sense that the reform plan was thoroughly thought out and time is needed to analyze the plan's effectiveness. Administrators are leaders, and must exhibit confidence and control. If a problem still exists after a reasonable amount of time, the reform plan should be amended. The emendations should then be communicated to the educational staff, implemented, and the results analyzed. This process should be repeated until effective change is observed.

Premature Contentment

One of the main impediments to successful educational change is complacency. When a district experiences significant success in school reform, it may become complacent, and fail to continue collecting data and adjusting the plan as necessary. If the reform is not continually implemented, the school district may revert to former ineffective practices. How the district responds to success, as well as to failure, is a good indicator of whether or not it has the capacity to sustain any successes.

School districts usually respond in one of two ways. The first is to focus on sustaining growth, which is at the heart of all educational change. When school faculty and staff have the will to sustain school reform, existing positive attitudes give the school district a fighting chance at continuous success. An alternate response however is complacency among district personnel who are given to basking in initial successes.

Many times schools see success and allow additional efforts to become mired in stagnation. The faculty and staff adopt an attitude of complacency, not willing to rock the boat in a successful environment. This in turn stimulates a cyclical and pernicious pattern of mediocrity which continues until an individual or group calls attention to overwhelming lapses in judgment concerning sustaining growth (Dawdidziak, 2010).

There appears to be no universally successful school reform. Education leaders have to determine what holds the most promise for their own school systems. Using researched-based strategies and time-honored traditions, school districts can develop their own formulas for school reform to meet the unique needs of their students, teachers, and administrators. Too often, Americans get in the habit of following the latest trend or fad, believing that what works for others will undoubtedly work for everyone. Administrators will need to choose educational trends that meet the needs of their particular students.

ADDRESSING PROBLEMS

Positive change can be achieved in any district. Building the capacity to sustain educational change, however, is difficult. Administrators focus on aspects of education they can change, and disregard insignificant issues. The desire and knowledge to effect change should be the cornerstones for school reform. Administrators who possess both qualities are more likely to succeed when implementing change.

Improving the ability of schools to sustain reform relies on the analysis of the data collected from agreed-upon evaluations. Teachers need effective professional development for any new or innovative mode of assessment that they will be required to administer. In order for continuous improvement to be possible, effective assessment has to be a catalyst. When administrators analyze data and formulate a decision as to whether school reform was successful and sustained, they must take into account all of the evidence that can be analyzed.

Not all evidence can be collected from standardized tests. Data can be collected from classroom observations, authentic evaluations/learning, and student surveys. When analyzing the problems that may occur when implementing school reform, administrators should consider outside influences on the school. Situations in children's homes sometimes create a distraction in the classroom.

Teachers having to address nonschool issues lose valuable teaching time, which has a negative impact on the learning process. Although schools work with children for a considerable amount of time during the day, these children also have to go back to their families and communities in the afternoon. Children today are faced with a multitude of issues once they leave the school building. Even in middle-class and upper-middle-class homes, family situations may not always be ideal.

In order to learn, all children must have their basic needs met. For students, it becomes difficult to concentrate on schoolwork when they are dealing with the effects of physical or verbal abuse, homelessness, or poor nutrition. These outside factors are not directly addressed in assessments, but should be considered when analyzing standardized-test data. If problems arise or improvements are minimal, stakeholders need to identify the problems hindering reform. Once the causes of problems have been ascertained, school-reform teams can determine what research-based practices and how much capital will be needed to achieve their goals.

Communication with, and the support of, faculty and staff are required before beginning the long process of school reform. Disagreement is fine, and can be constructive, but in order to continuously improve, the majority of a district's faculty and staff have to support reform. District leaders have to work hard at building consensus, but a dissenting minority cannot be allowed to impede the improvement processes.

Employees feeling stressed about upcoming changes will need to trust and respect the administrator leading the reform efforts. The process of consensus building is difficult. Administrators cannot simply deal with discontent by ignoring it and asserting their authority; they must make a conscientious effort to clearly articulate their vision of successful school reform.

Malcontents should be given a time to express their fears and frustrations, to improve communication between educators and administration. There may be times when a teacher feels upset over a diminutive detail that can easily be cleared up. Administrators should use caution to ensure all complaints are stated in a professional manner so as not to discourage others. When taking criticism from concerned educators, administrators must recognize genuine concerns and fear, and consider all suggestions. School reform is about fostering continuous improvement, which in turn will boost the academic performance of the American youth.

Administrators must also be cognizant that teachers throughout America already feel overwhelmed by the constant demands that are asked of them. The ominous cloud of standardized assessments is enough to stress a teacher. However, school leaders can alleviate some of this stress by aligning reform goals with state and federal standards. The connection between the two sets of standards should alleviate some of the stress on teachers and administrators.

Not only are teachers held accountable for their students' standardized test scores—administrators are also accountable. By combining the efforts of both administrators and educators, the pedagogical materials and curriculum will be appropriately laid out for teachers and students. Teachers will know what they are expected to teach, and students will know what they are expected to learn.

District leaders must rely on student-achievement evidence to determine the effectiveness of school reform. School districts may formulate their own theories concerning why the school reform implemented has not been effective. These may include incorrectly identifying the problem; identifying the problem correctly but choosing a strategy that does not address that problem; identifying the problem correctly and choosing the best strategy, only to fail in properly implementing the reform. Educators, parents, communities, and other stakeholders must engage in reform because something needs to change about our educational system.

Chapter 4

Family and Parental Involvement in Education

THE CRUCIAL ROLE OF THE FAMILY

Understanding the deep-rooted importance of family and parental involvement in education and its effect on the performance of a child requires recognizing the fact that parents are children's first teachers. Home is the first school, and as such, is the place where children learn an abundance of skills, knowledge, and attitudes, some of which supports what is taught in schools. In general, until age eighteen, children spend most of their time with parents and other family members (Walberg, 1984).

Children enjoy a better environment for learning and education in cases where family members get involved with their children's education. They tend to have higher educational achievement, and tend to perform better on exams. They miss fewer school days and tend to be more conscientious about completing school-related work outside of school. Conversely, children whose families are not as attentive toward their school experiences are often unable to compete academically with peers, their attendance is less regular, and they are less likely to graduate from high school (Funkhouser & Gonzales, 1997).

Because of the positive impact parent and family involvement in education has on the performance of children, schools often try to encourage parents and family members to increase their participation in the educational process. Many researchers, educational reformers, and politicians have tried to increase parental and family involvement in the educational system.

There are a number of obstacles that interfere with parents taking on a pivotal role in school-related issues and activities. In order to increase partnership of parents with schools, schools must create an environment that offers enough incentives and support for parents to take an active part in the educational process. Schools cannot expect that all parents and family members will increase their involvement with the educational system on their own. The total school staff, to include teachers, other school personnel, maintenance staff, and administrators, must work together to develop an environment that encourages parents to ask questions and share their feedback with school personnel. Some parents will need to be invited to schools, and learn to view schools as places where they may seek advice, receive suggestions on any number of school/student-related issues, and have their input and thoughts welcomed.

Some parents may be dissuaded from getting involved with what they perceive as a group of close-knit educational professionals who engage in language and practices meant to exclude parents from the work of educational systems. Schools often create an environment where it becomes difficult for teachers and parents to stand together for children and together help them carve out a better future.

Various governmental policies try to reduce the gap between teachers and parents so that they may come together to help students. The No Child Left Behind Act, for example, requires districts and schools to operate in a transparent manner, communicate with parents and other outside stakeholders, and share information and ideas that will lead to increased involvement of parents in the learning process.

NCLB explicitly requires that State Educational Agencies (SEAs) and Local Educational Agencies (LEAs) receiving federal funds have written parental-involvement policies. These policies describe how parents can be involved in the planning and review of educational programs. In order to fulfill local need, the act suggests integrating parental involvement plans with schools on local levels. Another important principle is to empower parents by providing them with training in valuable practices that may help their children achieve better academic results.

States and local school districts must also make sure parents understand state standards and assessments, so that parents can be more involved in monitoring the progress of their children. Schools are required to make sure that communications with parents are in language and formats that are understandable to parents. NCLB expands parental rights by allowing for more parental choice in the education of their children by increasing their public school options and by allowing for additional educational opportunities for eligible children in low-performing schools (Parental Involvement, Department of Education, 2004).

WHAT IS PARENTAL INVOLVEMENT?

Education leaders, teachers, and researchers have found that constructive communication between parents and teachers can increase the participation of parents in school activities. This formal participation offers a preferable degree of transparency in schooling and the education system, and allows parents to understand the requirements and expectations of the students by the school. Parents may make better use of such constructive meetings and communications with teachers to learn how to create a learning environment for children in their home (Desimone, 1999).

According to the Section 9101(32) of the Elementary and Secondary Education Act (ESEA), parental involvement in the education system can be defined as "the frequent participation of parents in a two-way and evocative or consequential communication with school staff about the subjects related with academic learning of their children and other school activities." The ESEA confirms that parents are an invaluable part of their children's learning process.

If parents are encouraged to take an active part in their children's learning process and extracurricular activities, better achievement outcomes will result. The ESEA notes that parents share responsibility with schools for the academic growth of children and need to be included in decision-making processes at appropriate levels. Schools should encourage parents to become members of school advisory committees designed to improve the education system to better serve the needs of children (Parental Involvement, Department of Education, 2004).

The benefits of parental involvement are not confined to education. When parents show valid concern about the overall improvement of their children and their well-being, children tend to perform well in their personal life, which increases their confidence levels. This increased self-confidence promotes their ability to learn well at school, and they perform better and achieve greater success. Often, when a child fails to perform well at school, teachers blame the child and his or her parents. The role of parents in children's school success or failure is beyond doubt.

Teachers need to recognize their own responsibility toward the academic success of all students as well. By blaming parents, families, and communities for low-performing students, teachers create an environment of mistrust that can be harmful to the overall school system. In addition, teachers are equally responsible for the failure of students, as it is their professional duty to help children succeed in the educational process and achieve better results. Teachers should realize the importance of adopting an attitude of shared responsibility between themselves and the parents of poor-performing children.

SCHOOL-HOME CONNECTIONS

Children from low socioeconomic backgrounds often fail to perform as well as students from upper or middle socioeconomic backgrounds. Low socioeconomic parents often fail to provide an environment conducive to the development of learning skills and good study habits. They often lack basic social skills, and find it difficult to negotiate or compromise. Their children do not function well in the school environments. Since they find it difficult to help their children, low socioeconomic parents feel responsible for their children's failure. Due to their own deficiencies, they tend to avoid schools and teachers.

Many teachers interpret the lack of contact from parents as a lack of interest. As a result, children in this situation suffer from a lack of focused attention from both parents and teachers. This predicament leads to dire consequences for the child's learning experience, and he or she may start to avoid classes or school. In order to reduce absenteeism and improve the performance of these students, teachers must find ways to reach out to and develop trusting relationships with parents. Parents who feel they will be judged by teachers will resist situations where they anticipate criticism and derision for their shortcomings.

Children need attention from all adults in their lives. Both teacher and parent will need to work together to ensure that the child will receive the social and academic supports necessary to turn around their attitude and behaviors toward school. Additionally, schools and other public institutions can play a major role in improving the social and family environments of students.

For example, the results of a study on the impact of initiatives taken by schools to promote a friendly environment for responsible fatherhood among black noncustodial fathers indicated that proper encouragement and other required services, along with student-friendly strategies, helped in improving the environment of students in their homes (Levine, Murphy & Wilson, 1998). Home-school connections that focus parents' attentions on the social and educational needs of children is an essential part of parental involvement.

HOW TO PROMOTE PARENT-SCHOOL PARTNERSHIPS

It is beyond any doubt that low-performing schools would benefit from developing strong parent-school partnerships to help students achieve better results and higher grades on school examinations (Adams & Forsyth, 2006). However, it is not always easy to promote such a culture of shared responsibility. Schools may face difficulty in attaining an efficient collaborative framework within the school groups, which include teachers, parents, students, and the administration.

Generally, education and school leaders try to generate a social framework that will help teachers, administrators, and parents solve differences in a peaceful and supportive manner. Parents and teachers must work together to create a collaborative relationship. Overall improvement of student performance can be the outcome of improved relationships between teachers and parents.

The Bureaucratic Nature of Schools and Parental Involvement

Education leaders can encourage parental involvement by improving the structural environment of schools that directly affects teachers, administrators, students, and parents. Historically, American culture has tried to promote a locally inspired, community-based school structure; however, most of the calls for decentralization of schools and school district systems have failed to remove the bureaucratic nature of schools. This includes a structural division of responsibilities, a strict set of laws and regulations, and hierarchical control over the functionality and operation of schools.

Almost all public schools in the United States feature specific bureaucratic characteristics. It is a general belief that schools, like any other public organization, cannot work properly without a bureaucratic structure. The bureaucratic nature of schools offers an excellent framework for effectual organizational activities. Bureaucracy existing in schools can prove to be detrimental to the performance and initialization of progressive operations (Hoy & Sweetland, 2000).

Bureaucratic systems often create barriers that prevent teachers from developing effective student-teacher relationships and discourage parents from taking part in helping students develop their learning skills (Hoy, Blazovsky & Newland, 1983). Researchers have found that centralized schooling systems under the burden of stern bureaucracies also cause alienation of teachers and obstruct student development (Bohte, 2001).

Other studies have revealed that the bureaucratic system supports teachers, school administrators, and parents to collaborate with each other (Jackson & Schuler, 1985), and helps teachers control and use their expertise to guide students effectively. Smith and Meier (1994) propose that a reduction in bureaucracy would increase administrative tasks among teachers, which would then have a negative impact on their performance.

The bureaucratic structure of schools can work in both ways. It is very difficult for an educational organization to work properly without a bureaucratic system. At the same time, the bureaucratic system may obstruct the proper functioning of the organization. To reduce such hindrances, it is necessary to formulate a bureaucratic system that may help the schooling system to achieve effective teaching and learning processes.

The bureaucratic system should be based on flexible formulae that will guide the teachers, administrators, and parents in promoting the learning skills of students and help them achieve better results. The centralized or hierarchical authority of schools can be used to implement these supportive regulations and policies to enhance parental involvement. On the other hand, the wrong set of policies and lack of flexibility or coerciveness of regulations may harm the process of teaching and learning (Hoy, 2003).

The Importance of Trust between Schools and Families

Another important factor that can help schools promote parental involvement and their attitude toward sharing responsibility for the performance of their children is the element of trust within different active groups, namely, teachers and parents. A healthy and congenial school environment, with an enabling and flexible structure, can help develop trust among teachers (Hoy, Sabo, & Barnes, 1996).

Impressive student performances also increase trust between teachers and parents, and help the administration improve the culture of parental involvement in education. In general, parents who are supported by regular interactive meetings with teachers often show greater trust levels in teacher-parent relationships (Adams & Christenson, 1998; Christenson & Adams, 2000). Schools can create an environment favorable for the development of teacher-parent relationships by sharing the responsibility of improving learning processes and the academic performance of children.

The goal of enhancing parental involvement can be achieved by creating teacher-parent collaborative decision-making activities that will also enhance the trust level between these two active groups. However, the administrative groups of schools often ignore the requirement of teacher-parent collaborative decision-making activities. Many schools that claim to support collaborative decision-making patterns hold complete decision-making authority in their own hands, which can reduce the positive influence of collaborative decision-making patterns (Malen & Ogawa, 1988).

Effective collaboration is characterized by decision-making opportunities by both teachers and parents at the school and classroom levels (Tschannen-Moran, 2001). The collaborative process can be instructional, including teachers and parents; or it can be structural, requiring agreement among administrators, teachers, and parents. Education reformers have found that it is not very difficult to implement instructional collaborative decision-making processes. Structural or managerial decision-making processes are much more difficult to implement, as parents have minimal influence over managerial decisions.

Parental involvement in schools and the education system can be increased through properly formulated bureaucratic policies that avoid any obstructions to parent-teacher collaboration, and strengthen trust levels within teacher and parent groups. The structural administration of schools can also help in promoting teacher-parent collaboration, supporting the goal of improving children's performance and educational skills by allowing parents significant influence over school and classroom decisions.

ROLE OF PUBLIC SCHOOLS IN ADVANCEMENT OF COMMUNITIES AND CHILD WELFARE

Public schools can play a significant role in the general improvement in their respective communities, and can operate as a major platform for enhancing child welfare in the community. Social reformers, politicians, and educational leaders have utilized various initiatives in the past to strengthen the relationship between schools and communities to achieve the common purpose of improving child welfare, and learning and developmental conditions for all children.

These initiatives suffer obstructions similar to those experienced by schools when they are focused on the work of educating. Detrimental poverty, racial and ethnic differences, socioeconomic differences, inactive families, low or no parental involvement, and insufficient political willingness and support for improvement all impact the efforts to advance the welfare of children. Any of these factors may obstruct the learning process of a child, and also may make it difficult to enhance the child's overall well-being.

Historically, schools have played a significant role in helping communities evaluate issues concerning child welfare and eliminating situations that impede children's progress. During the Great Migration of 1880–1924, a huge number of impoverished children moved into the schools of American cities. The majority of immigrants were poor and undereducated.

Social reformers and policymakers pressured public schools to work toward improving children's lives. Many schools devoted themselves not only to educating poor children, but also to providing them with proper nutrition and other amenities required for healthy living. Teachers devoted their time to teaching English to immigrant students. Many schools offered nonacademic services, including school nurses, gyms, playgrounds, and midday meals or lunches for poor students.

Some schools also started offering night classes for parents to help them learn English and other important parental skills that could assist them in caring for their children. Many schools encouraged teachers to improve school-parental ties by visiting students' homes and instructing parents on how to offer a better learning environment for children at home. However, such initiatives faced a certain degree of opposition from parents who were not ready to leave their ethnic and racial identities.

A major hurdle was the economic impracticability of sustaining such child welfare activities. Most of these initiatives were criticized as "socialistic," but many children enjoyed the benefits of programs intended to improve the overall situations of children and their families. Children not only experienced better living conditions; they also gained many opportunities to rise out of poverty. As a result, more immigrant children started coming to school regularly.

Ever-increasing fiscal burdens on schools created by child well-being initiatives caused political opposition and social criticism. In order to reduce costs, many state governments withdrew funding for social services offered by public schools. As a result, the upsurge in underprivileged children experienced in the late 1980s and early 1990s was met with reduced and nonexistent services emanating from schools.

The depressed socioeconomic conditions of underprivileged families were responsible for undermining the learning process and academic achievement of many children. Teachers again tried to find innovative ways to help students and tried to support the system of local public schools by taking part in improving social conditions and creating better learning opportunities (Crowson & Boyd, 1993).

Social reformers began making better use of schools to improve socioeconomic situations in different communities. Many full-service school programs were introduced to bolster the relationship between schools and communities, with the main objective to improve situations and provide better environments for children, their parents, and the community overall (Lugg & Boyd, 1993).

Most of these experimental policies for child welfare and social reform with the help of schools suggested that the efficiency of school-community relationships and their positive impact could be maximized by increasing parental involvement in schools. By encouraging parents to take an active role in the education system, policymakers tried to improve school services by making schools more accessible to parents. This also helped schools improve their relationship with parents, and helped them improve student performance (McGrath & Kuriloff, 1999).

Many researchers set out to substantiate analytically that parental involvement strengthened the school-community relationship by improving social conditions of students. Educational researchers suggested that parental involvement could positively improve the academic achievement of children. Studies revealed that those students whose parents were involved with their learning process were performing better, attended classes more regularly, and scored higher on school examinations than students who were lacking parental support and involvement in their learning.

Studies also suggested that low-performing schools could help failing students by trying to engage parents in the educational process of students. Researchers confirmed that schools could help students who had learning disabilities, or who belong to families from low socioeconomic backgrounds by interacting with and training their parents to help these students with their learning and schooling processes (Floyd, 1998).

FROM TRADITIONAL INITIATIVES TO THE OPEN SCHOOL SYSTEM

In order to increase parental involvement, many schools use strategies such as inviting parents for open meetings with other parents, arranging social programs, asking parents to volunteer during school social and sports events, issuing regular newsletters, connecting with parents through phone calls, and arranging for parent-teacher conferences. These strategies may seem manipulative, and often fail to offer to involve parents in the educational system. Still, school administrators and teachers may use these types of initiatives to stand as parental involvement, while excluding parents from serious decision-making processes.

Often school administrations do not allow parents to raise their concerns about ineffective administrative policies, substandard teaching, and faulty grading systems. Regulated initiatives by schools to involve parents in the learning process of their kids often remain lopsided and ineffective because such activities restrict parents from interacting with the education system in a meaningful way.

School administrators and teachers often exploit regular parent-school collaboration methods by providing limited and biased information. They rely on parents being unquestioning and passive, and believe that only education professionals can truly improve student learning. Often they ignore the rights and abilities of parents to make decisions, as well as the ability of parents to contribute information and suggestions for improving the schooling process. Additionally, some administrators are unwilling to make accommodations for parents unable to take part in regular parent-teacher meetings and similar activities because of their work schedules.

Many schools do not engage in unprincipled measures to restrict parental involvement. Most genuinely value the input parents potentially provide. In order to improve parent-teacher collaboration, many have experimented with innovative ideas and have open-door policies that allow individuals to observe school processes. Parents can visit at any time to scrutinize teaching methods, and how their children perform within the school structure. Such initiatives demand a flexible structural bureaucracy that allows parents to play a meaningful part in the decision-making process (Crowson, 1992).

EFFECTS OF PARENTAL EDUCATION

Parent education is used as a vehicle to encourage parental involvement in education. Parent education can be helpful in improving the home environment for children whose parents have a poor educational background. Schools offer parent education programs in order to enable parents to take positive action as advocates for school-parent collaboration and toward participatory decision-making in the educational process. Parent education programs try to improve the ability of parents to become actively involved in the education of their children.

In order to increase participation in education programs of parents whose native language is not English, parent education facilitators often provide instruction in the parent's native language. All relevant information is translated into the parent's native language. If the parent, for whatever reason, is unable to read this information, facilitators are expected to deliver the information and instructions orally (LEP, 2010). In the end, programs such as these are intended to encourage parents to share responsibilities with schools by acting as resident teachers and better nurturers in the home for their children.

Parent education programs have proven to be successful in improving parenting skills, as well as parents' ability to teach and coach their children. A model parent education program was designed at the University of Houston's Graduate School of Social Work and College of Education, in order to stimulate interest in school involvement among parents of students attending a low-performing school in the Houston school district.

The majority of the students were from families living in low socioeconomic situations, and all were black. Many black families live in poverty because of the failure of noncustodial fathers to provide for their estranged wives or partners, and their children. A large percentage of noncustodial black fathers are unwilling to take responsibility for proper nourishment and quality education for their children. As a result, many black children are living in fatherless, single-parent homes (Angel & Angel, 1993), and the parental attention to the child's education is solely the responsibility of the custodial parent.

The parent or parents of these children were invited to participate in an experimental parent education program that was designed to emphasize improving parenting skills in a specific cultural community. Extra efforts were made to create a trustworthy environment for parents, one in which there was parity between parents and researchers. At the beginning of the program, each participating parent was interviewed, so that researchers could learn more about their specific apprehensions and needs.

This detailed solicitation of information made parents realize that they were responsible for the educational programs at their schools, and they subsequently felt more confident about being actively involved (Norwood et al., 1997). During the parent education program, parents were encouraged to share their experience and knowledge about raising their children, and help them learn various life skills, including skills that could be helpful in an academic environment.

The program established the significance of the parents' knowledge base, and the value of parents sharing their knowledge and experience. The researchers were also able to demonstrate that by initiating two-way informational sharing processes, school practices would be enhanced as the transfer of information proceeded to parents from schools and from parents to schools.

This six-month program helped parents learn new parenting skills focused on improving the learning environment at home, and producing better learning skills in children. After six more months, researchers evaluated results and found that children of participating parents performed significantly better on standardized tests in mathematics and language. The Houston parent education program and its success confirmed that school administrations could greatly improve school and student performance by offering parent education programs that address the specific needs and apprehensions of impoverished minority parents.

Parents can be encouraged to become involved if their cultural, linguistic, racial, and socioeconomic environment is respected. This experiment also confirmed that schools could perform better by promoting two-way information sharing between parents and teachers, and by giving parents enough authority to influence the decision-making process of teachers and administration (Norwood et al., 1997).

SCHOOL-BASED MANAGEMENT TO PROMOTE SCHOOL-COMMUNITY RELATIONSHIPS

School-based management is another means of increasing parental involvement in the educational process, for the purpose of helping students achieve better results. Proponents of this approach believe it is better for schools to create a managerial group that possesses most of the decision-making power to influence the learning process of students at schools, rather than this power residing solely with the school principal.

The managerial group or committee should include teachers, parents, administrators, educational reformers, and community leaders. This school-based management strategy is based on the notion that people who are close to students can make better policy decisions to help real students perform better and achieve good results. School-based management is meant to improve in-class and in-school decisions that may positively influence students and help them increase self-confidence.

Such programs also increase the confidence level of teachers, making them feel more comfortable and able to help students properly (Smith & Piele, 1996). Teachers may also offer extracurricular activities to increase parents' participation in the education of their children. Such activities help parents from different socioeconomic, cultural, racial, and religious backgrounds come together on a common platform and share experiences and information. These activities also succeed in increasing the interest of students in school, and encourage their parents to influence them to attend school regularly (Alspaugh, 1998).

PARENTAL INVOLVEMENT PROGRAMS

It is difficult to suggest that any particular activities and programs will universally help low-performing schools improve and enhance student performance. Some school districts offer a higher degree of freedom for school management to try to reach students and their parents at a personal level, while others do not offer enough. Just as Tyack (1974) refuted the notion that there was one best system of education, so we must understand that different methods can be used to involve parents. Several programs have helped establish better collaborative relationships with parents. We will look at some of the features of these.

The basic idea of a parental involvement program is to provide many opportunities to increase mutually beneficial communication between school personnel and parents. Schools should encourage open and honest communication, and adopt an open school system to encourage school-community relations. Parental involvement programs should consider the linguistic, ethnic, religious, and racial identities of parents, and explore the apprehensions and requirements of parents facing specific problems such as physical disabilities, learning disabilities, poverty, single parenthood, joint families, and families with working parents.

Teachers should organize extracurricular activities that offer a practical platform for communication and relationship development between teachers and parents, and between parents of different students. Parents should be allowed to share their experiences, and to advise the school system and other parents about how to solve various parenting and schooling issues. Schools and social reformers should try to persuade politicians and bureaucrats to support the local public school system, as it is the primary platform for providing skilled human resources for an improved local, regional, and national economy.

In order to help students in poor communities, schools should try to implement stable reform programs. School authorities should be very careful when offering attractive programs for students to increase enrollment and reduce absenteeism—they need to ensure the sustainability of these programs. While school bureaucracy may create obstructions to implementation of student and community development programs, school administrations can often mitigate various problems.

School administrators must generate strategies to make these programs more viable and effective. In many instances, schools may fail to offer open and constraint-free conditions for teachers and parents to collaborate easily. The bureaucratic system can help by institutionalizing regulations intended to encourage mutual trust and collaboration between parents and teachers. School authorities need to remain flexible and innovative as they seek to implement the best possible set of policies for their unique district needs.

Strict bureaucratic rules may help school authorities keep things under control, but such rigidity will certainly decrease the potential teacher participation. It will also reduce the chance of parents voluntarily taking responsibility for their children's behavior and performance in schools. Conversely, if school authorities offer significant decision-making power for teachers and parents to improve classroom situations, teachers will feel more relaxed and able to influence students to perform better. Parents will also opt to become more involved in helping their children do better at schools (Adams & Forsyth, 2006).

FEDERAL SCHOOL-REFORM PROGRAMS TO PROMOTE PARENTAL INVOLVEMENT

Apart from overseeing practices and programs initiated by school authorities and state governments, the U.S. Department of Education also offers useful resources and research studies to be used by school reformers, education leaders, social reformers, school authorities, teachers, and parents to help them implement successful parental involvement programs. The U.S. Department of Education produces a television series, *Education News Parents Can Use*, which offers excellent tips and advice for parents about ways to ensure better performance by their children at school and promote stronger academic learning skills.

This monthly television series airs every third Tuesday during the school year. The program is aimed at helping parents by offering them tips, suggestions, instructions, and tools to help them take a more responsible and effective role in their children's educational experience. In order to help schools, state and local education agencies, teacher associations, parents, community leaders, and social organizations organize programs for developing parental involvement in the school system, the federal Department of Education offers volumes of published material concerning various education development issues.

The Institute of Education Sciences, which is affiliated with the Department of Education, is conducting a continuous project, What Works Clearinghouse (WWC). WWC offers information for school authorities, school-based management committees, teacher associations, and parent groups to answer some basic questions about the ways to offer better learning environment at schools, and what measures to take to help all children learn to read and write.

This program offers influential evidence gathered through the results of highly professional scientific research studies, directed toward education leaders, school reformers, policymakers, and school authorities. A primary goal of WWC is to help all educational stakeholders make better decisions and develop more effective practices for parental involvement programs and activities.

The Institute of Education Sciences also offers funds through the Southwest Regional Educational Laboratory to implement programs of the National Center for Family and Community Connections with Schools. These programs conduct studies into practices that improve educational processes, and help students achieve better educational skills. The National Center offers research-based information for use in implementing programs that will offer collaborative platforms on which to build close relationships among schools, teachers, parents, and communities (US Department of Education, 2004).

ROLE OF SEAs AND LEAs IN PROMOTING PARENTAL INVOLVEMENT

The success of various parental development programs and policies offered by policymakers depends on the ability of State Education Agencies (SEAs) and Local Education Agencies (LEAs) to work together with a congenial and collaborative attitude. In order to establish and sustain an environment of trust among teachers, school authorities, and parents in a school district, SEAs must remain in constant contact with LEAs, and LEAs must remain well connected with business owners and other community members.

When implementing parent education programs and other similar activities, local education authorities may wish to engage state authorities' assistance in attracting support from the business community for educational-reform programs. Positive relationships like these ensure that education reform, parent education programs, and parent involvement programs will attract sufficient funding to ensure success (Gordon & Louis, 2009).

The Elementary and Secondary Education Act outlines the function of SEAs in a number of school-reform efforts. SEAs, for example, are responsible for compiling and distributing high-quality evidential scientific research to LEAs and schools about best-in-class practices related to improving education. They are also responsible for disseminating information and research regarding parental involvement programs.

SEAs collaborate with LEAs to ensure consistent reporting of children's academic progress to parents, and distribute relevant school-improvement information to parents, public agencies, and the media. They examine the performance of different LEAs, identify low-performing LEAs and schools, and offer possible solutions and technical assistance to help LEAs change situations and conditions that contribute to subpar performance. Often this guidance strongly favors increasing parent participation to improve academic performance among students (US Department of Education, 2004).

The NCLB Act provides funding for LEAs to develop procedures, activities, and programs intended to increase the involvement of parents in schools and the education process. As mentioned earlier, all LEAs must develop written parental involvement policies that clarify expectations and the scope of participation of the LEA, schools, and parents. In order to maintain federal funds, a LEA's parental involvement policy must provide the opportunity for interested parents to work with their LEA to develop local educational plans and participate as part of the team that reviews the school's improvement over time.

LEAs, in turn, must provide technical support and other assistance to schools wishing to implement various activities promoting parental involvement. LEAs are required to review their parental involvement policies annually, with the reviewing team consisting of both educators and parents. During the policy review, LEA personnel and parents should try to identify obstructions that hinder the involvement of parents in the education process and offer suggestions to eliminate these hindrances.

LEAs are expected to further educational excellence by encouraging parents to participate in educational and extracurricular activities, and by informing parents about their right to know about the professional qualifications and performance of the children's teachers and other school personnel. LEAs also provide assistance to those parents who are not fluent in English and whose children find it difficult to learn because of linguistic differences (US Department of Education, 2004).

UNDERSTANDING PARENTAL INVOLVEMENT

When we discuss parental involvement in schools, we often concentrate on ways in which parental involvement can help schools perform better and how parents can help their children excel in learning. Another important factor to understand is the nature of impediments parents face in getting actively involved with the education system. It is a well-known fact that parental involvement can help students achieve success at schools. However, it is difficult to measure how much parental involvement is required of parents in order for them to help their children to improve their learning skills and performance.

Parental actions that obstruct the learning process and other educational goals are equally immeasurable. Comprehending the impact of parental involvement requires understanding deficiencies that reduce student performance, and providing parents with tools to diminish their effects. This same principle applies to understanding the ways schools, LEAs, and SEAs can encourage parental involvement in low-income communities (Gutman & McLoyd, 2000). Situations like these necessitate sensitivity to ethnicity, race, religious affiliation, linguistic challenges, single parenthood, and familial characteristics.

Parents are often influenced by their ethnic background when trying to help their children improve academically. It is imperative that school personnel understand the importance of family's cultural characteristics in the educational process. Schools should structure parental involvement programs that take advantage of the strong qualities individual parents bring to the schooling process, as a means for promoting improved relations between parents and the school. Interactions between parents and school personnel are meant to provide information and assistance to both the school and parents.

It is important to monitor how parents act on the instructions, information, and advice offered through such programs. Due to various cultural differences, some families may succeed in obtaining the maximum possible benefit of such interactional programs, while other families may fail to utilize these opportunities. Another factor to consider is the possibility of conflicts between parents' cultural and linguistic background, and the social, linguistic, and cultural values existing in the school.

Schools often promote common ideals of a capitalistic culture in American society and, in doing so, present the impoverished, minorities, the disabled, and immigrants as inferior (Delgado-Gaitan, 1996; Villenas & Dehyle, 1999). The success of parental involvement programs often depends on reaching parents living within different political, economic, cultural, and social realities. In order to help parents make better use of parental involvement programs, it is necessary to attend to these differences, and incorporate ways to meet the varied needs and expectations of parents within the parental involvement program.

The success of parental education and involvement programs depends on the ways parents can make use of their social, human, and financial resources to help their children perform better at school. Parents can also help their children improve their learning skills by providing attention to their children's studies and participating in meaningful collaboration with school personnel and authorities. Historically, schools have played a major part in improving social conditions. Collaboration between schools and parents can help alleviate the challenges facing students who are living in families that have a lower socioeconomic status. School reform will help our nation increase its skilled human resources. Policymakers must realize the importance of public schools and their role in achieving prosperity for our nation. Federal and state agencies have initiated various programs to improve the relationship between schools, parents, and communities. In order to increase parental involvement and reduce barriers that restrict parents from participating in the education system, it is essential to offer specific parent education for impoverished parents or parents with disabilities, so that they may learn better ways to boost their children's learning skills.

The value of parental involvement programs has been well established. Effective parent involvement programs are best achieved when the program originates with the study of the school community, and then proceeds to develop instruction, and provide advice and information that reflects the circumstances, needs, and potential contributions of families who are a part of the school community.

Schools must be prepared for the fact that one outcome of effective parental involvement programs will be the desire of parents to become partners in the decision-making process existing in schools. Thus, school personnel must possess a genuine belief that shared responsibility for multiple aspects of the educational enterprise will result in improved learning environments for children and youth.

Chapter 5

Community Engagement as an Impetus for School Reform

AN OVERVIEW OF PUBLIC-PRIVATE PARTNERSHIPS

Public-private partnerships have proven to be a popular solution to many public education challenges. The fact that they have been growing in popularity for decades suggests that relationships between public schools and private organizations are productive, but there is actually little evidence to support this view. Some scholars suggest increased civic and community engagement with schools as an alternative to these partnerships.

The National Commission on Excellence in Education's report, *A Nation at Risk* (1983), was the catalyst for an explosion in the number of public-private partnerships. Prior to 1983, only 17 percent of U.S. elementary and secondary schools had engaged in these activities, but by 1989, this participation had increased to as much as 40 percent (Marenda, 1989).

There were 140,000 partnerships between schools and businesses by 1991 (Rigden, 1991). Partners in Education (2000) estimated that there were several hundred thousand collaborations by the start of the new millennium, and private organizations had contributed around $2.4 billion to public schools. Despite these impressive statistics, there is not much in the way of empirical evidence to suggest that partnerships have had a positive impact on student learning. In fact, critics argue that they hamper democratic localism and civic voluntarism.

WHY PUBLIC-PRIVATE PARTNERSHIPS ARE POPULAR

External engagement in public schools is a good thing, particularly when that engagement comes from the private sector. People support the injection of private capital into public education. They also believe that positive outcomes are achieved through the mutual influence of school administrators and corporate executives, and that the public sector can do some things better than the private and vice versa. Those who support public-private partnerships hope that administrators will emulate the best aspects of the private sector, modernizing school administration.

During the previous century, many school officials were dubious about the idea of working with external organizations and agencies. In the 1980s, demands for reform overcame this reservation and so partnerships became more commonplace (Rist, 1990; Sipple, Matheney & Miskel, 1997). Board members thought that mixing with high-profile executives would increase schools' social capital and deflect negative criticism, making these partnerships more of a pragmatic venture than one founded on any democratic or moral belief.

Private organizations have their own reasons for partnering with schools, ranging from altruism to utilitarianism. Their motives may include a desire to serve society, improve community life, help students succeed, influence fiscal or curricular policy, and promote a better corporate image. One reason businesses want to partner with schools is to have the ability to promote themselves in, or through, the educational institution.

Some argue that the motive is to establish consumption as the ultimate expression of participatory democracy (Hewitt, 2007). This claim is supported by examples of businesses obtaining exclusive vending rights within schools. Since 1980, many schools have handed over exclusive rights to soft drinks companies to sell their products within the school in exchange for cash or other remuneration (Addonizio, 2000). This has led to economic concerns over the restriction of competition, as well as the ethics of promoting unhealthy products to students.

The success of public-private partnerships is hard to evaluate. The variety of forms the partnerships take makes them difficult to evaluate through standardized criteria and thus hard to compare. Vague goals set out at the start of the partnerships and little thought given to measurable outcomes of the projects leads to various partnerships claiming to be a success without any empirical evidence to support those claims. Public-private partnerships also have a tendency to focus on how to pursue a goal and sustain the partnership, rather than the success of the goal itself.

Several studies have investigated these partnerships. In 1989, researchers attempted to quantify how school-business partnerships had impacted school reform in a specific large, urban school district, discovering that out of 450 projects, only eight had produced instructional changes. A more recent study found that the resources acquired by schools in the course of such partnerships, such as prepackaged curricula, equipment, and enhanced facilities, hardly ever—if at all—made a significant impact on the day-to-day lives of students.

There can be unexpected negative effects from schools becoming dependent on private funds, as local and state officials may be inclined to give public money to schools that receive private funding (Fege & Hagelshaw, 2000). The most common difficulties in successful partnerships are inflexible goals, collaborators not trusting each other, lack of planning, unresolved conflicts, and the organizations having competing goals.

There are also many reasons why partnerships fail to deliver in terms of student learning. There is sometimes a tendency to focus on providing more resources, rather than on the reform of learning. Collaborators from incompatible organizational cultures, given that the beliefs of business executives and educators are not always compatible, can make it difficult to find consensus.

Business executives sometimes fail to recognize intangible assets, such as educators' inherent knowledge of how classrooms work. Reforms not tailored to specific schools or districts are ineffective because the micro-political context of neighborhoods and regions are ignored. Democratic deficits created by these partnerships may result in citizens feeling disempowered.

Criticism of public-private partnerships should not lead to their elimination. Rather, these partnerships should be used to supplement community engagement since they continue to enjoy public support. Abolishing them would impair the ability of superintendents to develop other forms of community engagement. Partnerships with the private sector also inject private money into public schools. Philanthropy is always beneficial when implementing reforms. Public-private partnerships can increase schools' social capital, which helps them to carry out local reforms.

COMMUNITY ENGAGEMENT IN SCHOOLS

In concept, citizen or community engagement is based on liberty, affording citizens the opportunity to have authority over government decisions. There has long been debate about the best conditions or prerequisites for inspiring citizens to try to influence public policy. However, it has proven quite complicated to conduct research into the subject, given the complex dynamics and intricate relationships involved, and the difficulty of validating or quantifying the data.

Citizen engagement and participation in the decision-making process is a fundamental right in a democratic society (Fishkin, 1991; Roberts, 1997; Skocpol, 1993). Community engagement with schools has a long history, dating back to before World War II, when "democratic localism" (Katz, 1971) was popular. Citizens expressed their views and altered directions of their schools through town hall or other meetings. The impetus for civic participation remains, even though the process fell out of favor in the 1950s as social and political influences changed.

Using Local Control to Facilitate Community Engagement

Community engagement in schools is often seen as impractical and complicated. It relies on involving individuals with the capacity to understand and willingness to learn school procedures in order to make reasonable decisions. With the growing complexity of the public school system, finding residents with the availability and inclination to do so is challenging.

In theory, electing representatives of the community to school board positions would provide for informed decisions to benefit the local community. In reality, state policymakers, along with business leaders, were able to take control of school reform between 1983 and 1989, presupposing that educators could not or would not act on their own to improve schools (Metz, 1990; Rubin, 1984).

They relied on a strategy of political-coercive change and intensification tactics in order to spur reform. Notably, they increased resources and altered policies that essentially required educators to do more of the things they were already doing well (Kirst, 1988). These efforts, however, were only partially successful. The reforms ignored variations in student needs and did not anticipate the number of teachers who would circumvent the reforms rather than comply.

In the early 1990s, school-reform efforts were shifted to the local level, with school officials accountable for improvement (Henkin, 1993). This allowed school board members and administrators to decide what reforms needed to be made, rather than just deciding how to implement those changes mandated by federal and state bodies (Kowalski, Petersen & Fusarelli, 2007).

This type of reform is complicated, as it involves managing the line between societal and individual rights. Decision-makers must fuse the wishes of individuals within the community with the need to reflect the values of society within a common school curriculum. The result is that teachers and other educators make decisions based on their professional knowledge, while still acknowledging the will of the people and ensuring that the community is engaged in school reform.

Approaches to Civic Engagement

Civic engagement in school reform can be approached in various ways, the most recognized of which are the adversarial, electoral, and communicative approaches. The adversarial approach can include groups of parents confronting incumbent board members, or criticizing public administrators over certain issues they have with the curriculum.

A group of parents may take exception to the inclusion of sex education, for example, or the theory of evolution in the curriculum. This approach to community engagement is risky. While it may produce results, it also often irrevocably destroys the relationships between school officials, parents, and other stakeholder groups (Feuerstein, 2002). It can also often lead to instability when board members are reelected, superintendents are fired, or there is other institutional unrest because of adversarial action from the community.

The electoral approach to community engagement is popular, particularly in relation to school board elections and referenda on tax (Edelman, 1985). While this is a better approach in terms of democratic participation, it isn't an ideal mechanism to encourage community participation. People often fail to exercise their right to vote and, in some communities, only 10 percent of voters cast ballots in school board elections (Grossman, 2005). In addition to being expensive, the electoral approach may discourage or detract attention from other, more efficient, forms of participation.

The communicative approach utilizes deliberative democracy, encouraging parents and stakeholders to express their opinions. Its aim is to engender open dialogue through support from superintendents and school officials in order to stimulate productive debate and encourage a consensus. While this is the most open and democratic approach, it is also notorious for being contentious and inefficient, due to inevitable differences of philosophical and political opinion within the community.

The Pragmatic and Philosophical Nature of Community Engagement

In order to enhance community participation in schools, reform efforts must be both practical and philosophical, to promote performance as well as civic participation. This allows reform to be undertaken locally, while remaining accountable to stakeholders. Education professionals and local communities should embrace community engagement as a normative standard in both school-reform activities and partnerships, which would encourage democratic localism, while promoting the spirit of civic voluntarism.

Partnerships should be made accountable through annual evaluations made towards predetermined project goals. The evaluations would focus on levels of democratic localism, social capital arising from the partnerships, the acquisition of relevant resources, and avoiding exploitation. This would allow public-private partnerships to foment school reform and engage the community, instead of existing to gain social capital for school officials and business executives.

REBALANCING THE RELATIONSHIP BETWEEN THE PUBLIC AND THE GOVERNMENT

The only way public education will achieve long-lasting systemic reform is through redrawing the relationship between the public and the government, and by fostering mobilization through public engagement. While public education is dependent on public money and is a civic responsibility, the crucial factor currently missing in its delivery is participation and engagement from the community.

There is naturally much debate, policy creation, and legislation passed with relation to public education, but often this is lacking the public voice. For education to be of good quality for students, communities must be engaged in all levels and types of decision-making. Decision-making must be structured so that public deliberation is built into its mechanisms, and the public can then utilize its knowledge to undertake its civic responsibilities.

The Public Education Network (PEN) advocates a modified forum of debate surrounding school reform to include the public or community voice that relies on the communication between the member organizations of PEN, local education funds (LEFs), and members of the community, in order to provide a robust dialogue on reform (Broun, Puriefoy & Richard, 2006).

LEFs are committed to local school reform, and are nonprofit organizations independent of the school system. They are typically made up of educational activists such as parents, advocates, and business and civic leaders, and provide the catalyst for encouraging community participation in school reform through the framework provided by PEN. They take the arguments of the public and shape them into clear arguments for reform, helping to create the conditions needed in the political sphere to enact and sustain necessary change.

It is clear that change is needed in U.S. public schools, in the areas of governance, curriculum, assessments, and professional development. However, there is no consensus on how to achieve such changes. It is widely agreed that standards-based reform is a good place to start, but there are many implementation challenges affecting school districts. Communities favor evaluating test scores that occur because of change. Communities are also largely in favor of reform, and are lacking not enthusiasm, but a means of access to influence the reform process.

CHALLENGES TO COMMUNITY PARTICIPATION IN SCHOOL REFORM

Community members find it hard to let go of long-entrenched values and listen to the views of others. As a result, community participation in decision-making is often accompanied by arguments and fraught with disagreements. Typically, school superintendents or school boards decide on enacted reforms. Education policy is often somewhat opaque to those it affects the most—the community. Top-down reforms are not always successful, as there is no guarantee a particular superintendent will be in place long enough to monitor reforms to completion.

Federal barriers interfere with greater community participation in school reform as well. Public education is not guaranteed under the federal constitution—rather is left up to the states. As a result, reform is often piecemeal or dependent on zip code or the appetite for reform in various localities. In addition, while measures such as NCLB make provisions for public participation in reform, many of these provisions are not being implemented.

PEN has found from its public hearings across the country that, while the public largely agrees with the goals of NCLB, there were objections to its implementation. This gap between the views of the public and policy implementation is leading to a growing skepticism of and resistance to the law on which these policies are based (PEN, 2005).

Some argue that public engagement is arbitrary, and that the focus should be on expert-driven school reforms, whether those reforms are to do with finance, accountability, or standards. These experts often include attorneys, policymakers, and education experts, who assume that the public does not have enough knowledge to contribute to the debate on reform. This method neglects the notion of public aspiration, essentially sidelining the desire for each generation to do better and be more successful than the last.

Lack of expertise is not sufficient grounds to exclude the public from the process of engagement with school reform, and debates between the public and "experts" should be encouraged. Debates that increase the knowledge and awareness of the public ultimately ready them to make decisions and hold intelligent discussions on reform, fulfilling its civic duties to demand universal access to quality public education and holding to account elected and appointed officials.

TYPES OF COMMUNITY ENGAGEMENT

There are multiple types of community-engagement opportunities, varying in degrees of time and commitment. The most effective of these are mobilization, constituency building, collaboration, involvement, and dissemination of information. Not all facets of engagement are necessary for every endeavor, but they all have their uses, as different forms of engagement are useful for achieving different goals of reform.

Mobilization

Mobilization involves citizens taking action in order to achieve systemic change. This requires a lot of commitment. Where other forms of engagement often produce small changes on a local level, mobilization is the category that facilitates broad, more fundamental changes. Mobilization is the hardest form of engagement to execute.

If, however, there is support for an issue—particularly relating to school reform, about which Americans are largely passionate—it is possible to make a change on local, state, or federal levels, depending on the type and scale of the issue. Mobilization is a means of redistributing power and expanding civil rights, as well as changing the relationship between public institutions and the public.

Constituency Building

Constituency building builds support or enthusiasm for an issue or cause, educating and energizing both individuals and organizations in order to help them understand why a particular course of action should be taken. It provides the means for engaging stakeholders from the wider community by finding a point of common ground to engender broader support for an issue. While these activities typically take place in person through meetings or forums, they are increasingly happening over the Internet through specialized issue websites.

Collaboration

Collaboration refers to people pooling their expertise, resources, and contacts in pursuit of the same goal—in this case, school reform. This process makes use of existing infrastructure, and is typically utilized by organizations with a stake in public education and the reform of schools. Collaboration has proved successful at a local level, although it has only a limited ability to produce change on a national scale (Puriefoy, 2005).

Involvement

Involvement relates to voting on school board issues, as well as other relevant forums, and the participation of citizens in school systems. This can include serving on the Parent Teacher Association (PTA), or taking part in an "adopt a school" program, and is a good way for community members to become more informed and play a part in reform.

Dissemination of Information

Dissemination of information is the simplest category, providing relevant parties with reliable literature about public schools. Community members are informed about the stake they hold and role they can play in school reform, and are educated on key issues. Policy or issues that need to be addressed are identified in detail. Information can then be disseminated through publications, meetings at town halls or schools, in local newspapers, or via community forums, depending on the issue at stake and the audience to whom the information needs to be imparted.

Public Groups and Community Engagement

To ensure the success of any engagement, it is vital to define what we mean by "public," so that the accurate demographic can be targeted and engaged more productively. Broun, Puriefoy, and Richard (2006) identify three public groups—policymakers, stakeholders, and the wider community—who are typically invovled in community engagement.

The wider community is naturally the biggest group, yet is the least utilized. It is comprised of "ordinary" citizens such as parents, particularly those whose children have typically not been well served by the education system and whose input regarding school reform is vital. While only 25 percent of adults have school-age children, the remaining 75 percent contribute to the improvement of public education by paying taxes that are used by schools, holding elected and other officials to account, voting for public officials who are relevant to public education, and voting for the school board.

Stakeholders are organized groups who influence policymakers through the control of vital resources such as money, votes, or political influence (Public Education Network, 2006). These are often the parties represented at the school board or other community meetings, and range from chambers of commerce to teacher unions, faith groups to civic organizations to parent-teacher associations. Stakeholders are a key part of community engagement in school reform, offering a coherent voice on specific issues, but this influence should not lead to the exclusion of the wider community.

Policymakers are elected officials such as legislators, governors, mayors, school board officials, boards of education, and school superintendents, who set the legislative framework for school reform and allocate resources to schools. Ideally, the wider community should have the opportunity to engage policymakers to put forward their views on specific actions or legislative matters, as well as the wider vision on which public education is based.

This is accomplished through sessions where discussions are held, as well as through collecting information from experts and using it to create a coherent framework for reform. This process requires excellent knowledge of school reform and poses a challenge for local education officials, who must shape the debate through relevant data and analysis without crowding out the concerns and wishes of the public.

Policymakers must adhere to a definition of quality public education that allows them to shape the debate and set parameters by which they can measure the response of communities. These parameters might include high expectations of students, standards-based curriculum and assessments, professional development, sufficiently qualified teachers, good preschool programs, support from the community and students' families, decent facilities, financial support, strong leadership, and good governance.

Ultimately, community engagement is a means of shifting power from its usual, more traditional positions—that is, elected officials and stakeholders—to the public at large, so that this group can play a greater part in school reform and make the process more democratic. For example, in New York, where communities were given a chance to say what they would like to see for education, residents reported that preparing students sufficiently for jobs was just as important as preparing them for civic duties (Broun, Puriefoy & Richard, 2006).

The New York example shows the productive, practical influence parents and the wider community can have when given the chance to participate in school reform. Essentially, while the public has no "real" power, it is a dormant force that can achieve a lot. Mobilization is the most important means of public engagement. School reform is a popular issue for communities to mobilize around. School-finance litigation in particular is an ideal issue that benefits from community engagement by ensuring that any court orders on the matter are properly evaluated and implemented.

COLLABORATION BETWEEN SCHOOLS AND COMMUNITY ORGANIZATIONS

Warren (2005) examines the different ways in which schools can engage with the community in order to best benefit each other. If school reform is going to be long-lasting and successful, it must involve the voices of the community. The regeneration of urban schools and communities are intrinsically linked, as it is difficult for communities to improve without good education, but it is also difficult for schools to improve without support from an energized, active community.

Districts have typically found it hard to improve schooling in poor districts, as these efforts are generally carried out entirely separately from other community-enhancing efforts. Linking these efforts is preferable, as children cannot be expected to achieve at school if they lack adequate housing, nutrition, safe communities, or if their parents suffer from stress due to low-paid jobs or unemployment.

It is unreasonable to expect that schools alone can make up for debilitating factors such as poverty and racism, although they must undoubtedly improve their efforts in teaching inner-city children. Community-based organizations that deal with issues such as housing, health, and regeneration would profit from partnering with schools and working together to improve the lot and the education of children living in these areas as a means of benefiting both schools and the community.

Engaging community groups with schools has the added benefit of helping teachers and other educators to better understand the communities and lifestyles of the children they teach, and thus to better adapt their style to meet their needs. This humanizes the student population, treating students not simply as a problem to be fixed, but as a group rich in heritage, culture, and traditions that adds value to the public education system. Community groups working with schools provide a vital link between schools and the families of inner-city students.

Marshalling the Power of Poor and Racial-Minority Communities

Racism, often fuelled by ignorance and isolation, is another problem faced by many inner-city schools. This often leads to teachers discriminating—however unconsciously—against students of color, and particularly against low-earning ethnic minority parents (Rioux & Berla, 1993), who are sometimes seen as being part of "the problem."

Financial and social resources are not enough to solve these issues; the entire culture of schooling needs transformation. Inner-city schools tend to be underfunded compared with schools in more affluent suburban areas. In order to achieve change in this area, it is necessary to create a political constituency around the issue of school funding made up of community groups who are passionate and motivated enough to force positive change.

Key contributions that community initiatives can make to school reform include helping children become better equipped to learn at school through improving the social context of education, and encouraging parents and communities to become involved with schools and participate in the education of children. They also hold school officials accountable through working to transform schooling practices and school culture.

Perhaps most valuable to the process is the fact communities are able to build a constituency around public education that can be mobilized to support the delivery of more and better resources in schools and address any other inequalities that may be found within the education system. Despite these obvious and comprehensive benefits, it is clear that in many urban areas, the reality reflects isolation and ignorance more than it does community participation and cohesion.

Teachers often report feeling isolated within these schools and many inner-city parents do not ever go into the school unless the school has a problem with their child. This results in a dearth of schools offering meaningful participation opportunities for parents. Urban schools still offer the greatest prospect for reform, even though public schools are the most democratically accessed institutions in the country, and are located in almost every neighborhood, serving 90 percent of American children (National Center for Education Statistics, 2002).

Focusing on social capital between groups of people better equips them to achieve common ends. This is substantiated by the finding that schools with greater amounts of social capacity—even though they might only have limited resources—make better use of the resources they do have, and use their social capital in productive relationships in order to obtain influence and further resources (Warren et al., 2001).

Social capital is developing good relations between parents and community groups within inner-city areas to improve the learning environment (Epstein et al., 2002). It fosters better relationships between adults and children, creating an atmosphere of transparency and trust within schools as well as between schools and communities, and among parents.

Social networking also helps to effectively mobilize groups and serves as a means for coordinating intended actions. When a network of trust is developed among teachers, principals, and parents, it allows them to work together to develop a common vision for school reform and implement that vision with fewer issues than they would have otherwise.

Power within communities impacts school reform. Communities with a high number of ethnic minorities are often poorer than average, and lack the means to challenge unfavorable views of them. Negative perceptions about the community, from those both inside and outside of the community, can lead to community decline and even school failure.

These pejorative views are exacerbated by powerful leaders who often redline these communities and burden them with environmental hazards (Bullard, 1990). As long as these communities lack the necessary power to mobilize in any great numbers, urban schools will continue to fail the children they serve. Greater community engagement in school reform will not correct this without comprehensive restructuring of inequality, particularly in the underfunding of schools in inner-city areas.

Lack of power causes problems between parents and teachers as well. Any effort to increase social capacity must also address this power imbalance, in order to ensure that the most productivity is being gained from the engagement of the community. If this does not happen, then any effort to push reform forward is likely to end in disagreement and unresolved conflict. If parents do not feel they are being given sufficient opportunity to participate or feel that their opinions are not being respected, they are not likely to be effective as agents of change.

In order for community groups to work with schools to implement change, the focus should be on relational power, which, in theory, should be a win-win situation. Relational power refers to the power of groups of people to get things done, as opposed to zero-sum power, where one group leverages influence over another. Focusing on relational power placates teachers and principals concerned that some community groups may try to make unreasonable demands that cannot be accommodated (Goldring, 1990).

Collaboration between groups and schools is the best option for working together and avoiding confrontation without ignoring confrontational issues, such as overcoming prejudices related to race or poverty. Working to build both social capital and relational power in order to form collaborations is arguably the best way to expand the capacity of school communities, while allowing latitude to build an electorate that can push for urban school reform.

School-Community Partnership Models

Three types of schools are best suited to developing school-community partnerships to promote school reform. Schools with a service model which operate as full-blown community schools; schools fitting the development model in which community groups sponsor schools; and schools built on the organizing model which involves school-community organizing, are all excellent candidates for school-community partnerships. Traditional, elite school reformers cannot complete their mission alone. They must work with communities looking to make a difference.

CASE STUDY OF COMMUNITY ENGAGEMENT IN SCHOOL REFORM

Engaging communities in school reform in order to make long-lasting, democratic, and positive changes for students is critical. Consider the case of a Mexican-American community that fought for their children's right to a good public education, irrespective of the language barrier. After much effort, they eventually achieved the right to a bilingual education, a diverse teaching staff, and training to equip teachers to deal with cultural issues specific to Mexican-American students. It is a classic example of a community successfully reforming its school system.

Salinas, California, experienced a massive population growth during the last two decades of the twentieth century. There was extensive urban development, as well as a shift in its ethnic composition. In the 1970 census, the town had a population of 60,000, about a quarter of which was Mexican-American. By 2000, the population had grown to around 151,000, 53 percent of which was Hispanic.

This demographic shift naturally led to big changes in school population, particularly in the Salinas Union High School District. Given the ethnic population growth that had begun in the 1970s, educators and officials could no longer ignore the cultural, social, and linguistic needs of students who had previously been in a minority.

The Mexican-American community initially met stiff resistance from school officials and felt shut out of the process for change. Inquiries and requests made by community leaders were largely ignored. A number of incidents led community leaders to seek legal help in order to become more knowledgeable about their rights. In the 1970s, an increase in school violence was attributed by many educators to children's behavioral problems. Community leaders argued that violence had more to do with curriculum and instruction than behavioral issues.

Often, children from Mexican-American backgrounds were pushed out of high school and into work, as many as half of them between 1970 and 1983. Many Latino students in the district were labeled "mentally retarded" because they were tested in English, which they did not understand. In order to address these issues, the Mexican-American community mobilized and initiated a lawsuit.

In order to promote a more inclusive learning environment, community leaders demanded that there should be Mexican-American teachers and principals proportionate to the number of Hispanic students within the school district. A taskforce recommended a system through which to achieve parity in terms of the ethnicity of the teachers the district employed. The board of education rejected this proposal. It wasn't until 2003, almost twenty years later, that anything approaching parity in recruiting teachers and other education personnel was achieved within the district.

In an effort to speed up this process after it had first been rejected, parents mobilized to form an informal grassroots organization, La Mesa Directiva, to coordinate parental action within the community. They began by lobbying officials and integrating themselves into school life in order to raise their profile and champion their cause.

When their message was ignored by the school board, they resorted to more extreme direct actions. They arranged school walkouts based on their knowledge that schools were dependent on attendance in order to receive funding. Eventually, the organization filed a complaint at the U.S. District Court. This lawsuit took years to make its way through the courts, but ultimately the court found in favor of the parents. Change can be bought about through the persistence of a sufficiently passionate and mobilized community.

The Salinas case study illustrates that achieving reform instigated by communities is not just a case of numbers: communities in and of themselves do not hold much power as a collective, as they are not elected or automatically part of key stakeholder groups. Even though the Salinas district had rapidly increasing numbers of Latino students, their needs were not automatically addressed. It was only when the community mobilized at the grassroots level and set up an organization through which to channel its activities and shape its actions did it begin to achieve results.

The will to carry out good and enduring school reforms exists in the American public, and communities are willing to get involved and stand up for changes, particularly when those changes have an influence on their families. There needs to be provision for schools and communities to open constructive dialogue with each other in order to avoid conflict and the breakdown of negotiation (which can lead to legal action, as in the Salinas case). Overall, community engagement in school reform is promising, if there is a mechanism through which it can take place.

•

Chapter 6

Recruiting, Retaining, and Fairly Compensating Our Teachers

STAFFING SCHOOLS WITH COMMITTED AND COMPETENT TEACHERS

In order for school reform in the United States to be successful, we must recruit, train, retain, and fairly compensate teachers. School districts continuously engage in the complementary processes of recruiting and retaining teachers. The current economic downturn however has forced many states to make painful reductions in their public education expenditures—which in turn impacts the ability of school districts to hire and sometimes to retain high-quality teachers. It makes sense, then, for districts able to hire to proceed with the most prudent polices available that relate to teacher recruitment, and to engage effective strategies to retain excellent teachers.

Based on their belief that districts should be aware of the advantages and disadvantages of different recruitment and retention policies, Guarino, Santibanez & Daley (2006) conducted a review of literature to determine which strategies best support teacher recruitment and retention. Although the availability of literature on the areas identified varied, the authors proposed that districts attend to: characteristics of individuals who enter and remain in the teaching profession; school and district characteristics that affect recruitment and retention, to include compensation polices; and policies that affect both preservice and inservice teachers.

Teacher Entry, Mobility, and Attrition

The highest number of new teachers in any given year are female, with white women accounting for higher numbers than women in ethnic minority groups. There is evidence, however, that in the early 1990s the number of new minority educators increased. At the same time, college students graduating with high academic achievement are less likely to enter teaching

93

than other graduates. Teachers, both in their early years of teaching and when nearing retirement, show a similar trend in high turnover and dropout rates, producing a pattern related to age or experience.

Higher attrition rates have been noted in whites and females in the fields of science and mathematics, and in those who have higher measured academic ability. Location of teaching position also impacts mobility and attrition rates. Most studies demonstrate that suburban and rural school districts have lower attrition rates than urban districts. Public schools, on average, are found to maintain higher teacher retention rates than private schools. Not surprisingly, higher salaries are associated with lower teacher attrition, while dissatisfaction with salary is associated with higher attrition and a waning commitment to teaching (Guarino, Santibanez & Daley, 2006).

Compensation and Working Conditions

Entry, mobility, and attrition patterns discussed above indicate that teachers seek increased salaries, greater rewards, and improved working conditions. Educators tend to transfer to teaching or even nonteaching positions that meet desired criteria. Higher compensation results in lower attrition. These findings suggest teacher recruitment and retention is dependent on the desirability of the teaching profession in relation to other opportunities. The inherent appeal of teaching depends on "total compensation" which compares the total reward from teaching, both extrinsic and intrinsic, with possible rewards determined through other activities.

Schools with high percentages of minority students and urban schools are harder to staff, and teachers tend to leave these schools when more attractive opportunities become available (Guarino, Santibanez & Daley 2006). Certain factors, which can apparently be influenced by policy change, may affect individuals' decisions to enter teaching, as well as teachers' decisions to transfer within or leave the profession.

Lower turnover rates among beginning teachers are found in schools with induction and mentoring programs, and particularly those related to collegial support. Teachers given greater autonomy and administrative support show lower rates of attrition and migration. Better working conditions, intrinsic rewards, and higher salaries remain the most compelling elements of concern to teachers.

Research conducted by Mathematica Policy Research for the U.S. Department of Education examined the compensation process for public school teachers, calculated, an element of teacher recruitment and retention that has been relatively ignored for many years (Glazerman et al., 2006). The traditional system, whereby teachers are paid based solely on their years of experience and level of education, has caused many critics to claim that it does not promote good teaching, or is not as fair as other systems that determine pay based on performance, skills, or willingness to teach in areas of high need.

Proponents of the traditional system argue that teachers' experience and education are crucial indicators of their performance, and that because of its open and fair assessment it is the only logical choice. To reach an optimum balance, educators and policymakers have created numerous methods for revising how teachers are compensated, each seeking to adjust teacher incentives differently.

As the scientific evidence on these methods' effectiveness is extremely limited, it is difficult to choose among them. Historically, implementing any pay reform, let alone directing a critical study of one, can be a demanding issue. A number of ambitious and interesting reforms have folded, often within a few years, under opposing political pressure or from fiscal restrictions. Attempts to study the few surviving reforms have yielded little usable data to date.

Preservice and Inservice Teacher Policies

Literature on the influence of preservice policies on teacher recruitment and retention are limited, however there are two important points that should command attention of school districts. One of the recommendations of the National Commission on Teaching and America's Future (1996) in its report *What Matters Most: Teaching for America's Future* was that teachers be licensed based on demonstration of knowledge and skills.

This edict led states and teacher education programs to require teachers to pass a battery of tests before they exited teacher education programs or before they were licensed by states. These actions resulted in a reduction of the number of minority students entering and completing teacher education programs. Therefore school districts seeking more diverse teaching staffs will see a limited number of minority candidates available for recruitment.

A second preservice teacher policy to which districts should attend is the difference between candidates completing traditional teacher education programs and those completing alternative route programs. According to the Guarino, Santibanez, and Daley (2006), review of literature, teacher candidates completing alternative-route teacher education programs tend to be older and more diverse. Further, they tend to have higher retention rates than candidates completing traditional programs. Recruiting teacher candidates from these programs could address both the needs for more diverse teaching staffs and the desire to retain good teachers.

Districts wanting to retain their best teachers should strongly consider what matters to teachers who remain in their teaching positions. Mentoring and induction programs tend to matter to inservice teachers, as does class size, autonomy, and administrative support. It is also interesting to note that state accountability practices also impact teachers' decisions to remain in their positions (Guarino, Santibanez & Daley 2006).

Financial circumstances notwithstanding, districts have control over some of these issues. They should consider publicizing situations favorable to inservice teachers, as a tool for both recruitment and retention. As districts develop their reform agenda, they should put at the forefront a vision for the type of teaching force needed to support their plans for reform, and use empirical studies such as those reviewed by Guarino, Santibanez, and Daley as a guide to recruit and retain teachers.

TEACHER ENHANCEMENT PROGRAMS THAT WORK

It is often easy to focus on the negative aspects of the educational system, but there are a number of exciting new programs that have produced demonstrable change. One of the most promising of these new initiatives is the Teacher Advancement Program (TAP). TAP's goal is to attract skilled and talented individuals into the teaching profession and retain them by promoting availability of higher salaries and career advancement without the need to leave their classrooms. The TAP model sets teacher pay and their further advancement to correspond to student achievement growth, noted classroom performance, qualifications in high-demand subjects, and willingness to contribute to mentoring duties. This model also seeks to enhance teacher quality through ongoing professional development and performance accountability. In the late 1990s, the Milken Family Foundation in Santa Monica, California, developed TAP as a comprehensive school-reform model.

TAP is a schoolwide program that provides teachers with opportunities for enhanced pay for performance (calculated through expert observers and analysis of student test data) and future career advancement with related pay raises and continued professional development, simultaneously holding teachers accountable for student learning. TAP's strategy for recruitment, motivation, and retention of the most effective teachers promoted four principles: Multiple Career Paths, Ongoing Applied Professional Growth, Instructionally Focused Accountability, and Performance-Based Compensation.

Teachers have the option to remain in the classroom as career teachers or become mentor or master teachers through the Multiple Career Paths principle. Mentor and master teachers, and the principal, become the leadership team overseeing all TAP activities. They receive enhanced compensation for additional responsibilities, which include supporting the professional growth of other teachers, and working with the principal to plan achievable goals for teacher evaluation. Mentor and master teacher promotions are based on a performance-based selection process. Final decisions are made by the principal with input from administrators and a teachers' committee.

Ongoing Applied Professional Growth provides for time to be built into the school week, using TAP, for school-based teacher learning that can address identified student needs. Mentor or master teachers lead weekly "cluster group" meetings for teachers. An individual growth plan with specific goals and activities is determined for each teacher. Mentor and master teachers provide other teachers with ongoing classroom support.

Instructionally Focused Accountability provides opportunities for certified and multitrained evaluators to assess each teacher at least four to six times over the school year. Teachers are evaluated both individually (based on a given teacher's students' learning growth achievements) and collectively (based on the learning growth of the total number of students in the school).

Performance-Based Compensation allows teachers to earn annual bonuses related to both individual teaching performance (as determined by multiple teacher evaluations), and growth in student achievement. Classroom-level and school-level achievement growth both impact performance pay. Districts are encouraged by TAP to pay competitive rates for teachers working in high-need subjects and schools.

Charlotte-Mecklenburg Schools in North Carolina applied TAP principles to their Pay for Performance pilot program in order to improve student achievement in low-performing schools by rewarding staff based on their attendance, professional development, and student performance. All staff members working in the pilot schools were eligible for participation in the program, and received cash bonuses for reaching certain goals.

In the first year (2004–2005), the bonus was conditional, based on staff members attaining individualized goals for student achievement. Teachers' goals were based on raising student test scores on North Carolina's End of Grade and End of Course testing, in addition to local tests. Nonteaching staff members were assigned goals related to student outcomes in their area of expertise. For example, social workers were expected to reduce dropout rates for their students. If achievement goals were met, teaching and nonteaching staff had the opportunity to earn a bonus of fourteen hundred dollars. They could earn an additional bonus of six hundred dollars if they missed four or less days during a school year, and attended at least thirty hours of teacher professional development. An average of two hundred certified teachers were paid the bonus in the first year, which amounted to approximately 25 percent of educators participating in the program. Approximately 50 percent of these received the student achievement bonus only, and did not qualify for the added attendance/professional development bonus.

The California Certificated Staff Performance Incentive Award Program set out to use TAP principles to encourage greater standardized test score growth in low-performing schools throughout California. This statewide program was operated by the California Department of Education (CDE). Cash bonuses were paid to all certified staff in low-performing schools who were able to raise students' test scores over one year, as measured on the Academic Performance Index (API).

Schools had to meet two criteria for their staff to be eligible to compete for the award and to be subject to the incentive. They had to be in the lower half of the API distribution as per its baseline score, and had to have shown test score growth in the previous year. In order to qualify for a bonus, schools had to meet three additional criteria. They had to at least double the API growth rate; 80 percent of the growth had to be realized in numerically significant subgroups (e.g., racial/ethnic minority groups); and the school's students had to have attained a 95 percent minimum test score participation rate in relation to elementary and middle schools, or 90 percent in high schools. Of the approximately four thousand schools initially deemed eligible (that is, in the lower half of the base API score distribution) during the first year of the program's operation, about thirteen hundred schools (or one-third) met the additional criteria. All qualified schools were ranked by CDE by their API growth scores, and by the number of Full-Time Equivalent (FTE) certified staff. Bonuses were distributed according to rank, with the first thousand FTE- certified employees receiving a twenty-five thousand-dollar bonus; the next thirty-five hundred, ten thousand dollars; and the last seventy-five hundred, five thousand dollars.

The California Certificated Staff Performance Incentive Award Program included about twelve thousand FTE staff comprised of classroom and other teachers, plus ancillary staff sharing in a bonus pool of approximately a hundred million dollars. During the year that this program was in effect, about three hundred schools had staff that qualified for this bonus, accounting for less than 25 percent of the staff on the qualified list. The program commanded substantial national awareness during its brief run, including several feature articles in *Education Week.* National interest in the program was most likely attributable to the size of the bonuses.

Another successful program, the Cincinnati Evaluation and Compensation System, seeks to enhance teacher professionalism and boost student achievement levels by relating teacher pay to teacher skill and performance as measured by classroom observations and teachers' portfolio reviews. Cincinnati has now replaced the traditional teacher salary structure of regular automatic advancements based on teachers' experience and graduate degrees with a system tying promotions to teacher evaluations.

Assessments are based on sixteen criteria encompassing four domains: preparation for student learning, creation of a suitable environment conducive to learning, instruction for learning, and strict professionalism. To determine the teachers' ratings, evaluation teams review lesson plan portfolios and observe classroom practices. Annual ratings then provide formative guidance to teachers. "Comprehensive" reviews, generally occurring once every five years, grade teachers into one of the five decreed mastery levels, thus determining their salary range.

The program design seeks to replace the uniform salary schedule, tying permanent pay increases to career advancement where this would not be automatic, rather than offering bonuses in an existing seniority-based salary schedule. It also rotates annual and total reviews, which consist of a complete review in all four domains for each teacher. Once the teacher has advanced past the apprentice level, the review takes place every two to five years.

These are "high stakes" reviews to determine a teacher's mastery ranking, and therefore his or her salary range. "Low stakes" annual reviews are conducted in two of the four domains in all years when a teacher has no comprehensive review. Annual reviews determine teachers' proficiency and provide them with constructive criticism to further their improvement. Teachers must meet set proficiency standards in order to qualify for experience-based pay-step growth within their mastery rankings, independent of student test scores. Their performance is assessed by peers, based on professional pedagogical norms deemed to contribute to student learning.

The Missouri Career Ladder program is unusual in that it combines teacher performance, tenure, and extra responsibilities to determine monetary incentives. It seeks to enhance student achievement levels by providing opportunities for teachers to earn extra financial rewards for completing increased work and furthering professional development. Eligibility for participation in the program is determined by teachers' noted performance and portfolios. Policymakers anticipate that by incentivizing educators, academic services, and student learning opportunities will improve. This program began in the fall of 2004 as a three-year pilot program.

In theory, teachers advance along the Career Ladder based on their position and progress in classroom performance as rated by observers; in reality, however, the bonuses are directly related to increased responsibilities. Progress on the Career Ladder is determined solely by increased responsibility and the rate at which any extra work is paid. Teachers meeting statewide and district-level performance standards become eligible to receive pay enhancement for Career Ladder responsibilities. This can be in the form of increased work, or involvement in professional development programs.

The program does not replace teachers' regular salary schedule. Career Ladder responsibilities must be of an academic nature and directly related to improvement of programs and services for all students. There are three stages to the Career Ladder, based on years of experience and other criteria. Progression up the Ladder involves teachers being assessed at each stage via periodic observations and evaluations of documentation.

Each successive stage offers an opportunity to acquire extra pay enhancements for taking Career Ladder responsibilities. In Stage I, teachers are eligible for up to $1,500; Stage II, $3,000; and, Stage III, $5,000. Out of more than 65,000 teachers in 524 statewide districts in Missouri, over 17,000 teachers (26 percent) in 333 districts (64 percent) participated in the Career Ladder program during the 2005–2006 school year.

CAUSES OF TEACHER ATTRITION

According to the report *The Influence of School Administrators on Teacher Retention Decisions Across the United States* (Boyd et al., 2009), when given the opportunity, many teachers choose to leave schools that serve greater percentages of low-income, low-performing minority and ethnic-group students. While this phenomenon has been well documented by substantial research literature, far less research has been put into understanding which specific features of the working conditions in these schools might result in this somewhat elevated turnover rate.

Extremely high teacher turnover rates can be financially draining and are damaging to schools' educational cohesion. Therefore, in an effort to interrupt teacher attrition in schools with high turnover rates, mentoring programs and teacher retention bonuses have been initiated. These initiatives will prove less effective than anticipated at reducing damaging attrition unless schools have a clearer understanding of why teachers leave.

Almost half a million teachers leave their posts each year. Only 16 percent of this teacher attrition is related to retirement. The remaining 84 percent is due to transfer of teachers between schools, and teachers who leave the profession all together (Alliance for Excellent Education, 2008). In New York City alone, more than five thousand teachers left their posts in 2005. Eight percent transferred to a different school, and 10 percent moved out of the New York City school system. Current studies are drilling down to better understand the complexities of teacher turnover. For example, they are distinguishing between permanent and temporary exits from teaching, and are making distinctions among transfers within districts, across districts, and exiting teaching completely (DeAngelis & Presley, 2007; Johnson, Berg & Donaldson, 2005). Generally, previous research on teacher retention has either dealt with the parallels between turnover and teachers' characteristics (types of teachers more likely to leave), or between turnover and school characteristics (types of schools affected by greater teacher turnover rates).

A consistent predictor of turnover is found in teacher characteristics and their work experience. Turnover is greater among young and old teachers compared to middle-aged teachers, and among less experienced teachers in comparison to their more experienced peers (Ingersoll, 2001; Marvel et al., 2006). Previous research that links teacher gender, race, or ethnicity to turnover proves less consistent (see Allensworth, Ponisciak & Mazzeo, 2009; Guarino, Santibanez & Daley, 2006; Johnson, Berg & Donaldson, 2005). Teachers' preteaching experiences and pathways into teaching also reflect attrition behavior. Evidence suggests different attrition patterns for teachers who complete traditional teacher education programs and those who follow alternative routes to teaching. It appears that, generally, teachers appointed via early-entry routes (e.g., Teach for America and the New York City Teaching Fellows) show a greater tendency to leave posts than teachers entering via more traditional routes (Boyd et. al., 2006).

Attrition patterns and teacher quality measures have been linked, but not consistently. Teachers with stronger qualifications as measured by self-test scores, and those who received their degrees from an undergraduate institution with a strong reputation, show increased tendency to leave teaching (Boyd et al., 2005). Teachers who are measured as more effective by their students' test-score gains show less likelihood of leaving teaching (Boyd et al., 2007; Goldhaber, Gross & Player, 2007; Hanushek, Kain, O'Brien & Rivkin, 2005).

Research on teacher retention and school characteristics has primarily investigated measures relating to the student composition of the school. Schools with greater concentrations of students from low-income groups, nonwhite and ethnic minority groups, and with low-achieving students are predicted to experience greater teacher turnover rates (Boyd et al., 2005; Carroll et al., 2000; Hanushek, Kain & Rivkin, 2004; Scafidi, Sjoquist & Stinebrickner, 2005). In New York City, for example, first-year-teacher attrition in the lowest performing schools was 27 percent, compared to 15 percent in schools with the highest student achievement.

The relationship between teacher turnover and certain district or school factors is evident in certain state databases. Imazeki (2005) evaluated data from Wisconsin and determined that higher teacher retention is directly related to higher salaries. Loeb, Darling-Hammond, and Luczak (2005) examined data from California and determine that, although a school's racial makeup and the proportion of low-income students may predict teacher turnover, pay rates and working conditions, including increased class sizes, problems in facilities, multitrack schools, and shortage of textbooks, proved noteworthy factors in forecasting high rates of turnover.

Allensworth, Ponisciak, and Mazzeo (2009) found that low student test scores in elementary schools was an indicator of low teacher retention from year to year. Their study transcends student makeup by also taking into account measures of school working conditions such as teachers' reports regarding how they interact with their principal, parents, and other teachers.

The researchers discovered that school working conditions assist in explaining a great degree of the variability in decisions relating to teacher retention. The researchers used administrative records from over fifty thousand teachers, plus survey responses from a sample of teachers and students. Ladd (2009) investigated administrative and school-level responses to surveys of school climate data in North Carolina schools to illustrate that teachers' perceptions of school leadership is very predictive of their decision to remain at that school or seek alternative posts.

ATTRITION IN CHARTER SCHOOLS

According to Miron and Applegate (2007), while several other studies have researched the reasons teachers seek employment in charter schools, few have actually asked why teachers leave these schools. There are considerable performance differences among charter schools, both among and within states (Gill et al., 2001). The quality and stability of the teaching force is one factor increasingly viewed as important to charter school success, but research about charter school educators remains limited.

In addition to providing more choice for families, charter schools intend to offer new opportunities to teachers. Teachers are able to assist in inaugurating a new charter school, and often they have the freedom to teach using the methods they prefer. The charter concept assumes that managing value conflicts among personnel will be notably reduced when teachers' beliefs and interests approximate that of the school's educational mission. Research suggests that providing teachers with school choice might also promote shared professional culture and greater professional autonomy, and ultimately improve student achievement vicariously (Lee & Smith, 1996).

Charter school proponents often use the argument that charter schools encourage teachers to innovate, are providing a better match between teacher preferences and the school's desire to be innovative. Innovation is influenced by teacher satisfaction with facilities, autonomy, and opportunities for professional development. Literature on organizational innovation strongly suggests that people innovate when they have sufficient resources, appropriate incentives, and professional autonomy (Mintrom, 2000).

Substantive frustration with working conditions, dissatisfaction with salaries and benefits not meeting expectations, disappointment with administration and governance—are all issues that almost universally contribute to teachers leaving their posts. This erosion of the teaching force each year is an indication that many charter schools will experience difficulty establishing professional learning communities that can propagate a difference in children's education. Consequently, a high rate of teacher attrition in charter schools is one of the greatest barriers to successful charter school reform.

It can be argued that a certain amount of attrition can be positive, as it corrects a mismatch between teacher and school. On average, charter schools' attrition rates are between 20 percent and 25 percent; however, for new teachers, the attrition rate is nearer to 40 percent annually. This extensive attrition is disturbing. School resources (human and financial) are consumed by high attrition that undermines comprehensive staff training programs and efforts to consolidate effective, stable learning communities. It is likely to undercut the legitimacy of the school as viewed through the parents' eyes.

Age is the primary background characteristic that strongly predicts teacher attrition. In charter schools, younger teachers are more likely to leave than older teachers. There are no significant attrition differences noted between the sexes, or in relation to ethnicity or cultural background. The grade level taught is also a strong indicator, with attrition rates being greatest in upper grades, particularly grades six, seven, ten, and eleven. There is only a slightly greater chance of special-education teachers leaving charter schools than teachers of mainstream classes.

Teachers with limited experience are significantly more likely to leave charter schools. Many of these inexperienced teachers are presumed to have moved to teaching jobs in other schools. Certification also carries significance: attrition is higher for noncertified teachers and for teachers teaching outside their certification areas. This factor may be related to pressure on schools from NCLB to ensure that their teaching staffs meet the definition of "highly qualified."

Other prominent teacher attrition factors include teachers' relative satisfaction/dissatisfaction with the school's mission, their perception of the school's ability to attain that mission, and their confidence in the capacity of the assigned school administration to lead the cause of the school's mission. Most teachers who leave are routinely less than satisfied with school curriculum and instruction, available resources and facilities, and salary and benefits.

Proponents of charter schools would be well advised to focus their efforts on reducing teacher attrition, particularly the excessively high turnover of young new teachers. Discrepancies between teachers' expectations for charter schools and those schools' realities should be identified, and strategies for reducing the gaps should be designed and implemented. Strengthening teachers' sense of security should be paramount, as it will increase their overall satisfaction with working conditions, salaries, benefits, administration, and governance.

THE DEARTH OF MALE TEACHERS

Roughly one-quarter of all classroom teachers are male (Johnson, 2008). Why are there fewer male than female teachers? Generally, the majority of men do not view teaching as a viable career option, and many influences, including guidance counselors, steer them away from working with children. Also, traditional gender roles specifically restrict career options for men who are reluctant to challenge dominant definitions of masculinity. Some of the main reasons for the low recruitment and retention of male teachers include low salaries, lack of prestige, and our society's innate misgivings about men having ongoing contact with children not their own.

Low salaries may have a differential effect on men because of the perception that they need to be a family's primary wage earner. Teaching is certainly not esteemed for its financial benefits, and the opportunity cost of teaching may be higher for men, since better-paying jobs are disproportionately available to them. One way to mitigate this problem might be to extol teaching as a vehicle for social mobility, or provide multiple opportunities for promotion and salary increases (Lortie, 2002).

The unintended consequence could be what is called the "glass escalator effect," whereby keeping men in education leads to channeling them out of the most "feminized" areas—the classrooms—and into administration. Despite an overall consensus that teacher salaries are low, the wage issue is complicated and a simple solution to the problem is elusive. Not only would an across-the-board salary increase be prohibitively expensive, it would fail to recognize overall quality of teachers, or target those most effective in their jobs, regardless of gender.

Communicating teaching's low status in the professional world is difficult. Teaching's lack of prestige is counterintuitive. After all, teaching professionals are responsible for the education of subsequent generations, arguably a laudable vocation. Few would disagree, however, that educational professions do not have the same cachet as, for example, doctors or lawyers. If conventional definitions of status or reputation are taken for granted—that is, relative social standing of a profession—then the social standing of teaching has suffered greatly throughout history due to its close association with two marginalized groups: women and children.

Teaching's low status resulted in a number of restrictive policies that took control of the profession away from educators and placed it in the hands of middle-level administrators. It has been argued that teaching has undergone intensification in recent decades, with teachers becoming overloaded with nonteaching duties. Excessive paperwork and child and health care duties not central to the process of teaching subsequently cut them off from professional growth in their fields.

A preponderance of support for curriculum and pedagogy comes almost exclusively from administrators, which positions them as the educational experts and implies a greater status for them over teachers. Devaluation in comparison to administrators' eroded respect of teachers over time. Males and females who want to stay in education compensate by taking better-paying and higher-status administrative positions. In fact, it is fairly common for male teachers to be encouraged to leave the classroom for administrative positions (Thornton & Bricheno, 2000). A preponderance of men in managerial positions taps into the same wellspring of stereotypical gender roles.

Both at work and away from school, men experience undue pressure to avoid physical contact (or allow themselves to be alone) with young children for fear of a perceived impropriety. Evidence from research suggests that male teachers are under greater scrutiny from peers or the school community, and that this suspicion is stressful for men who enjoy working with children (Sargent, 2001).

Apprehension about caring for young children is especially problematic for preservice and new teachers, although it appears that this anxiety abates somewhat as teachers become more experienced (Hansen & Mulholland, 2005). Mistrust of male caregivers for younger children is sometimes part of a pervasive societal homophobia, or avoidance of behaviors inconsistent with stereotypical masculinity. Anxiety about being perceived as gay, or a "soft male," continues to confront male teachers and likely discourages others from teaching (Sargent, 2001).

Care is a problematic concept in education. Various definitions and applications of care abound, and other professions that involve caring, such as nursing, tend to experience similar issues and are historically women-dominated vocations. Within education, caring for children professionally is for men a taboo that many are unwilling to challenge out of fear of social repercussions within the larger society. The cycle perpetuates itself to some extent, because children do not observe men in caring roles. Acceptance of the status quo by America's public school teachers continues to teach children stereotypical views of gender (Gutmann, 1987).

A number of programs aim to increase the number of men in teaching professions. MenTeach is a nonprofit organization striving to provide information and support to those who are interested in teaching, or who are encouraging others to work with children. The organization was established in 1979 in Minneapolis after its founder, Bryan Nelson, recognized a need for a more diverse educational workforce. Since then, MenTeach has provided a resource on the Internet for information about teaching and a platform for male teachers to share their unique experiences.

A number of retreats and conference presentations for men in education resulted in a variety of independent publications about fatherhood and other educational issues. The organization also conducted comprehensive research about the dearth of male teachers, suggesting a few policy interventions, such as male-specific recruitment programs or initiatives to combat sexism and gender bias in schools (Nelson, 2002).

Mizzou Men for Excellence in Elementary Teaching (MMEET) is organized and directed by Dr. Roy F. Fox at the University of Missouri-Columbia. Its primary mission is to inform and support male teachers at various stages in their careers. MMEET consists of monthly seminar meetings where participants discuss educational issues relevant to the male-teacher dilemma. Those eligible for the program must either be teaching or on a path to certification. MMEET emphasizes collaboration among education professionals and provides an essential opportunity for young educators to be mentored by more experienced teachers.

The Call Me MISTER program is a recruitment initiative established at Clemson University in South Carolina to promote diversity in the teaching profession. The program does not specifically seek out men, but focuses on overall diversity and is especially interested in teacher candidates from impoverished backgrounds. The assumption is that the latter will be more effective reaching youth from similar economic conditions. MISTER combines resources from a consortium of historically black colleges in South Carolina to provide scholarships, tuition assistance, and social and academic guidance to prospective teachers.

Similar to the MISTER initiative, the Troops-to-Teachers (TTT) program strives to recruit highly qualified teachers for schools that enroll a preponderance of at-risk students or are in low-income communities. One crucial difference between TTT and the other outlined programs is that TTT's fundamental mission is to support the transition of military personnel into civilian life via employment as teachers in targeted public schools. While improving diversity in the teaching profession is not really a part of their mission, approximately 86 percent of active duty personnel are men, which makes this program a pool for recruiting male teacher candidates.

In order to further increase the number of male teachers, collaborative relationships should be established between teacher preparation programs and school districts. Gender issues should be explicitly addressed so that traditional gender relations chains are broken before new teachers reach the schools. Colleges of education, in collaboration with local districts, can work closely with K–12 teachers and administrators to place male preservice teachers in classrooms with veteran male teachers. They could also conduct special chats or panel discussions so that new and veteran male teachers have a chance to share their experiences.

Local school districts must do their part in this collaborative arrangement by sending teachers and administrators to college campuses to meet with students, especially men, who are considering a major in education. Additionally, men considering education as a major could be identified by university databases and subsequently contacted by an academic advisor or a practicing male teacher to discuss their interest in education.

This proactive relationship between the school district and colleges of education would likely require the assistance of a special "men in education" liaison—perhaps a graduate student or a team of students and education professors specifically dedicated to the male-teacher problem. Tuition assistance or stipends should be made available to practicing teachers who participate in the collaboration. A partnership between schools of education and local districts is essential to the effective and well-intentioned implementation of programs to attract and recruit male teachers.

Generally, the majority of men do not view teaching as a viable career option, and many influences, including advice from guidance counselors, steer them away from working with children, even when men are greatly motivated to do so. Additionally, traditional gender roles specifically restrict career options for men who are reluctant to challenge dominant definitions of masculinity.

THE IMPORTANCE OF TEACHER QUALITY IN THE RECRUITMENT AND RETENTION PROCESS

Goldhaber's (2006) work, which reviews education research that dates back to the Coleman Report (Coleman & Campbell, 1966), demonstrates that teacher quality is the most important school-related factor affecting student achievement. This is confirmed by more recent micro-level findings (Rivkin et al., 2005; Rockoff, 2004), which also suggests that quality varies considerably among teachers. Some studies suggest that having a good, rather than a poor, teacher may translate into an additional year's growth in learning (Hanushek, 1992). There is great deal of interest in understanding teacher quality and how it can be affected by education policies.

In an attempt to guarantee a minimal level of teacher quality, a primary screen used by all states is the teacher licensure system (commonly referred to as "teacher certification"). Those wanting to become public school teachers have to meet certain requirements. All states, for example, require teachers to hold a bachelor's degree and to have had some training in pedagogy to be licensed to teach. Most also require teachers to have had training in the subject they teach, as well as some type of student-teaching experience.

Teachers also have to pass background checks and state-mandated tests before they can work in a classroom (Rotherham & Mead, 2004). States deem candidates ineligible to teach if they cannot meet or exceed a "cut score" on a licensure test. Despite the popularity of teacher testing as a policy, there is much uncertainty about using these tests as an indication of quality. Both theoretical work by Stigler (1971) and empirical work in other contexts (Kleiner, 2000) suggest that, in general, licensure is not a guarantee of service quality and there is relatively little empirical work that links teacher test scores to student achievement.

The pass/fail cut score for teacher content or other licensure-related exams varies by state and is typically set by expert consensus panels, not by empirical evidence. In the absence of evidence about the relationship between teacher tests and measures of teachers' classroom effectiveness, there is no means of judging the extent to which states' use of these tests allows ineffective teachers into the classroom or screens the potentially effective teachers away from the workforce.

Evidence demonstrates that states face significant trade-offs when they set particular performance levels as a precondition to becoming a teacher. In spite of testing, many teachers who might not be desirable in the teacher workforce, based on their contribution toward student achievement, nevertheless become eligible based on their test performance. Conversely, many individuals who would be effective teachers become ineligible due to their test performance. This situation does not necessarily mean that states should not be demanding these tests; they may provide important information for local hiring authorities to assess, along with other teacher attributes, in making their hiring decisions. However, it does indicate that in the hiring process, there are other factors that should be considered in the hiring decision-making process. It is this category of "other factors" that school districts must find ways to tease out, as they hire new teachers and retain effective teachers.

Chapter 7

The Impact of Effective District Leadership on School Performance

THE IMPORTANCE OF QUALITY LEADERSHIP

Until recently, there was very little evidence regarding effective leadership and how it functions at the school, district, and state levels. Questions remain concerning how leaders can best influence learning, and the type of training needed to meet increasingly tough job demands. Additional questions focus on state and district policies that help leaders and those that get in their way. Attention is also directed toward the best ways to evaluate the behavior and performance of school leaders so that effective practices can be documented and rewarded, and ineffective ones remedied.

Leadership in education is vital to reform efforts, and has often been referred to as "the bridge that crosses the divide," enabling teachers to approach reform from the front line of learning. While teachers are naturally vital for education, school principals and district superintendents are advantaged by being able to construct the vision and expectations needed to deliver better teaching and learning experiences. They have the position and capability to enable everyone involved in the education system to realize that vision.

Conditions for Effective School Leadership

Improved training is not enough to get the leaders we want and need in every school. State and district officials also need to set expectations of what leaders need to know, and actions they need to take to improve both teaching and learning. These standards should form the basis for holding leaders accountable for results. Data should be available to leaders to inform their decisions. Also, they should have the authority to direct resources to schools and students with the greatest needs. All districts should establish policies on the recruitment, hiring, and placement of school leaders, as well as policies to evaluate them.

It is important that states and districts work together to create supportive leadership standards, training, and work conditions. To create, in other words, what we have come to call a "cohesive leadership system." Rather than engage in isolated efforts on single elements of leadership improvement, collective action is the most likely pathway to lasting change throughout the system. Collaboration has not been the historic norm in education policy. Efforts at state-district policy coordination remain relatively new and are yielding both early successes and cautionary lessons about the challenges of maintaining the momentum of positive change.

The Imperative for High-Quality Leadership

First-class leadership is essential to make a genuine, positive difference for all students. This is underscored by the fact that there are virtually no examples of troubled schools reversing their circumstances without the presence of high-quality leadership. While other factors clearly play a part in improving overall school performance, leadership acts as the catalyst for change (Leithwood, Louis, Anderson & Wahlstrom, 2004). The national conversation has shifted from *whether* leadership really matters or is worth the investment, to *how* to train, place, and support high-quality leadership in schools and districts where failure remains at epidemic levels.

A more deliberative approach is required in identifying future leaders and providing them with training to not only administer and manage, but also to lead. School reform calls for leaders who can set a vision for student learning, create a climate where teachers effect high-quality instruction, and build policies to support both. The right leadership can make measurable differences, as evidenced by Capitol View Elementary in Atlanta, Frankford Elementary in Delaware, and in entire urban districts like New York City, where bold school- and district-level leadership has been a major factor in dramatically lifting the performance of children.

Leadership training is essential, but training alone is not enough. New principals need mentoring, but mentoring should be more than just a sympathetic ear. Effective mentoring for new leaders results from real guidance from knowledgeable professionals who have exhibited proven success as educational leaders over time. Even veteran leaders and their teams need support however.

Ongoing professional development is needed that reduces isolation, builds skills, and provides time for leaders to receive additional training on their roles as instructional leaders and effective managers of school resources. Given the focus on data collection in today's educational environments, they also need additional training on how to best use data to make decisions and accurately guide their teachers.

Partnerships between Central Office and School-Level Leaders

District central offices that play limited roles in leadership professional development and support likely lack the capacity to participate in such work. Many urban districts operate under conditions that frustrate central office participation. These conditions include the threat or reality of state takeover (Elmore, Ableman & Fuhrman, 1996; Goertz & Duffy, 2003; Katz, 2003a), severe budget shortfalls (Bach, 2005; Katz, 2003b), state control of resource allocations, and desegregation and special-education consent decrees that focus on compliance with external mandates, rather than learning support (Boghossian, 2005; Chute, 2007; Haynes, 2007).

Ambitious district office centralization efforts seek to strengthen student learning by engaging the central office in learning-focused partnership relationships with schools. The "best of breed" programs invest substantially in the development of central office administrators as key reform participants, support them in developing new forms of participation in reform on the job, and involve external support to assist central office administrators' support roles. Central offices in these districts boast successful records in learning improvement and productive school *partnership* relationships rather than limited, managerial, and compliance-oriented bureaucracy.

These partnership relationships involve a variety of activities that are spelled out in a range of research literature. For example, Honig (2003) talks of "building policy from practice" and "organizational change," while Kennedy (1982) writes about valuing "working knowledge." Hubbard, Mehan & Stein (2006) discuss "reform as learning" while Copland (2003) explains why these relationships may be more successful than managerial ones, through references to "inquiry-based practice." Burch and Spillane (2004) put it even more succinctly: one of the main activities in a partnership relationship is "leadership."

However they are described, one of the main ways these partnerships work is by central offices providing a dedicated group of administrators who work closely with individual school leaders. Together they engage in joint work as they identify problems of practice. They concentrate on situations that hinder student learning and develop solutions to correct them. This allows district and school administrators to develop blueprints for action that incorporate collaborative justifications based on specific educational contexts.

District and school administrators engaged in building school partnerships develop central office and school policies to put agreed-upon ideas into practice, revisiting them regularly, and refining them when necessary. An environment is created for building on lessons learned, reviewing evidence, and ensuring that there is a framework in place so all parties are accountable.

These partnership relationships are created by substantial district investment in central office staff development, as they play a pivotal role in reform. One of the reasons reform has not been as successful as it could have been—or in the worst cases failed—is because central office administrators have not been actively involved in their implementation (Malen, Ogawa & Kranz, 1990).

Strengthening how central offices support student learning is not solely or even mainly a technical matter of developing better policies and formal governance structures. Rather, central office support involves helping administrators throughout central offices build their capacity to participate productively in improvement efforts. Such an approach requires significant investments not only in schools but also in the professional development of central office staff.

Central office administrators are encouraged to be innovative when it comes to determining what it means to engage district-central office partnerships. Beyond the general guidance that central office administrators should support learning, research-based models of this professional practice are virtually nonexistent.

Even extensively documented cases, such as that of New York City's Community School District 2 in the 1990s (Elmore, 1997), reveal little about how administrators' functioning in central office changes when they incorporate support for learning improvement into their daily practice. Even if detailed models of central office practice were available, such practices would invariably involve some degree of context-specific "real time" strategies, as central office administrators work in partnership with schools to continually gauge how to deepen schools' capacity for sound learning techniques (Honig, 2006).

External support for central office administrators seems essential to enabling their productive participation in dynamic learning-support partnerships. Research demonstrates how community agencies and reform-support organizations can significantly assist not only with school change but also central office participation in learning-improvement initiatives (Corcoran & Lawrence, 2003; Gallucci, Boatright, Lysne & Swinnerton, 2006; Honig, 2004a; Honig, 2004b; Marsh et al., 2005; Smylie & Wenzel, 2003). In these arrangements, fellows or coaches from the external organization assist central office staff in their own transformation efforts.

THE WALLACE FOUNDATION REPORT

As educational research has demonstrated for decades, many school-improvement efforts post disappointing results, in part because of limited central office participation in the implementation. However, as a wealth of recent research shows, the importance of engaging central office administrators as key participants in educational improvement suggests that ambitious central office reinvention initiatives may prompt meaningful central office change in support of positive learning outcomes.

The Wallace Foundation commissioned a report to study what it takes to promote and support powerful, equitable learning in a school, and the district and state systems that serve the school (Honig et al, 2010). The purpose was to analyze central offices and determine what role administrators were taking as part of the transformation process. The study found that administrators' work essentially involves four aspects.

Administrators are responsible for developing learning-focused partnerships with school principals to deepen instructional leadership practice, as well as assisting in partnerships between principals and central office, reorganizing and changing the culture of central office units to better support the principal-central office relationships and, therefore, improve teaching and learning. In addition, administrators are expected to take the lead in transforming the overall central office process and supporting the continual improvement of both working practices and school relationships by collecting relevant evidence.

The Wallace Foundation report focused on three central district offices and found that the heart of the transformation effort lay in creating personal relationships between central office administrators and school principals that focused on helping principals become better instructional leaders. Central office administrators also worked directly with teachers and interacted with schools in a range of other ways. The most striking feature in all three central offices was that transformation efforts were most successful where the capacity of principals to lead was developed through relationships with individual central district administrators.

In many districts, there is a growing emphasis and interest in principals' instructional leadership. This is a promising shift because it moves principals toward effective leadership in learning improvement, as well as efficient building and staff managers. School districts routinely bring in external groups to help principals make these shifts in leadership. In the three study districts, however, the central office staff, collectively known as Instructional Leadership Directors (ILD), provided ongoing support to help principals improve their practice. The partnerships created were further reinforced by other central office administrators.

CHANGES IN THE ADMINISTRATION PRACTICES AT THE DISTRICT LEVEL

Currently, additional central office units are beginning to take steps to alter their practices to best support the improvement of teaching and learning. They do so by adopting new approaches to their own work, such as using case or project management to accomplish their work. On the face of it, case management entails simply assigning individual staff from areas such as Human Resources, Budget, and Facilities to work with small groups of schools directly. These structural changes help guide district staff working with schools toward more productive ways to improve teaching and learning. When staff in the three study districts adopted a case-management approach, they worked to provide high-quality, responsive services to individual schools by looking at individual needs, goals, strengths, and character. They identified the individual principals in the schools for which they were responsible, outlined what they were trying to do to improve teaching and learning, and described the kinds of resources they needed and how to secure them.

Another essential aspect in the transformation of central offices is stewardship, which is essentially leadership to guide overall processes. This practice requires administrators to develop a "theory of action" to support their efforts and involve others to make sure their theory is understandable. They must make it clear to office staff, school principals, and others specific activities that are taking place to transform the central office, and how those activities will work to improve teaching and learning at the individual school level. This process helps to increase participants' understanding by providing time to discuss and grapple with what is actually involved in the transformation of central offices.

Stewardship also helps on a strategic level, in terms of employing external resources and developing relationships that would support the central office transformation process. One way this was done at districts that were a part of the Wallace study was through leaders proactively seeking and honing relationships with a range of financial contributors in order to deepen their understanding of the transformation process and seek their support for it. If leaders received offers of support or other outside assistance that did not match the strategic direction of the project, they turned them away.

Participation in evidence-based decision-making is vital for all staff in the central office. Evidence such as student-performance data was used by central office administrators to inform their decisions about their own work and actions. They participated in the ongoing collection of evidence from their own experiences of the transformation process in order to improve the quality of their own practices, which ultimately had a positive impact on the process. They also drew on their own experience to alter and improve the way in which they interacted with all other aspects of central office transformation.

There have previously been calls for district leaders to rely almost exclusively on standardized test results and other forms of scientific-based research to make their decisions. The findings from this study form something of a departure for evidence-based decision-making. The three districts in the study show how, like innovative private firms, rapidly changing urban school systems achieve the best results through regularly capturing and evaluating their own experiences of ongoing work, and then deciding how those lessons can be used to further assist in their continual improvement efforts.

The results and arguments of the study suggest that those interested in the district-wide improvement of teaching and learning, such as district leaders and policymakers, among others, need to move beyond old debates in education. This means moving past the question of whether schools or central offices should be driving reform and developing an understanding about the systematic problems that require improvement on a district-wide basis. This challenge requires both schools and central offices to take key leadership roles in the transformation process in order to achieve the change necessary for continuous teaching and learning improvement.

Overall, the Wallace Foundation study highlights the vital role that central offices play in developing district-wide systems of support to encourage improvement in teaching and learning. In recent years, some policymakers have questioned the importance of central offices, calling for their functions to be outsourced to private management organizations. They have also called for funding allocations to central office administration to be subject to severe cuts, in order to channel more resources directly to schools.

The study, however, suggests that such action sorely underestimates the vitality and importance of good central office leadership in helping to bolster the capacity of schools to improve. District offices can potentially improve schools throughout the district's system, rather than a handful of individual institutions improving in isolation and independently of other schools in the district.

IMPROVING STUDENT LEARNING

Increased attention at both the local and national levels on improving student learning has resulted in a growing expectation in some states and districts for principals to act as effective instructional leaders. Consider these statistics: nearly seven thousand students drop out of U.S. high schools every day and every year approximately 1.2 million teenagers leave the public school system without a diploma or even an adequate education. A large number of students will have attended one of the two thousand high schools in America in which less than 60 percent of students graduate within four years after entering ninth grade.

The situation is not much brighter for students who do persist, earn a high school diploma, and enter two-year or four-year institutions. In community colleges, approximately 40 percent of freshmen (and approximately 20 percent in public four-year institutions) are in need of basic instruction in reading, writing, or mathematics before they can perform in college-level courses (National Center for Education Statistics, 2010). It is vital that principals advocate for these students and provide leadership to reverse this appalling educational outcome, which stifles the aspirations of too many young people and prevents them from achieving their potential.

The failure of many public school districts to provide the working conditions that well-trained principals need in order to prosper is often identified as a central reason for these ongoing graduation and future-preparation issues. By having access to resources and being committed to school reform, principals are able to work with teachers to create school environments that facilitate excellence in learning and have a profound influence on student achievement.

The issues that principals need to work on with teachers include aligning instruction with a standards-based curriculum to provide a good measure of achievement, and improving both student learning and classroom instruction through effectively organizing resources. At the outset, however, principals must engage in sound hiring practices, ensure professional development is available at their schools, and make sure that they keep abreast of issues that may influence the quality of teaching in schools.

While having good leaders in place is undoubtedly crucial, it is not always enough. If principals do not have good work environments to support their improvement efforts, then even the most talented and best-trained individuals may find themselves overcome by the challenges they face on a daily basis. The Southern Regional Education Board (SREB) has investigated the working conditions of principals to better define what is missing in terms of support from the district.

The SREB surveyed principals about the conditions under which the district expected them to perform, asking whether this oversight was conducive to improving school and student performance. The research was supported and lent credence by SREB's extensive school-improvement experience. The aim was to determine high school principals' perception of the conditions their districts are providing in support of school improvement.

Principals presiding over the most-improved high schools responded positively, stating that they felt their working relationship with the district was positive. They were able to give detailed descriptions of the responsibilities of district staff in helping to improve student achievement, and could describe the support they were given by the district. District offices centralized most of their reform initiatives in the least-improved high schools. School leaders felt they were not real players in the school-reform process and that the district was not concerned with empowering them or building their capacity to play a bigger part in reform efforts.

Typically, districts where no major high school improvements have been made suffer from a lack of a cohesive agenda for improvement. Such an agenda would be expected to specify clear goals, research-based practices, improvement-focused accountability, and strategies to support implementation. In practice, schools without such an agenda can often be characterized by incoherent actions. Many of the principals in such schools report that they are not involved in defining existing instructional issues in their schools.

These principals are also not involved in developing viable solutions to address problematic issues. The district (or state) makes these decisions instead, meaning that principals have little ownership of their problems or the proposed solutions to them. They also report having little support or motivation to find solutions, and that they do not feel there is a well-designed system of improvement. Rather, they feel that "improvements" are undertaken in a fragmented manner, or in a series of random acts.

When decision-making is decentralized by district, leadership roles are redefined at all levels. Principals are supported by district staff members, not circumvented by them. District staff members make frequent visits to schools with the intention of providing coaching, technical assistance, and staff development. Teachers benefit from continuous professional development, enabled by principals who have sufficient autonomy and resources to engage and develop junior staff. Professional development may target groups or individual teachers, and the teachers are given opportunities to work together on curriculum and instruction.

In contrast, many districts focus not on such educational leadership, but on educational management. The support provided to improve instruction in these districts is not grounded in research on effective teaching. In addition, these districts lack a systemic approach to improvement and, as such, fail to provide principals with the guidance and support they require to reform processes and put into place effective instructional practices.

Many principals find they spend much of their time finding ways to work around the district office, rather than with them. To obtain the support they need, they often decide that they must circumvent hiring protocols and develop "underground" relationships with individual staff in the district office. Supportive district leaders understand the challenging work principals must do, as in many cases they have been successful principals themselves.

These district leaders support principals' focus on instruction and acknowledge that priority by publicly focusing on curriculum and instruction in school board and superintendents' meetings. Rather than micromanaging staff, they routinely involve school and teacher-leaders in developing and using tools such as walk-throughs, pacing guides, and research-based instructional practices.

The best districts have developed a collaborative "lattice" approach between the central office and the school. This entails districts providing good principals with the support they need to enable their schools to succeed. When given the space by the district to focus on improving their schools, principals can then support their teachers to do the same. The focus of districts must be on raising standards and achievement, and improving instruction by supporting and enabling principals to develop their ability as instructional leaders.

STATE LEADERSHIP AND THE DISTRICT

New legislation and widespread demand for education reform has highlighted the fact that federal leadership has been ineffective in ensuring school improvement. In their efforts to improve teaching and learning, states have come up with a patchwork of tests and standards by which to abide. This variability predated NCLB, but the trend continues. If state policy is going to impact student learning, it has to pass through a host of school and district leadership values, behavior, and beliefs, as well as policies. It is hard to measure the effect of the state on student learning. Local processes can either blunt those effects or enhance them.

Still, state actions will have significant implications for other players able to create change by taking a leading role in educational policymaking. These "other players" might include the local districts, whose own policies incorporate both local and state laws. Districts are required to respond to state leadership initiatives, but they are also involved with the legislative process through their relationships with professional associations. District leaders can shape policy through interacting with legislators via professional associations, emphasizing points of interest, and demonstrating ways their district's agenda incorporates state policy.

The reactions of districts and schools to accountability requirements vary considerably. Smaller districts generally see themselves as instruments of implementation for state policy and capable of utilizing that state policy to meet local priorities. Some medium-sized and large districts see the state policy as a framework and a context that they can use as a guide when deciding which local priorities should take precedence. Still other districts, including large districts that have poor student-learning profiles, see themselves as victims of state policies. This sense of oppression can lead to an unfair assessment of the quality of education in these districts.

Research on school districts has been dormant for a long time, but is now entering a new phase of activity. This has led to several important investigations examining the role of the district in educational improvement (Marsh, 2002; Togneri & Anderson, 2003; Iatarola & Fruchter, 2004). Many recent studies attempt to illustrate the complex struggles of districts in creating and sustaining school improvement by focusing on internal organization and decision-making processes (Honig, 2003; Coburn & Talbert, 2006; Firestone & Martinez, 2007; Anderson & Rodway-Macri, 2009).

Other research seeks to highlight the link between decisions and the potential effect they have on students by examining how district personnel work with schools (Stein & Coburn, 2007). While a great deal of early attention was given to the ways in which the district acts as a (re)interpreter of state policy, relatively few works focused on the role of the district in interpreting state policy initiatives (Youngs, 2001; Spillane, Reiser & Reimer, 2002).

Much of the research into school districts focuses on medium-sized or large districts, which have complex organizational settings. Although there are studies of rural school districts (Keedy & Allen, 1998), there is a lack of extensive study districts in these areas, apart from those relating to school finance. One key reason that rural and small districts receive less attention is undoubtedly because most students in the United States are part of large districts, even though small districts make up the vast majority of districts in the country.

Jimerson (2005) studied the fact that small districts—particularly those in rural communities—are often disadvantaged in their abilities to implement state and federal policies. Often, small and medium-sized districts have limited resources and must rely on their partners in order to achieve their improvement goals. Larger districts benefit from offices relating to curriculum, testing, and professional development, which can exceed the resources available in state agencies.

According to most observers, large districts are also powerful delegates in the education- policy system. They do not just respond to state action; sometimes, they can drive it, too. While smaller districts find it harder to influence policy, they do find it easier to apply state policy uniformly as they may only have a small number of schools and all have similar characteristics.

By contrast, larger districts tend to have disparate populations within their schools, which can lead them to adopt nonuniform policies in order to increase standards and accountability (Elmore & Burney, 1998).

IMPACT OF STATE POLICIES ON DISTRICT BEHAVIOR

Locally defined priorities tend to reflect local community contexts, while at the same time adhering to the framework of standards set by the state regarding accountability policies. Policymakers should also work with education agencies to comply with, and exceed, the expectations set by state policy in light of local needs and priorities by finding ways to disseminate innovative ideas developed by local districts.

Both state policymakers and education agencies need to take more notice of legitimate district concerns, so that the implementation of well-meant government policies does not lead to so many unforeseen inequities. Quality performance benchmarks need to be developed by district authorities—and particularly superintendents—to work alongside whatever the state mandates as minimum standards. Nationally standardized tests should be used as a base for additional standards, as well as those issued by the state.

District authorities should also engage more constructively in the development and adaptation of state policy through advancing consistent networks that meet the varying needs and priorities of districts, and reflect their differing capacities and demographics. District leaders should be given space to shape local understanding of policies set by the state, so they can more effectively define and pursue local goals and priorities.

Once district leaders have had the opportunity to contextualize state policies, local education priorities, policies, and services should then incorporate this understanding. This will foster a change in culture among state policymakers and enable them to consider the fact that one size does not fit all in terms of how the state can help school and district leaders to meet accountability challenges.

FUTURE AVENUES AND DIRECTIONS FOR REFORM

In order to better understand the link between student achievement and district central offices, direct indicators of student performance and achievement should be the focus. For example, "teacher qualifications" such as expertise, knowledge, skill, education, certification, and experience have been shown to have a large impact on student achievement, after home and family factors have been considered (Armour-Thomas, 1989; Ferguson, 1991; Greenwald, Hedges & Laine, 1996; Sanders & Rivers, 1996).

Citing this research, Darling-Hammond and Ball (1998) argue in favor of state-level policy reforms when designing teacher education and certification requirements. The recommendations they make also relate to the recruitment and training of principals, and include suggestions for professional development and reward structures. They point out many important roles that should be carried out by central office administrators until the teaching force is significantly more professionalized and schools no longer need such capacity-building support from the district, suggesting that there is research to be done on how this can be achieved.

Those who seek to reduce or eliminate the role of district central offices in school-reform efforts often cite individual schools (such as charter schools) that move forward on reform efforts without help from a district office. Still, many external partners involved with helping schools achieve results highlight areas where central office logistical support is needed for ongoing success. While individual schools have achieved success on their own, most schools, especially those with low-income populations, require outside help to improve instruction and achievement, whether this help comes from an external partner or the district office.

A Vision for Schools

The district—including the school board, the superintendent, key staff, and influential stakeholders in the community—must have the capacity to develop and articulate both a vision and a set of practices that send a clear message regarding the mission of schools located in the district. This should be a message not only for educators, but also for the community-at-large. Messages that articulate a clear vision for a district's schools create public understanding of what the school system is trying to accomplish.

The authenticity of a message is affirmed through the district's development of a strategic plan that manifests the vision, then by district actions that establish the conditions necessary for principals and teacher-leaders to create different kinds of schools. These conditions include aligning all policies and resources to the plan and creating a collaborative and supportive working relationship with each school. Other expectations include supporting the principal to become the school's instructional leader and communicating the vision and strategic plan to the public in a highly visible way.

An explicit vision provides the context for principals to make decisions supported by parents and the larger community. Engaging parents and the larger community in ongoing dialogue about the changes needed to prepare more students for success is essential. In order to support high schools in creating greater motivation among all groups of students through positive learning experiences, awareness must be developed among parents, businesses, and community leaders.

Districts must work continually with parents and community leaders to ask and answer a variety of questions related to the common vision for school improvement. These questions should guide the community in realizing a vision for schools that requires students to think, solve problems, and produce high-quality work. The school and the community should work collectively to help students see a connection between their studies and their future.

To fully understand the causes of low achievement and low motivation, schools need more information about how students perceive their school experiences, the beliefs school faculty hold about students, and about the purpose of the high school and the ways in which at-risk students receive (or do not receive) extra help. Once schools understand why students are failing, districts may assist schools in defining how to address the problems using proven practices.

Ongoing Professional Development

Effective districts invest in learning not only of students, but also of teachers, principals, district staff, superintendents, and school board members. Low-performing schools are not likely to turn around unless educators who work in these schools have extensive opportunities to learn and implement effective practices designed to engage students in a challenging curriculum. Because many students enrolled in low-performing schools have trouble reading, these schools must initially make literacy the centerpiece of professional development.

Districts can help themselves and their schools by investing in professional development to prepare future school leaders. The first step is to identify (early in their careers) talented teachers who have the potential to become principals. The district should develop collaboration with a university or approved outside entity to provide potential leaders with learning experiences designed to prepare them to lead and improve the district's most challenged schools. Principals and teacher-leaders of low-performing schools need flexible resources and the ability to redirect resources to adopt a comprehensive school-improvement design aligned with the district's strategic vision. This flexibility can help them improve the school's climate, organization, and practices. Too many low-performing districts try to solve their problems by bringing in new superintendents every two to four years and removing principals from schools that do not make

AYP. Without different policies, practices, resources, and additional operational flexibility these districts are destined to maintain their low performing status.

Cooperative and Collaborative Relationships

Districts must define schools' core values for achieving identified goals. The cross section of the community creating this educational vision must include perspectives of less-educated and less-affluent residents, whose children make up a growing proportion of students. Districts must also communicate expectations for a level of instruction that engages students in intellectually challenging and authentic learning experiences that foster student motivation. Districts must also develop collaborative structures for working with principals and school leadership teams to create school environments that improve student engagement and learning.

States must assist every district in working with its community to shape a bold vision for improving schools. States can provide external facilitators and consultants to work with districts in developing their district plan and involving the community and others in that process. States can also assist districts in performing resource audits and offer ideas for redirecting resources to better support a school-improvement framework.

States should ensure that principals have autonomy to select their faculty, discretion to allocate resources for school improvement, and authority to select professional development aligned with their school-improvement plans. For schools that show significant improvement in meeting new accountability indicators, a system of incentives should be put in place to reward success. These indicators might include increasing the percentage of students leaving grade eight ready for high school, reducing the failure rates in grades nine and ten, and increasing the percentages of students on track to meet college standards at the end of grades nine and ten.

Resources to Support Reform Efforts

Many districts have limited resources available for discretionary use in supporting improved learning. Consequently, schools and principals have limited resources to help them raise student achievement. After accounting for salaries, facilities maintenance, technology needs, and transportation, resources that are left for schools and principals to use in addressing critical problems unique to the school, including achievement, promotion rates, graduation rates, and school climate, are severely limited. The chief financial officer for one district estimated that schools in his district have discretionary control over only nineteen or twenty dollars per student.

Some schools receive revenues from parking passes, athletics ticket sales, vending machines, or other limited sources. In most cases, however, schools lack the resources needed for significant changes. Generally, principals control about 6 percent of their school's budget. Decentralized districts such as Chicago and New York City have provided principals with discretion over 85 percent of their school's budget. Schools under decentralized management were more likely to make decisions conducive to improved learning outcomes such as reduced class sizes (Viadero, 2003).

Archer County, Texas, has found innovative ways to allocate significant resources for schools to use for their greatest needs. In an effort to differentiate between the needs of different schools, the district has a system in which schools are assigned points according to how many of their students are eligible for free or reduced-price lunches, student mobility, and other factors indicative of a high-need school.

If, for example, 70 percent of a school's students qualified for free and reduced-price lunches, the school would receive two points for additional staff positions. One point earns a school one full-time-equivalent teaching position. The principals have flexibility to use points to hire additional staff of their choice or to modify teacher contracts to provide time for program planning, professional development, mentoring, and data analysis, as long as their decisions are consistent with their school-improvement plans.

Archer County also has a safety-net program that allows schools to apply for money to address the needs of at-risk students. This budget item was created specifically to meet the needs of at-risk students and to provide schools with programs to help them meet AYP. The source of the safety-net funds is the "extended day" money for tutoring and student support services received from the state, plus about $250,000 added by the school board. With an economically disadvantaged population approaching 50 percent, Archer County is not particularly affluent, yet the district learned to better manage and allocate its resources to support its schools.

The points and safety-net programs provide principals with flexibility, while also offering additional resources to schools with the greatest needs. The safety-net program costs an additional $250,000, and the points program about $3 million out of the $131 million annual budget. Despite the relatively modest funding, the superintendent and district leaders see these programs as critical in empowering principals and giving them the tools to meet their school-improvement goals.

Principals should be given a voice in budget decisions. A truly collaborative budget- planning process improves district efficiency and culture by enabling each principal to articulate his or her school's unique needs within the context of the district strategic plan. This allows new and creative ideas to emerge from educators who are most familiar with the problems. Principals and district leaders have a platform for ongoing dialogue on the district's vision and plans to address specific school problems. An environment of mutual understanding, respect, and ownership is created when principals and district leaders work with each other in this way.

A radical and promising model of giving schools control over their own budgets is currently being implemented in New York City's Empowerment Schools Organization. The Empowerment Schools are given a budget for specific district support services, and then allowed to either purchase services from the district, or go outside the district to purchase them. This practice gives principals the opportunity to develop a thoughtful plan about what their school needs in order to better achieve district goals, and requires district staff to understand the schools' needs (M. Copeland, personal communication, December 3, 2008).

Changing Roles for District Offices

In order to achieve the maximum number of successful schools, school districts need to participate as key players in reform (Foley & Sigler, 2010). There are a number of questions and critical issues facing schools as districts evolve from their bureaucratic roots. These questions include the roles that should be kept at the district level, those that should be eliminated, or those that should be passed on to others. Districts also have to look at new functions they may wish to take on and the capabilities needed to assume these functions. At least initially, they will need to determine whether decisions should be centralized, made at the school level, or made elsewhere.

There is also support for districts to take action to discover common interests between schools and the community through ongoing outreach. Districts need to find ways for people to meet and discuss how to further common interests and work on them collaboratively in order to break down barriers. This type of outreach empowers families and communities, and positions them to be useful assets to school systems (Foley & Sigler, 2010). Building relationships within the education system and holding open conversations are excellent ways to foster engagement.

The Urgency of Resolve for Low-Performing Schools

Darling-Hammond postulates that our political leaders have finally begun to recognize the importance of education to the survival of individuals and societies in the twenty-first century (2007). This is gratifying news. The other aspect of this conversation is all too familiar: while our children do learn, not all of them are learning as much or as well as they should to meet the demands of the new century.

In the United States, there are low levels of achievement among students from low-income backgrounds and students of color. This is in contrast to the fact that students in educationally supportive states and those from advantaged backgrounds easily rival students from across the world. To put this into context, nine-year-olds from white, advantaged backgrounds read as well as thirteen-year-old black and Hispanic students. In addition, even though funding has increased, it has done so unequally and the achievement gap has grown. Typically, schools that serve a large number of "minority" students face big issues, which put them at a disadvantage when compared to other schools. They have to deal with lower budgets, larger classes, and often less-qualified teachers and school leaders. The effect of this has been to create an "educational debt" that adversely affects the students in these communities. Major efforts need to be undertaken to address this issue. Recruiting great teachers is important, but it is not the whole answer. Systemic elements are needed to support the work of talented educators. It is not the people who are at fault: it is the system that needs an overhaul.

As Ted Sizer once put it, "The people are better than the system." We have come a long way in understanding how to create more effective school leaders and build a national commitment to educational leadership. However, we are not there yet. We need leadership to forge all of the various elements of school reform today into well-functioning systems that make sense for those working hard to achieve results for children. A well-functioning system requires not only improved training but also, as Knapp et al. (2003) tell us, "a more coherent web of support for strong, learning-focused leadership in schools and school districts."

Chapter 8

Benefits and Disadvantages of a Year-Round School Calendar

KAI ZEN EDUCATION

Education may very well be the single most important ingredient in allowing a person to achieve success in life. The ascendancy of each individual defines the prosperity of our society; hence, education is the backbone of a continuously developing society. As G. K. Chesterton once said, "Education is simply the soul of a society as it passes from one generation to another." Education is a continuous process of converting information into knowledge that can help students develop and explore further information.

In order to learn, one must take new information and process it in a way that relates it to what is already known, and in the process form a newer, deeper understanding of the material (Mesizrow, 1991). Just as learning involves changing one's understanding of concepts and ideas over time, social phenomena such as education must also be subjected to ongoing scrutiny, evaluation, and change. It is necessary to recheck policies and practices upon which education systems are based, and continually strive to make improvements.

The purpose of this book is to consider ways in which our educational system can and should grow, change, and continuously improve in ways to best serve our children. In order for the United States to continue to progress toward a knowledge-based society, it is necessary to reform and streamline our education system to enable the development and assimilation of information as knowledge. Our schools are the primary institutions to facilitate transference and conversion of information into students' knowledge base. It is our duty to keep a watchful eye on the schooling processes, and to change educational policies and practices to ensure improvement.

The Japanese have a philosophy of continuous quality improvement called "kai zen," which they apply to many areas of their life. Kai Zen (sometimes written as Kaizen) is the idea that one does not need to wait for something to be broken in order to fix it. Rather, one should always look for opportunities to improve upon current processes, making things incrementally better as time passes. This drive for continuous improvement should apply to our educational system; we need to constantly be striving to make things better, reevaluating how we do things, looking at the results we are achieving, and taking steps to improve things incrementally.

Study after study has shown that the American educational system is not just in need of regular, continuous quality improvement. Before we get to that point, something very different is needed since the system is in a state of fundamental disrepair. Our children are performing poorly compared to other developed countries. Children from low socioeconomic backgrounds are performing even worse.

Whether you believe that continuous improvement is good for our educational system or not, what is certain is that our educational system needs to change. However, any change requires leveraging available resources in ways that promote the desired change, and our educational system is no different. In education, one of the most readily available resources to be leveraged is time.

MOVING TOWARD MAJOR CHANGE

In 2005, the National Task Force of Public Education (NTFPE), which included prominent politicians, businesspersons, and education leaders as members, issued a report on the required methodological changes in our education system. The report, *Getting Smarter, Becoming Fairer: A Progressive Education Agenda for a Stronger Nation*, emphasized that the most important resource of the education sector is time. The report discussed how our current system of a short school year with a long summer originated in the 1800s, when children were needed to help work in the fields in the evenings and summer.

Our educational system also began at a time when most students were expected to have primary schooling, then go on to a life working the family business, in manufacturing, or in other ways contribute to the family's economic well-being. During this time, only about 20 percent of children were actually being groomed to attend college. Today, however, things are much different. The family is no longer a cohesive economic unit that requires the work of children to help with the family's income.

We have also moved beyond the point where in a majority of homes one parent (most often the mother) was home to attend to children. The traditional family unit of a working father and stay-at-home mother is no longer the norm. Rather, 32 percent of children are raised in single-family households (NTFPE, 2005) where the parent presumably has to work full time. Similarly, over 60 percent of school-aged children in two-parent families live in a situation where both parents work outside the home (NTFPE, 2005).

Changes are also apparent in our economy; our information-age society will result in a reduction of jobs requiring minimal levels of education. Many jobs today require a college education or the ability to acquire and adapt skills for high-performance workplaces of the twenty-first century. We must make changes in our educational system to better prepare our children for the jobs of today—and jobs of the future. In order to increase the reach of the public education system, it is necessary to increase the amount of time used for schooling, as well as to improve the efficiency with which we use the time allotted for educational endeavors (Silva, 2007).

USING TIME TO IMPROVE STUDENT PERFORMANCE

Proponents of a year-round school year suggest that a shift in the time designated for teaching and learning will help students achieve more by minimizing summer learning loss, allowing for innovation and implementation of creative programs, and providing the time needed to assist children who need extra help (Costa, 1987). Many school districts around the country are in fact working toward increasing both the hours in each school day and the number of days schools are in session.

Many education leaders are open to the idea of increasing the number of days per school year up to an additional month, and some support year-round school programming. Some leaders suggest an extended school day and/or school year for schools that are failing to perform well. This suggestion seems to have some foundation in research, as data show that certain groups (including students from low socioeconomic backgrounds) are negatively impacted by the traditional summer hiatus. The proponents of year-round schooling claim that with extended time to teach, teachers will be able to help all students attain better performance results (Silva, 2007).

It is easy to understand why education reformers put so much emphasis on time spent teaching and learning. Research shows that time may be the most essential resource of the education system (NTFPE, 2005). However, it is important to recognize that merely increasing the amount of time students are in school is not a panacea for improving student performance. It is necessary to utilize the available time in the best possible manner. If teachers fail to convert the available time to quality teaching and learning time, the increased school hours will not improve student performance.

Parents have a stake in school hours as well. Some parents are already concerned with their child's academic progress, and thus prefer to employ additional educational services for their children that may offer better after-school educational opportunities. Still other parents prefer to spend their own time educating their children after school. In these cases, the idea of increasing school-day hours may not be supported by parents of students from affluent backgrounds, and may not be necessary. Still, by increasing high-quality education time, schools can provide help for students who cannot afford learning opportunities outside of school.

While there are many positives of a longer school day or year, there are also a number of concerns. Cost, for example, is an issue that must be considered. Increasing the number of hours and days in school can prove expensive since there are personnel and facility-use issues that must be taken into account. This leads some educators to believe more emphasis should be placed on increasing the utility of available school time.

Some education leaders suggest that instead of increasing the hours and days in a school calendar year, it would be better to spread out the available number of school days in such a manner that the school services may remain available for the students throughout the year. This might mean offering three short breaks rather than one long summer vacation, or simply offering various classes or tutoring programs during the summer downtime. Either way, this will add up to increased costs in facility usage and likely increased staff costs as well.

Despite some perceived negatives and specific issues that would need to be addressed, the idea of year-round schools is continuously gaining support in the United States. There has been a 544 percent increase in the number of public schools adopting year-round school options. A total of 3182 schools in forty-six states have involved 2.3 million children in this year-round schooling structure (Everhart, 2003).

HISTORY OF THE YEAR-ROUND SCHOOL CALENDAR

School schedules of the past varied significantly from community to community. Schools in rural areas offered a short calendar year and a relatively short school day, which included a long summer break, so that students were able to help their families with farm work. Gradually, rural schools started extending the number of school days, while urban schools were reducing the total number of hours in the school schedule (Silva, 2007).

While rural areas preferred a short calendar, the idea of long school calendars became popular in the nineteeth century in urban schools. In 1840, most of schools in Detroit, Philadelphia, and Buffalo followed a schedule of 251 to 260 days per year (Weiss & Brown, 2003). New York City schools closed for only about three weeks during the entire year. Many influential families opposed the idea of longer periods of schooling, and supported the idea of a long break for students during the months of July and August. Due to this desire for a shorter calendar and to accommodate natural weather patterns, many New York City schools began offering a two-month summer holiday for student in 1889. At this time, most of the United States was on a short calendar year schedule.

School schedules were also influenced by the surge in the immigrant population in the early twentieth century, as time was needed to offer a proper education to the children of these new Americans. In some communities, summer-break sessions provided the opportunity to teach English to immigrant students, while other communities preferred to offer extra classes during summers to allow students to graduate early and join the workforce sooner (Silva, 2007). Thus, it appeared the short calendar year served multiple purposes, as well as differing needs of various sectors of society. As a result, long summer breaks were institutionalized.

The idea of a year-round school became a topic of serious discussion in the United States in 1904, in Bluffton, Indiana. Even then, concern over student achievement was growing. The longer school year calendar was proposed to improve student achievement (Glines, 1995). Over the years, other reasons to offer year-round schooling surfaced. During World War II, many schools offered year-round schooling to help women who worked outside the home, but who needed childcare. When the war was over and husbands overseas returned home, the pattern changed again and school days were reduced.

By 1960, most American schools accepted a norm of 170–180 school days per year, five days a week, with six and a half hours in each school day (NTFPE, 2005). Since then, almost all schools in the United States offer no less than nine hundred hours of schooling per year for American students. Most educators realize that this relatively small amount of educational time makes the task of helping students perform better more challenging. Thus, in order to improve the standards of education, teachers throughout the nation have once again begun to consider the option of increasing school hours and the number of days in a school calendar year.

While some educators focus on incorporating ways to increase the quality of time spent in school, most teachers recognize the need for extending school hours and days in the school year, so that they would have more time to reach and teach their students. But, as in the past, there are reasons other than education that prevent some from embracing a longer school year. Conversely, there are also many reasons for some to advocate for year-round schools.

REASONS FOR YEAR-ROUND SCHOOLS

In the 1970s, Heyns (1978) suggested the possible benefits of extended school days on students' academic performance. She tried to establish that, while students enjoy a better cognitive environment during school days when they remain in touch with their school, family and community, they suffer a definitive lack of cognitive development during the summer days when they remain away from schools while enjoying their holidays with family and community. In short, during the school year, real learning is occurring, but the long summer break takes its toll by seemingly erasing some of what has been learned.

This loss of learning is even more pronounced among students from low socioeconomic backgrounds. Heyns also suggested that the difference in achievement of students from families with different socioeconomic statuses (SES), ethnicities, and races, while not widely observed during the regular school year, increases during the summer vacation. Heyn's views have been supported by studies that suggest that children from higher SES families learned more over the summer than did their less advantaged counterparts (Burkam et al., 2004).

The unequal learning opportunities for students of different SES backgrounds and community environments are major reasons for this achievement gap among students. During the school year, when students are placed in common situations for education and development at school, the disparity between students' opportunities outside the school is diminished because both groups are learning enough at school to help minimize the differences outside of school. The environment within the structure of school appears to reduce the effect of SES differences among students, and may help the students belonging to lower SES families perform better.

Some students still fail to take advantage of equal opportunities for learning at school. Still, it is difficult to believe that school resources are equally distributed among various students within schools (Dougherty, 1996). In theory, school resources compensate for the differences between learning opportunities and disparate home environments. Realistically, it is impossible for schools to compensate completely for these differences. While we cannot eradicate differences between learning opportunities and disparate home environments, we can significantly reduce the effect of these differences by improving the quality of the school time.

School time is a complicated concept. The quality of school time differs from school to school, and, of course, not all of the time spent in school is of equal benefit to each student. Part of the reason for this is because not all time at school is spent on educational endeavors. There is time throughout the day that is purely administrative, managed "downtime": lunch, assemblies, announcements, changing classes, and various other breaks are examples.

We have established the fact that improving students' achievement scores can be accomplished by increasing the amount of time spent at school, but the best results are realized only by increasing the amount of time allocated to quality teaching and the amount of time students are focused on learning. It would be of little consequence to keep students in school longer if teachers fail to maximize this extra time by offering learning experiences for students that they cannot receive at home.

This brings us to the idea that a longer school year may not be a "one size fits all" solution. There may be students whose parents succeed in providing better educative experiences after school hours. The extended school hours may improve the chances of students belonging to lower SES families to learn better, but other students may actually face situations of reduced learning opportunities while remaining in school.

In order to make better use of school resources, it is important to not only increase the amount of consistent time spent concentrating on academics, but also to provide teachers with the training and resources to maximize their teaching opportunities and create an environment in which students are motivated to learn. Studies have revealed that students who attended longer school hours made slightly better performance results than those who spent less time in school. However, students who received more quality instruction time enjoyed significantly better achievements, regardless of the amount of time spent in school (Fisher et al., 1978).

Studies have established that extending the number of school days in the year improves the chances of learning for all students, thus year-round schools can improve students' learning experiences. Research also suggests that students suffer during longer summer breaks. Not only do they fail to accumulate new knowledge over the summer months, they also forget some of the previous year's learning material. Students offered several short breaks during the year, rather than an extended summer break will forget less (Everhart, 2003; Harp, 2000).   •

Younger children who arguably have the most to learn, can be the most damaged by these short school years. In his analysis, White (2000, p.15) mentioned that " the three-month summer break is a particular hardship for younger children who are just beginning to build foundational skills and for students whose parents can't afford fancy vacations or summer camp." A longer school year, in addition to helping prevent information loss, may allow students to achieve more during the year if they have more frequent brief breaks, allowing them time to assimilate what they are learning and get refreshed for the next session.

Another area to consider when looking at the potential benefits of year-round schooling is its potential impact on No Child Left Behind. The main objective of No Child Left Behind is to help every American school reach 100 percent proficiency for all students in math and reading by the 2013–2014 school year. As schools work toward this goal, they are required to illustrate "adequate yearly progress," showing that they are steadily moving towards proficiency year after year. Sadly, most schools are far behind the proficiency strides necessary to reach 100 percent proficiency in the allotted time.

Long summer breaks are likely taking a toll on school's efforts to reach the required performance mark. While students may make adequate progress during the school year, much of that learning could be lost during summer breaks. As a result, the learning bar has to be reset to a lower level at the start of the next school year. Year-round schooling would contribute to the success of No Child Left Behind.

By offering extended school hours and school days in a year, teachers could work in an environment where continuous learning would be possible. Teachers could also use the extra hours of school to work with students who take more time to learn and who face problems in keeping up with the other students in the class. Children and youth who are experiencing more difficulties with academic success would be exposed to more teacher time, which potentially provides them more opportunities to strengthen their skill development and knowledge base.

Year-round schools may also prove to be positive for children who are nonnative English speakers. Immigrant students would learn English much faster, as they would be exposed to the English language continuously throughout the year, rather than being immersed for a few months, then sent home, where they speak their native language, for the long summer. Extended quality instruction from their teachers would obviously speed their language acquisition (Haser & Nasser, 2003; Opheim, Mohajer & Read, 2001). Improved language skills would then help them continue to learn more effectively in all areas of their education.

Year-round schools provide relief for families that require help with daycare (White, 2000). In many families both parents work full time outside the home, making it difficult to ensure adequate supervision of children during the summer months. In fact, the current school calendar—which includes the long summer break with little parental supervision and presumably less adult interaction—could be part of the reason that so much learning is lost and no new learning is accumulated. Extending the school year to include the summer months would ensure both adequate supervision and continued learning for these children.

Many teachers have suggested that the quality of instructional time at school can be improved by employing a year-round school calendar because it offers continuity in the process of education (Kneese, 2000). This is not to say that the only possible answer is a full, required year-round school calendar. It might be possible to achieve the goal of improving overall student learning through variations of year-round schooling that would cater to those who most need the extra time in class. White (2000) observed that schools might offer intersession classes for weak students, many of whom come from low socioeconomic backgrounds.

Some schools already offer free intersession courses, while others require minimal fees and offer financial aid for those in need (Haser & Nasser, 2003). By allowing some creative enrichment classes during the intersession periods, schools may also succeed in attracting high-achieving students, students from families in higher SES groups, or students whose parents do not need daycare. A wide variety of these courses could be offered so that they appeal to various groups. Intersession classes may include regular course classes, specifically in mathematics, computer science, or creative arts and sports (Atalig, 2003).

In an educational climate that focuses so heavily on standardized testing, while at the same time makes use of a rather short school day and year, some teachers may find it difficult to offer extra time for needy students. Extending the school year could be a great asset to those teachers. However, teachers themselves could experience some negative impact from an extended calendar.

Year-round schools with extended school hours may fail to allow teachers to take care of their own families and children. In the absence of long summer breaks, teachers may find it impossible to attend professional development and higher-education courses to maintain their education certification or to attain promotions (Atalig, 2003). A flexible school schedule that would allow more needy children to have a separate calendar could solve many issues, but could also entail new problems.

ADVANTAGES OF YEAR-ROUND SCHOOLS

Supporters of a year-round schooling system often suggest that policymakers should adopt this schooling format because students in other countries often outperform their counterparts in the United States. Research shows that students in twenty-four other developed countries outperform American students in math and science (Weber, 2010). Why are students in other countries doing so much better than our own? One reason may be that most international schools offer longer school years with more hours per day (U.S. Department of Education, 1983). According to a report funded by the National Commission on Educational Excellence, most European schools offer 190 to 210 days per year, and schools in Japan offer 240 school days a year. Compare this to the average 170–180 days a year that American children spend in school. Noticing a strong correlation between achievement and the number of days spent in school, the commission recommended that schools hours be extended to seven hours a day, while the school year should include at least 200 to 220 days. The report also recommended establishing eleven-month contracts for teachers in public schools.

According to Silva (2007), while children belonging to middle-class families enjoy higher learning opportunities even during the longer school breaks, children from low-income group families do not. Thus, the extended school days or intersession classes may help low-income students achieve more learning throughout the year, and lose less of this new knowledge between years. However, as was pointed out previously, it would be of minimal benefit to make intersession classes compulsory for students belonging to affluent families who have experiences during their long summer breaks that prevent extensive loss of learning.

Year-round schools offer a variety of specific advantages in addition to increased learning. Some of the significant advantages include better student performance, reduced absenteeism among students and teachers, better discipline, diminished stress on teachers, and better learning opportunities for students. Schools following multitrack programs also enjoy easing of problems due to overcrowding, proper utilization of resources, and cost savings (Brekke, 1992). The following sections discuss some of these specific advantages in more detail.

Various research studies reveal that students attending year-round schools often perform better than students in traditional schools. Differences in performance among traditional and year-round students from similar home environments are particularly important to note. Much has been written about the achievement gap between students from middle-class backgrounds and those from low-income backgrounds. However, low-income and middle-income students appear to make comparable achievement gains during the school year.

When low-income students spend time away from school, the achievement gap widens. In fact, the rate at which the achievement gap widens between children from different socioeconomic backgrounds actually accelerates when low-income students are not in school (Alexander, Entwisle & Steffel Olson, 2007). Research shows that performance among students from low-income backgrounds improves when they attend schools with modified calendars (Cooper, Valentine & Charlton, 2003). It appears then that modified school calendars should be considered as one of the viable options for reducing the achievement gap.

Teachers and students experience a closer relationship in year-round schools than they do in traditional schools. In the absence of any long-term break from school, students do not feel detached from the school environment. Furthermore, the additional time allows teachers to offer students time to achieve better results, creating a sense of excitement and interest in students, and a sense of unified effort between student and teacher. Elsberry (1992) found that, likely due to an increased sense of belonging and accomplishment, the attendance pattern of students was much better in year-round schools than in traditional schools.

Some have expressed concern that teachers will have problems attending to their own family life if year-round schools are instituted. However, year-round school systems have shorter but more frequent school breaks, allowing teachers more regular time during which they may concentrate on personal and family needs. As a result, many teachers in year-round schools actually feel less work stress.

Research suggests there is less teacher absenteeism in year-round schools (Barron, 1993; Kocek, 1996). Teachers feel less of a need to take "mental health" days at year-round schools because they enjoy frequent breaks that give them a chance to recharge regularly throughout the year. In addition, teachers are able to schedule professional development opportunities during the intersession periods, in order to compensate for missed classes during the summer (Haser & Nasser, 2003). Research focused on teacher attitudes in year-round schools revealed that teachers found more satisfaction in the year-round school schedule (Fardig, 1992; Nygaard, 1974).

Low-income students have opportunities to develop habits for improved learning skills while attending year-round schools. The experience of immersion in learning offered by year- round schools, with more time spent in classrooms, proves to be beneficial to many students from low socioeconomic backgrounds, including those for whom English is a second language. Many second-language learners who have difficulty mastering English are advantaged by the opportunity to be immersed in English during intersession classes. They also develop better relationships with other students, and begin to feel more part of the school culture.

In addition to improving their academic standing, students at year-round schools may also have opportunities to develop creative talents they might not otherwise have explored, such as music and art. These classes work as a catalyst to improve personal growth. Results from research studies conducted on student behavior in year-round schools as compared to traditional schools suggest that there is a significant difference between the two in terms of self-confidence and self-concept. Other studies have found that year-round students have fewer inhibitions (Herman, 1991), and feel positive about their schooling experience (Fardig, 1992).

DISADVANTAGES OF YEAR-ROUND SCHOOLS

Along with significant advantages, there are also distinct disadvantages associated with year-round schools. The major disadvantage is the assumed detriment to family structure. American families have become accustomed to the traditional long summer vacation. Parents may find it difficult to schedule vacations and family reunions. This concern is not to be dismissed, as it is important to children's development to spend quality time with their families. Childcare could also become a concern, particularly if multiple, shorter school vacations were scheduled throughout the year, at times when parents are working.

Year-round schools can also prove to be disruptive to family life when children in the same household attend different schools. If one child in a home is a student at a traditional school while another attends a year-round school, the children may not have holidays together. Families could end up in a situation where one child is on a lengthy vacation while another is required to attend school.

Despite these potential problems with family scheduling, research studies have shown that, after implementing year-round schooling, parents found it not as hard to deal with the new schedule as they had anticipated (Pelavin, 1979; Shields, 1996). Another possible drawback, however, is the impact on the families of teachers in year-round-schools. Teachers whose children attend traditional schools may have difficulty spending time with their children during summer vacations. Because of these potentially negative effects on the family life of students and teachers, the year-round school system was discontinued by some schools, including the Seminole County, Florida, school district (Harp, 1996).

Extracurricular activities are another dimension of schooling that can be negatively influenced by year-round schooling. Teachers managing extracurricular activities observed difficulties adapting these activities into a year-round schooling schedule. Extracurricular activities can put stresses on all students, even those who might not be attending a specific school session. Students at year-round schools who were interested in sports activities found it essential to attend practice even when they were not part of that session. Similarly, teachers were required to perform their coaching duties even if it was not their session to teach. The problems in maintaining extracurricular activities in secondary schools were more complicated, and so in some areas, year-round schooling has been offered only for primary schools, where there ar fewer extracurricular activities (Opheim, Mohajer & Read, 2001).

Another area of concern when adapting to a year-round schooling schedule is administration. School administrations have sometimes found it difficult to deal with licensure and contractual issues of teachers when working out schedules for year-round schools. It can also be difficult to plan optimal usage of school buildings. Of course, a serious issue is finding ways to best leverage this new extra school time and to increase quality instruction time. In short, year-round schools require the administrative blocks of schools to keep working throughout the year, which increases the administrative burden (Atalig, 2003; Kneese, 2000).

Situations become even more difficult in multitrack schools, as the administration is required to manage different students in the same school at different times (Opheim, Mohajer & Read, 2001). Multitrack year-round schools require more use of buildings, educational equipment, and other facilities, which creates further insufficiencies and increases expenses. Time is often wasted, particularly in mundane activities such as moving equipment from one class to another (Carter, 1999).

CONCLUSION

In this chapter, we explored how students' experiences can be enhanced by implementing a year-round schooling system. Overall, the potential for increased learning opportunities that year-round schooling brings is at least somewhat tempered by concerns with scheduling vacations, allowing proper family time for students and teachers, dealing with administrative costs and concerns, and ensuring that this new time is used to maximum effect. Year-round schools can offer students more engagement, more learning time, and less lengthy downtime during which learning may be lost.

Year-round programs can be especially beneficial for low SES children, who have been statistically shown to suffer most from long school breaks. Low SES students' home and community environments may not support continued learning once the school closes for summer vacation. Students who need more time to learn may benefit from the extra help teachers are able to provide when increased school time allows them to do so. Increasing the time spent in school would bring the U.S. education system more in line with other developed countries, helping our children to be better prepared to compete in a global community.

While a major advantage of year-round schools is more quality instruction time, the administration of year-round schools requires extra effort when it comes to managing students, teachers, and the structural requirements of schools. Schools may find it expensive and challenging to manage the cost of extended-day education. Clearly year-round schools have some disadvantages.

Research shows that as parents, students, and teachers grow accustomed to the year-round schooling system, they inevitably find it more satisfactory when compared to schools operating under traditional school calendars. To enable our children to be truly competitive in the global marketplace, and to give them the opportunities that they need to succeed, our educational system needs to grow and change. Year-round schooling should be strongly considered as one part of the answer to better educating America's youth.

Chapter 9

Superman Would Hold Everyone Accountable

PROMOTING RESULTS THROUGH ACCOUNTABILITY AND ASSESSMENT

Educators, parents, politicians, and concerned citizens agree that the American educational system is in poor shape, and that far-reaching changes are needed for improvement. One illustration to support this fact is that in today's junior high schools, more than 80 percent of black and Latino students say they intend to go to college; for those who get to college, up to 60 percent require remedial work to prepare them for college courses; furthermore, 25–50 percent of these students drop out of college after only one year (Dubois, 2007).

Facts like these are evidence that our educational system simply is not preparing students for success beyond high school despite numerous attempts at school reform. We still find ourselves lagging behind other developed countries when it comes to educating our youth. Recent efforts, including NCLB, have focused on accountability in school reform. While one may debate the judiciousness of implementing No Child Left Behind and other reform attempts, it has to be admitted that results are what we need, and to know when results are achieved requires assessment and accountability.

Accountability in education refers to the practice of holding school districts, school administrators, educators, and students responsible for demonstrating specific academic performance results. *Accountability* has become a word that embodies a whole host of educational activity (Accountability, 2004), and is held up as a banner by some and feared by others. Throughout the country, policymakers are moving toward systems designed to reward educators for achievement and punish them for lack of improvement.

Historically, school system reform was guided by "inputs" into the system. Essentially, schools were given more resources, more funding, more staffing, and in some cases added more school days to the school year, in an attempt to improve learning outcomes. The focus on inputs, however, did not necessarily lead to noticeable improvements in student achievement.

Today, attempts at performance improvement center around changes in assessing students, reporting results, and holding schools and teachers accountable for those results. Under the No Child Left Behind Act, each state was required to submit an accountability plan, and they are now responsible for demonstrating continued improvement in student learning (Accountability, 2004).

There were a number of problems with the push toward accountability. For example, many states have difficulty developing adequate accountability systems, as they failed to incorporate solid academic standards and proper assessments. States' adoption of the Common Core State Standards, and their potential acceptance of assessments being developed by the consortia of states, will hopefully eliminate this problem. However, there are still states that have not adopted the Common Core State Standards.

There also remains a paradox where low-performing schools are having the most difficult time making significant improvements (Accountability, 2004). As a result, these schools risk losing funding and support so desperately needed in their improvement efforts. Of course, many people are worried about the validity of making such huge decisions about funding and support based on a single high-stakes test. Clearly, there are no easy answers to fixing our education system, but accountability and assessment are the current avenues that we are taking.

When discussing how to improve our educational system, it is imperative to understand the language and the relevant issues. In this chapter we look at issues of accountability by defining it, considering the role of the states in accountability efforts, analyzing the debate sparked by the No Child Left Behind Act as related to accountability, exploring the use of technology to facilitate accountability, and examining the role of various types of student assessments, including the use of value-added assessments, when it comes to accountability.

AN OVERVIEW OF ACCOUNTABILITY

Rewards and punishments are a part of everyday life. A prime example of this is an employee who decides not to show up for work. As a result, the employer decides to deduct money from the employee's wages—hence the worker's negative behavior is punished with an equally negative action. A number of sociologists and psychologists have done extensive research into the correlation between rewards and sanctions and the essential role they play in the performance of individuals (Cooper & Robertson, 1986; Latham & Pinder, 2005; Lawler, 1973).

The way that rewards and sanctions operate has drastically changed over time (Sennett, 2006). Take the "company men" that worked in various private or public corporations. With a high rate of work effort, dedication, and company loyalty, they could look forward to moving up the ranks of the organization. Not being picked for promotions or pay raises, however inconvenient or embarrassing, did not mean immediate removal from the workforce.

Things are different today, and much more is at stake. Employees with essential knowledge and contemporary skills are capable of reaching higher positions than those who cannot keep up with the extremely competitive nature of businesses. Current systems of rewards and punishments in today's organizations provide alluring bonuses for some, but create devastating problems, including job uncertainty and stresses, for others. This may all sound like reflections in psychology, or strategies for big business, but these ideas apply just as strongly in education today.

Historically speaking, schools have functioned a lot like the multimillion-dollar corporations of today, though with considerably shorter career ladders. Like corporations, they operated on the basis of hierarchies and stratification. Permanency and social rank led to a growth in job longevity, and factors such as insecurity, opposition, and staff turnover were decreased.

The "apprenticeship of observation" (Lortie, 1977) made new teachers understand the standards of performance in place at schools. The social unity between teachers allowed for collective expectations of the performance of students; the bad performance of a few students was tolerated and the high achievements of others were, for the most part, ignored. The highly competitive and aggressive systems of operation in the business world infiltrated the school system with the formation of accountability. This accountability increased with NCLB.

Many early efforts at educational reform concentrated on providing schools and teachers with more resources, particularly schools dealing with disadvantaged students (Hanushek & Raymond, 2004). Unfortunately, these additions of tools and assets had little real effect on student achievement. NCLB came to be in this type of environment, along with policies based on standards, testing, and accountability and an emphasis on performance objectives and teacher responsibility for student learning.

ACCOUNTABILITY AND THE STATES

NCLB forced states to develop and implement accountability standards. Policymakers remain committed to reform through accountability, and most parents, citizens, and educators support general NCLB principles. Opponents of accountability assert that it is poor practice to base so much on a single test. They argue that this practice weakens the curriculum, as teachers may teach to the test and encourage cheating. Further, an unfair burden is placed on teachers who teach students who have traditionally performed lower on standardized measures (Accountability, 2004).

These critics further assert that states have rushed into accountability without adequate preparation, including things such as revising the curriculum, training teachers, and acquiring necessary resources. While some states, such as Florida and New Mexico, have held teachers accountable by using standardized-test scores as part of their evaluations and the consideration for pay raises, many educators feel that it is unfair to hold teachers accountable in this way when so many aspects of student learning are beyond the teacher's control (Accountability, 2004).

As NCLB mandates continue, many state educators resist rigorous standards and expectations in an effort to meet NCLB annual performance requirements. Separating and identifying the effects of accountability policies of individual states is an unavoidably arduous task. As the accountability of a state is measured at one moment in time, the varying features and factors of all the state's schools cannot be accounted for when assessing the levels of accountability, thus making the examination of state-level variation an essential activity when analyzing student outcomes.

Other features that can lead to skewed and disproportionate estimations of accountability besides state policies include demographic differences and dissimilar assessment procedures among schools. Noticeable performance growth may coincide with implementation of an accountability system in a state. Nonetheless, it is unclear how accountability systems directly impact student performance.

Reward and punishment schemes as a result of school accountability have led to questions about the true impact of accountability systems on schools, teachers, and students. Questions also abound regarding the possible link between accountability and cheating, and the unnecessary classification and fragmentation of students into special-education categories has surfaced.

When schools do not perform adequately on state assessments, there are usually two immediate responses at the district level. The first inclination is to make adjustments in the curriculum, educational program, and teaching.

This does not take into account the high rates of staff turnover at certain schools or the difficulties surrounding changing school policies and the time needed for such changes to be effective.

The second response strategy is more immediate, and involves schools being more selective about the students that are accounted for in the scores. This strategy could support or totally replace the former. It involves allowing schools to remove students who performed poorly on assessment, so as to boost the school's overall performance levels without actually making improvements.

THE NO CHILD LEFT BEHIND DEBATE

The NCLB Act was certainly designed with the best of intentions. The act sought to create performance expectations by which schools, school districts, and states would be judged, with the intent of ensuring that all children were learning and receiving a quality education. However, academics continue to argue about whether or not the law has had the desired effect on schools.

NCLB was passed amid debates over whether external, test-based accountability actually improved student performances (Amrein & Berline, 2002; Carnoy & Loeb, 2002; Haney, 2000; Hanushek & Raymond, 2004; Lee, 2006, 2007, 2008; Lee & Wong, 2004; Raymond & Hanushek, 2003). Research on the effects of accountability policies and high-stakes testing after implementation of NCLB mandates were mixed and ambiguous. Information about the methods by which the new accountability systems would affect the performance of students and achievement gaps was also minimal (Lee, 2007, 2008).

One requirement of NCLB is that sanctions be imposed against schools not meeting established goals. Whether or not sanctions work is unclear however. Available information on two key options possible in the early stages of improvement by failing schools—supplemental educational services, and school transfers—suggests most parents ignore these choices for improved educational situations for their children, or districts are reluctant or quite simply incapable of catering to the needs of the parents.

School districts that are compelled to provide transfer options often lack replacement schools that are an improvement from the schools the students aim to transfer from, making it difficult for the districts to successfully execute replacement school policies (Kim & Sunderman, 2004). Whether having transfer options equates to better performances is questionable, as the number of students (approximately 1 percent of those eligible) who take advantage of the option is too small to determine the efficacy of this policy.

Supplemental educational services have been taken advantage of by a greater number of students (14 percent of those eligible in 2005–2006), thus the response to this option has been limited as well (Hoff, 2007). Insignificant and barely noticeable effects have been found by third-party assessments in relation to their improvement of student performance (Chicago Public Schools, 2007; Heinrich, Meyer, & Whitten 2008; Heistad, 2006; Potter et al., 2007; Rickles, Barnhart & Gualpa, 2008; Zimmer et al., 2007).

Restructuring options and corrective actions made available through NCLB, including charter school conversions or takeover by education management organizations (EMOs), may work in select cases, but they do not seem to be successful on a bigger scale, and are also accompanied by unwanted side effects. In Maryland, for example, certain reconstitutions intensified the capacity problems of some schools and led to a reduction in the social equilibrium in others.

A few schools did, however, take advantage of and benefit from newly organized schools (Malen et al., 2002). The effect of reconstitutions in Chicago and New York's Schools under Registration Review program were also inconclusive (Hess, 2003; Brady, 2003; New York State Education Department, 2003).

Research from Philadelphia and Baltimore suggested that takeovers by education management organizations were successful in some cases but unsuccessful in others (Blanc, 2003; Bracey, 2002; Saltman, 2005; Travers, 2003; Useem, 2005). Districts that were taken over by whole states also produced unequal results. The most probable factor of success in district takeovers by states can be attributed to financial management (Garland, 2003).

Not much is known about the conversion of charter schools as a means of corrective action and school redesign, however research on this topic is expanding. Still, changing district-administered schools into charter schools appears to have had unequal outcomes (Brown Center, 2003; Gill et al., 2007). There are actually a disproportionate number of charter schools on the list of failing state schools as compared to normal public schools (Brown Center, 2003).

Despite the apparent failures of NCLB to create widespread improvement in all schools' ability to improve performance among all students, some researchers have seen improvements resulting from accountability. Researchers at Harvard University suggest introducing systems of accountability into school systems often leads to increased achievement (Hanushek & Raymond, 2004). In fact, they assert that student improvement could not occur without required accountability.

Hanushek & Raymond (2004) caution that their analysis showed that simply reporting results has little impact on student performance, and that it was the sanctions and rewards associated with accountability that made the real difference. According to the authors' findings, rewards and punishment support improvement, and in fact lend credence to aspects of No Child Left Behind that so many have contested. If this assertion is true, and accountability for results is what matters, then the conversation must by necessity turn to the area of how to assess such results.

TECHNOLOGY-BASED ASSESSMENTS AND ACCOUNTABILITY

Students live in a world that is rich with rapid technological advancements, sophisticated mobile phones, games, and electronic gadgets. Today's generation will avoid the learning curve that adults had to undergo to come to grips with these tools. Public organizations such as hospitals and schools have begun to incorporate various technologies into their systems.

In this modern age there is one day in the year when schools go back to the way things were: computers, laptops, and other gadgets are switched off, electronic devices are silenced: this is on testing day. Some states are slowly incorporating new technologies such as the Internet into their tests. Computers are being used to deliver sections of the yearly state testing programs as directed by the No Child Left Behind Act by just over half the states (Bausell, 2008).

For the most part, the use of technology by these states has not drastically changed any fundamental approaches to testing. These technological advancements have merely made traditional approaches to test assessment more organized and efficient. Among these states, the most technologically advanced have only served to produce computerized counterparts of conventional multiple-choice, paper-based tests. All in all, the different versions of tests and what the results show remains unchanged.

Technology can do more than change the efficiency of current testing. Teaching and learning are areas that can be dramatically improved through technology. In elementary and secondary education, technology can widen and enhance assessment and various skills and concepts within it. Testing procedures that incorporate technology can do more than decipher whether or not students got a question right or wrong.

The use of technology can also identify individual patterns of thought and problem solving, using various forms of media that make room for more complicated and multifaceted questions and collection of data made available by the students as they answer the questions. Various technologies allow educators to gain a deeper understanding of how students solve problems, and whether or not students understand the concepts behind the questions. Teachers are thus armed with information on students' cognitive processes that then allows them to vastly enhance the quality of teaching.

Changing the fundamental dynamics of educational assessment by introducing technology will not be without challenges. Difficulties, including the associated finances, administration, and maintenance of technological networks, must be considered. Underfunded schools and schools located in low-income communities will likely have the most difficulty accessing new technologies.

Technology-enhanced approaches to testing would also need to be included in existing professional development in order for teachers to understand how this approach to testing can impact their teaching, as well as the curriculum. Too many teachers resist the incorporation of technology into teaching and learning, and more effort must be exerted in order to overcome what is actually a complex and multifaceted problem.

Groff & Mouza (2008) organize teacher resistance to technology use into six separate factors that must be addressed: student factors, teacher factors, nature of the technology factors, nature of the project factors (e.g., technology-enhanced assessment), district/school factors, and legislative/ policy factors. The partnership between pioneering technological advancements and ongoing growth in cognitive science provides a potential opportunity to significantly enhance teaching, and teaching in ways that make efforts to remove barriers to incorporation of technology into the nation's schools imperative.

In the late 1990s, Randy Bennett, who was responsible for the Technology-Based Assessment Project for the National Assessment of Educational Progress (NAEP), suggested that there would be three stages by which technology would help improve educational assessment. The first of these was the ability for technology to increase the efficiency of testing by mechanizing existing processes.

Secondly, questions—the available methods of response and the ways in which they are assessed—would become more sophisticated and complex, which would allow for more comprehensive old and new skills. Performance assessment would play a key role as technology enabled a brand-new generation of simulation. Lastly, assessment and instruction would work hand in hand to alter teaching for the better and to enhance student performance (Bennett, 1998).

NCLB AS AN IMPEDIMENT TO INNOVATION IN ASSESSMENT

Attempts to create new styles of testing were made more difficult when NCLB passed in 2002. The act, which states that yearly tests must be given in reading and mathematics in grades three to eight and once in high school, led to a significant spike in the number of annual standardized tests. More than forty-five million tests are now taken each year, which makes test maker and policymakers scurry to get the tests ready for teachers and students (Toch, 2006).

The growth in test taking, as well as the restricted capacity of the assessment industry and state educational departments to be fully prepared for the assessment season, has created a situation whereby assessment companies and state testing officials stick to the traditional types of tests instead of developing new methods of assessment. Testing models suffered greatly as a result of NCLB requirements and the infancy of new assessment technologies.

NCLB does not stop the use of computer-adaptive assessments, in which the level of difficulty of the questions is determined by the previous answers given by the students. However, it does state that assessments should be in line with state content standards and that each student should be assessed at their official grade level (Borja, 2003). This is to allow the comparison of results from student to student and create equal standards for students without taking into account any information about their backgrounds.

South Dakota and Idaho had already begun using technology-adapted testing for elementary and secondary students by the year 2002. The tests used by the states were altered to test the performance of low-scoring students by using questions below their grade level. The testing process also suffered from technical issues and, as a result, the U.S. Department of Education requested that computer-adaptive assessments used by these states to meet NCLB requirements be discontinued.

In the year 2007, the U.S Department of Education agreed to allow Oregon to use a within-grade-level computer-adaptive assessment for NCLB-mandated state tests. Other states were not able to take advantage of this shift in policy, since many had agreed to multiyear contracts and spent millions of dollars supporting traditional and fixed-format assessments (Madaus, Russell & Higgins, 2009).

State budget shortcomings made possible by the dot-com crash in the early 2000s reduced interest in computer-based innovations for student testing. Despite the hindrances, test experts still suggest that assessment will soon be delivered by computers and the Internet, particularly as a method to gradually increase the effectiveness of testing systems (Ash, 2008).

Problems such as test storage, provision of test books, papers, pens, and the physical distribution of these items will be eliminated as a result of computer-based testing. The rate at which tests are scored and analyzed will be greatly increased as well. In 2008, twenty-seven states delivered at least one of their assessments by computer (Bausell, 2008). Virginia administered over 1.4 millions tests using the Internet in the spring of 2008 (E-testing at the State Level: Lessons Learned, 2008)

EXAMINING THE EFFECTIVENESS OF COMPUTER-ADAPTIVE TESTS

Computer-adaptive tests offer a different type of efficiency. These tests can produce a more reliable estimate of student achievement using fewer items than required for a traditional test (Madaus, Russell & Higgins, 2009). Since the test quickly adapts to a student's skill level, this form of testing eliminates the need for test items that don't yield information about a student's ability.

Answers to easy questions offer little information to help assess a high-achieving student's specific level. Similarly, overly difficult questions provide little guidance on a low-achieving student's specific level. Seventy-five questions might be needed to get noticeable and relevant data on students at various educational levels (for example, twenty-five questions at low, medium, and high levels); a computer-adaptive test could offer fifty questions instead.

Since questions on computer-adaptive tests are focused on the student's particular achievement level, the test can provide more specific evidence about that student's performance. While computer-adaptive tests are only used for NCLB-mandated assessments in Oregon, they are increasingly used at the district level as practice and benchmark tests.

The efficiencies gained from computer-adaptive testing don't merely reduce the time and money used to administer testing programs. Incorporating automated essay scoring, a technology already in use on standardized tests such as the GMAT, the standardized test used for business-school admissions, enables assessments to test conceptual understanding and writing skills through open-ended essay responses.

More efficient tests make for development of more flexible testing programs. Rather than yearly testing, portions of the test could be given throughout the year. This provides a more accurate sample of students' progress over time. Teachers, administrators, and district officials have more immediate access to classroom or school-level assessments. Stronger links to teaching are created as teachers use test data to guide future instruction. Students also receive automated feedback, which can more readily be used to improve learning and performance.

More periodic, flexible, and efficient testing allows teachers to more easily embed assessment into current instructional processes. At the same time, a few researchers are starting to find ways in which technological advancements can enhance assessment in more fundamental ways. They suggest that the technology-enabled assessment systems Bennett and others envisioned are indeed possible. These systems would be able to test knowledge and skills more thoroughly, test skills and concepts that haven't been measured in the past, and reflect more fully what we know about how students learn.

Among the efforts to pioneer forms of technologically based testing is the Problem Solving in Technology-Rich Environments (TRE) project. The project began in 2003, when a sample of two thousand nationally representative students took part in a study to explore how information technology could be involved in the nation's "gold standard" for testing, the National Assessment of Educational Progress, by creating situations "that would feature . . . the kind of exploration characteristic of real-world problem solving" (Bennett et al., 2007).

Skills such as data retrieval, self-monitoring of effort, organization, interpretation of results, and the capacity to communicate interpretations coherently were measured by the project. One scenario required eighth graders to solve problems about complex relationships between mass, volume, and buoyancy. Links between balloon altitude and payload mass needed to be discovered by the students. Students conducted experiments using balloons with different payload masses, gathered information, and reached conclusions using a mixture of multiple-choice and open-ended responses.

TRE shows the existing potential in technology-based testing. There are more complicated and multistep questions for students to answer. Various forms of media, such as instruments and animated balloons, allow for interesting ways of presenting questions to students. Complex questions can be presented in ways suitable for elementary school students (Ridgway & McCusker, 2003). Visual and graphic representations are made available to students so they can see each step of their solutions, as with the balloon during their experiments.

Another example of technology-enabled assessment being used in science education is Floaters, a test given to students as part of the World Class Tests optional assessment program in the United Kingdom. The international initiative uses highly visual, engaging questions, enabling young students to be tested on an aspect of scientific method in ways not possible using paper and pencil. Students use an interactive simulation to weigh a variety of foods and observe whether the food floats in water. Students must then develop a hypothesis about the patterns they observe (Boyle, 2005).

The questions in TRE and Floaters can be dynamic, and they provide new data and challenges that are based on the actions of the students. The students are allowed to try out various methods and even attempt multiple solutions. Computer databases can record and store the strategies and methods used by the students. More incisive judgments can be made about the steps taken by the students to solve the problems as a greater range of data is made available.

The buttons pressed by the students in the TRE exercise, the choices they made, and the order of the values they chose is stored in a database. The quality of their choices and their actions is measured using a set of rules that are evaluated and scored based on existing statistical frameworks. These statistics are then linked across multiple skills and allow the students to be scored based on various points of evidence.

Since the steps taken by the student have been stored and can be analyzed, their choices can be observed and their reasons for choosing certain responses can be studied—which aids in the process of identifying gaps in their skill level and fundamental misunderstandings. This information can then inform future instruction (Bennett et al., 2007).

Instead of one-dimensional right or wrong answers, technology-based assessments can provide a multitude of data points regarding students' actions and responses. Their ability to understand complicated infrastructures can be assessed by simulation exercises. Since these models are closely tied to classroom instruction, and measure process and content simultaneously, widespread use is problematic. As the NAEP cannot assume that all the nation's fourteen thousand school districts have studied identical science content, the TRE exercise restricted its problem solving to technology, rather than science.

On the other hand, the Calipers project, which is funded by the National Science Foundation, is interested in developing performance assessments of a high quality that can be used for testing on a large scale in classrooms and informing instruction. With a focus on physical-science standards relating to motion and forces, as well as life-science standards relating to ecosystems and populations, the project requires students to solve problems that include measuring the correct speed and angle at which to rescue an injured skier trapped on an icy mountain.

Much like TRE, the Calipers project collects descriptive information about the students' choices and approaches to solving the problems presented to them. The project also makes use of multiple-choice answers and open-ended responses. The aim of the Calipers project is to couple the descriptive data with students' self-assessment activities in order to produce information to aid learning and instruction for the students and teachers (Quellmalz et al., 2008)

Education is a complicated and decentralized system in the public sector, which is financed and controlled at various levels. In order to successfully make enhancements to assessment, carefully controlled and monitored changes will have to be made, including revisions to curriculum, standards, and teacher training. If educators and policymakers do not pay attention to these sectors, there can be no guarantee that core practices and methods in the notoriously rigid education system will be changed by the introduction of technology.

Education historian Larry Cuban of Stanford University warns that the "persistent dream of technology driving school and classroom changes has continually floundered in transforming teaching practices" (Cuban, 1996). If technology is introduced without taking into account the content and methods of instruction, the only change that will occur will be to automate the existing systems.

COMMONLY ACCEPTED STUDENT ASSESSMENT PRACTICES

While technology may be better leveraged for accurate testing, types of assessment are even more important. Historically, education has used two types of assessment: norm-referenced assessment and criterion-referenced assessment. Today, a third option, value-added assessment, is receiving much attention. Following is a discussion of all three forms of assessment.

Norm-Referenced Assessment

Norm-referenced tests are the most traditional assessments used for accountability. In this instance, students are compared to each other. These assessments require that half of all students be ranked "below average" (Evergreen Freedom Foundation, n.d.). Norm-referenced tests have been criticized over the years. While it is true that some valuable information can come from norm-referenced exams, they are of limited use in truly ensuring academic learning and improvement. Unfortunately, these tests often illustrate a school's socioeconomic divisions more than the effectiveness of teachers and the school (Evergreen Freedom Foundation, n.d.).

Criterion-Referenced Assessment

Criterion-referenced testing has historically been preferred by educators over norm-referenced assessment (Evergreen Freedom Foundation, n.d.). In this type of testing, students are tested to ascertain how they fair in demonstrating specific knowledge and abilities. Rather than being compared to other students, the results are compared to previously developed levels of knowledge and achievement.

Value-Added Assessment

Value-added assessment is designed to ensure that students are learning, by comparing their current knowledge and skills against their previous knowledge and skills. In essence, this type of assessment focuses on student growth, rather than comparisons to other students or accomplishments of specific achievement levels (Evergreen Freedom Foundation, n.d.). Value-added assessment provides an objective way of evaluating teachers, and is less about who a student is than about what goes on in the classroom (Evergreen Freedom Foundation, n.d.). Value-added assessment can be done at the student level, classroom or teacher level, or school level. It offers a variety of advantages over norm-referenced and criterion-referenced assessment, including the following (Evergreen Freedom Foundation , n.d.):

- Value-added assessment moves the focus from statistics and demographics to asking of essential questions such as, "How well are students progressing?"
- Value-added assessment focuses on student growth, which allows teachers and students to be recognized for their improvement. This measurement applies equally to high-performing and advantaged students and under-performing or disadvantaged students.
- Value-added assessment provides results that are tied to teacher effectiveness, not student demographics; this is a much more fair accountability measure.
- Value-added assessment is not a stand-alone solution, but it does provide rich data that helps educators make data-driven decisions.
- Value-added assessment assumes that teachers matter, and recognizes that a good teacher can facilitate student improvement.

PROGRAM EVALUATION AND ACCOUNTABILITY

School reformers know that program evaluation strategies can be used by schools to collect and study information that will ultimately aid in continuous enhancement decisions. Five steps can be used by practitioners in any contexts to gather and analyze data effectively:

Set the stage and clarify goals: The optimal time to make choices about assessment is in the developmental stage. Writing sessions and meetings can produce opportunities in which to share ideas about the suggested program, and the reasons for its use and proposed effects. A voluntary after-school program in mathematics and English can be used as an example. The staff should consider the students they wish to target, how the program will run as a whole, and the goals of the program, which may include proficiency on state tests and higher pass rates, as an example. The more defined the goals, the easier the measurement of its effects will be. Allowing staff participation at the beginning of the program will also ensure their active participation during the assessment stages.

Create evaluation questions: Creators of informal evaluation systems can use their target goals to create suitable questions that the evaluation will answer. Questions include whether or not the program was executed as it was planned, if the execution supported the goals that were initially set up, the number of participants in the program, and if the program had a positive effect on the students. Other questions could include the growth of students who participate in the program and whether or not the program improved their opinion of school.

Analyze and interpret data: The efficiency and goals of the program can be measured by studying data collected. Methods of teaching and the various activities can be analyzed. Test scores and patterns can also be examined. Percentages and other statistics can be used to evaluate trends in student participation. Reasons students participate can also be measured and possible improvements to the system can be made. Data can be examined during program operation times to make slight modifications and at the end of the program to make decisions about future efforts.

Use the results: Members of the program staff will need to decide how they will use information gathered from the analysis of program data to make changes in implementation of the program. The data analysis will likely show improvements as a result of program implementation, but it will also show areas that are in need of further development. The staff needs to establish which revisions they will make for the following term and how they will continue to make changes based on the data collected.

Key role of Evaluation: Lastly, district staff must identify the key role of evaluation strategies in aiding improvement planning in schools. The staff is presented with useful information about how well a program was executed, needed modifications, and ultimately, the impact of the program on students. Evaluation removes ambiguities and presents an unbiased framework that can effectively judge the importance of any initiatives taken by a school. Well-informed decisions can be made by schools with the data gained from the evaluation of programs.

MOVING FORWARD BY TRACKING PAST PROGRESS

School reform can no longer rely mostly on inputs—that is, giving schools more resources and more support. Time has shown that inputs have no real impact on student performance. Federal edicts, such as NCLB, have enforced protocols based on standards, testing, and accountability. Standards emphasize performance objectives and require high levels of accountability from educators.

Required reform and accountability, particularly those that impose sanctions similar to those imposed by NCLB, often create much stress and anxiety. This certainly has been the case since NCLB went into effect. Many educators ask whether it is fair to hold schools accountable for student achievement. And, even if it is "fair," how are we to measure such achievement? What testing and evaluation formulas will be used? The answers to questions like the above are not easy. Obviously, achievement can only be guaranteed if we assess it in some way. However, current assessment models are flawed.

Research exists to suggest that standards and accountability may improve learning for some disadvantaged students, particularly those with disabilities. McLaughlin and Rhim (2007), for example, found that when some schools implemented accountability guidelines, they promoted an environment of increased collaboration among educators and created an environment where teachers expected disabled students to perform better, which in turn encouraged better learning outcomes.

Some countries have been able to show effective and useful outcomes based on their use of certain accountability policies. However, American policymakers and researchers still do not have any real evidence that these latest accountability reforms are working to improve the performance of the vast majority of students (Hofman, Dijkstra & Hofman, 2009).

Conversations around school accountability have been polarized. Politicians and parents often want to hold schools and teachers completely responsible for student achievement. Teachers point to disinterested students and uninvolved parents, saying that there is only so much they can do. But studies have shown that if teachers and students work together, and schools hold themselves accountable, great strides can be made. All of this discussion of accountability and standards is intended to bring us to a place where schools are performing better and our children are learning.

Researchers at Sam Houston State University in Huntsville, Texas, observed positive strides toward improved learning outcomes among a variety of middle schools (Jackson & Lunenburg, 2010). The researchers believed that improvement strategies must not only improve learning, but also develop responsiveness and social equity. While studying middle schools, they found that teachers at high-performing schools were using teaching strategies that required students to think critically, and strategies that involved the use of real-world problems.

These teachers were not simply teaching abstract ideas or teaching to the test. They noted that student achievement can be improved when students receive recognition for efforts such as note taking and doing homework, as well as having the opportunities to work collaboratively in groups and engage in active learning like the testing of hypotheses.

These findings show that the type of assessment or accountability that NCLB brings is not the be all and end all of the teaching equation. Rather, the quality of instruction is the biggest part of learning. It is paramount that we continue to work toward a more balanced solution, finding ways to encourage quality instruction, while also monitoring results.

Chapter 10

Strategically Allocating Resources to Support Teaching and Learning

ALLOCATING RESOURCES TO IMPROVE STUDENT LEARNING

Providing every child with an equal opportunity to learn has been a central challenge in public education. In fact, at its inception, universal public education in the United States was viewed as the "great equalizer." Education was perceived by some as the vehicle through which individuals could rise above the social and economic circumstances that may have created longstanding barriers to reaching their potential as individuals and contributing citizens.

As the test of time has proven, education alone cannot address entrenched social problems—multiple institutions, policies, and support systems are necessary to level the social and economic playing field (Levin & Kelly, 1994; Rothstein, 2004). However, education is and will continue to be one of the primary means by which inequity can be addressed. Public funds will continue to be allocated in support of educational programs, and the rationale for these investments will likely continue to be that education creates social equity.

The purposeful and practical allocation of resources to support equitable access to high-quality learning opportunities is a major component of education policy at the federal, state, and local levels. Leaders at all levels of education are charged with making decisions about how to effectively distribute and leverage resources to support teaching and learning.

Resource allocation consists of more than assigning dollar amounts to particular schools or programs. Equally, if not more important, is the examination of the ways in which those dollars are translated into actions that address expressed educational goals at various educational levels. In this respect, leaders are concerned not only with the level of resources and how they are distributed across districts, schools, and classrooms, but also with how these investments translate into improved learning.

It is critical for resource allocation practices to reflect an understanding of the imperative to eliminate existing inequities and close the achievement gap. All too often, children who are most in need of support and assistance attend schools that have higher staff turnover, less challenging curricula, less access to appropriate materials and technology, and poorer facilities.

Leadership and Resource Allocation

Allocating and developing resources to support improvement in teaching and learning so critical to school-reform efforts are fundamental leadership challenges. Education policymakers must be informed about emerging resource practices and cognizant of the ways incentives can be used to create conditions that support teaching and learning.

Resource allocation in education does not take place in a vacuum. Instead, it often reflects policy conditions that form a context in which opportunities for effective leadership can be created. For example, effective leaders know how to use data strategically to inform resource allocation decisions and to provide insights about how productivity, efficiency, and equity are impacted by allocated resources.

The roles, responsibilities, and authority of leaders at each level of the education system also impact whether and how they are able to allocate resources to particular districts, schools, programs, teachers, and students. Further, the type of governance structure that is in place also affects decisions about resources and incentives. Governance issues arise as leaders become involved in raising revenue and distributing educational resources. These activities involve multiple entities, including the voting public, state legislatures, local school boards, superintendents, principals, and teachers' associations. Each of these connections can provide insights into how best to allocate resources and provide incentives that powerfully and equitably support learning, for both students and education professionals.

Resources necessary to operate a successful school or school district cannot be confined to dollars alone, however. Indeed, the resources needed to actively and fully support education are inherently complex and require an understanding that goes far beyond assessing the level of spending or how the dollars are distributed. Educational leaders must be able to examine the ways in which those dollars are translated into action by allocating time and people, developing human capital, and providing incentives and supports in productive ways.

Principals, district officials who oversee and support his or her work, and state policymakers whose actions affect the resources the principal has to work with are all concerned with three basic categories of resources:

1. Money. Activities at several levels of the system, typically occurring in annual cycles, determine both the amount of money that is available to support education and the purposes to which money can be allocated. No one level of the educational system has complete control over the flow, distribution, and expenditure of funds.
2. Human capital. People "purchased" with the allocated funds do the work of the educational system and bring differing levels of motivation and expertise developed over time through training and experience.
3. Time. People's work happens within an agreed-upon structure of time (and assignment of people to tasks within time blocks) that allocates hours within the day and across the year to different functions, thereby creating more or less opportunity to accomplish goals.

These resources are thus intimately linked to one another. Each affects the other and even depends on the other to achieve its intended purpose. An abundance of money and time, for example, without the knowledge, motivation, and expertise of teachers (human capital) does little to maximize desired learning opportunities created for students.

Furthermore, an abundance of human capital without money or time to distribute it does little to alter practice in classrooms or to share expertise with others. From their position of influence over the acquisition, flow, and (intended) use of resources, educational leaders thereby undertake a massive attempt to coordinate and render coherent the relationships of the various resources to the goals they set out to achieve.

Relating Resource Allocation to a Performance-focused Agenda

As the focus on the improvement of learning becomes more central, what educational leaders are expected to do and accomplish through the allocation of resources has changed. Historically, supporters of education were more concerned with the dollar amount allocated per pupil, and they spent much of their political capital advocating for increases from one year to the next.

Educational leaders were responsible for creating balanced budgets with the dollars they had available and accounting for expenditures in a responsible manner —a complex task in large school districts. Little attention was paid to how resources were related to performance or what type of performance was expected. The standards-based reform movement of the past several decades changed the situation fundamentally, by prompting new questions about what the learning standards should be and how educators should be held accountable for improved performance.

In response, educators have become more focused on results, while taking the stance that higher performance cannot be accomplished without adequate resources. Thus, a sea change has occurred, prompting educational leaders to consider how resource allocation is related to building high-performing systems that work for all students. As they take seriously the charge to become more learning focused, leaders critically examine the equity, efficiency, and effectiveness of existing resource allocation policies and practices and make decisions regarding ways in which resources might be reallocated in more productive ways.

This resource reallocation challenge is as important in the present era of standards-driven reform and accountability for results as it is difficult to realize. Given the considerable variation in the needs, capacities, and contexts of schools, it is striking—though not surprising—that for the most part, resource allocation patterns in K–12 education are relatively uniform (Nakib, 1995; Monk, Pijanowski & Hussein, 1997; Miles & Darling-Hammond, 1998).

The uniformity of leaders' responses to these varying needs may simply signal a safe course: the most easily defended set of decisions in a context of competition for scarce resources. Beneath the surface of this course of action, however, conflicting expectations, tensions, and barriers may be impeding leaders' ability to think more creatively about how to organize and allocate limited resources and act strategically. These barriers exist at all levels of the educational policy system.

In such a situation, leaders might wish for definitive understanding about the impact of particular investments on student learning, yet the state of knowledge here is incomplete (National Research Council, 1999). The highly contextual nature of schools, the variations with which any particular improvement strategy is implemented, the motivational conditions that are present, and the need to adapt strategies to fit specific circumstances all interact with the resources brought to bear on learning-improvement goals.

Consequently, leaders act in response to particular needs and learning challenges with limited evidence of performance. In such a context, and despite differences among states, districts, and schools, educational leaders face some common problems of practice with respect to resource allocation. Four of these are central to leadership that focuses on learning:

1. Making resource-related decisions that seek to close achievement gaps and have good prospects for enhancing the equity of educational outcomes, as well as organizing schools and districts to enable the alignment of resources with learning- improvement agendas.

2. Structuring time, the nature and assignment of staff, and programs so that they collectively emphasize learning-improvement priorities; managing the politics of learning-focused leadership.
3. Mediating the political pressures associated with decision-making about resources that emphasize learning improvement and with the redistribution of authority to act; developing the human capital of the school or district.
4. Providing supports, incentives, and opportunities for learning that build motivation and expertise, thereby fostering higher performance.

DECIPHERING THE INTRICACIES OF SCHOOL RESOURCE ALLOCATION

There are two components to understanding what controls district and school resources. The first component traces every one of the dollars spent in order to determine who controls what is purchased. The second step unravels the barriers to schools changing the ways in which they use the resources so they appear to "control." District leaders often are surprised to find they do not share the same views of how much control schools have. District leaders also learn how their departments unwittingly combine to limit school options (Miles, 2004).

When school leaders are included with district leaders in the assessment, they are frequently taken aback to find that district leaders believe they have more control over resources than they actually experience. Although districts may think that schools have budget control, the actual flexibility schools experience is often defined so narrowly that they really have few options. Even in districts that have implemented versions of "school-based budgeting," schools will often have a very limited ability to make changes in staff. Districts might give schools "control" over their substitute dollars, instructional supplies, and equipment. Worse, the purported "control" frequently comes with specified governance structures or various approval processes that drain valuable group time and sap energy by debating marginal changes having little to do with instruction. This is why so many reformers argue that districts need to move to more complete solutions. Student-based budgeting is often cited as one such solution (Miles, 2004).

School-based Control of Resources

As schools begin to change the way they use staff to support their unique designs, districts will find they need to move toward giving schools dollars based on the number of students in their school instead of allocating funds based on specific staff positions. This change is important for management and equity reasons. Logistically, as more schools want to change the way they use staff, it becomes confusing to keep track of all the trading in and converting of staff. Trying to free up only certain funds for flexible solutions can create further complication and raises troubling equity issues (Miles, 2004). Giving schools more autonomy does not guarantee improved achievement automatically. Without incentives to improve school performance and an understanding of alternative possibilities for organizing resources, increasing school-level control over resources usually results in limited change (Wohlstetter, 1995). Worse, the first changes that schools tend to make in the use of resources can have very little to do with improving the achievements of students, and more to do with the needs of adults.

As districts move to create flexibility in the use of resources, they will need to ensure that schools meet legal and funding requirements. The district may, for example, encourage schools to combine staffing resources from special programs, including bilingual, special education, and Title I, in order to create a more integrated, individualized instruction for every student.

In order to support more comprehensive programs and still be able to ensure that schools are meeting the specific needs of special-education students, the district will need to set up a dedicated system for accountability integration. Schools will need proactive district action and guidance to make many of the more significant changes in resources and organization. In some cases, dramatic improvement in achievement will require schools to make difficult or large-scale personnel changes.

Gradual changes in staff due to attrition may not help a school implement new strategies quickly enough for them to notice desired changes in outcomes and improvements. It may prove necessary for a school to alter the teaching staff mixture and hire more academic teachers and fewer nonacademic teachers and support staff. Or the school may decide to eliminate instructional aides and invest the dollars in professional development or certified reading instructors instead. A school cannot change dramatically the composition of its staff. And it is extremely unlikely that a group of teachers will recommend changes that result in lost jobs without district directives and support.

Allocating Resources for Comprehensive School Reform

Across the United States, districts looking for greater results in student performance desperately need more funding to support four crucial requirements. Primarily, they are in need of investment funding to allow the introduction of new curriculum and teaching practices. Secondly, districts need dollars to create time and purchase the expertise to support principals and teachers in planning and learning the new strategies. Thirdly, they must find ways to ensure teacher salaries that will attract and retain powerful teachers.

Finally, they need to provide more individualized attention and time for students in academic subjects. Many districts will benefit from new dollars in increasing the standards of student performance, but not if they are added on top of flawed programs, practices, and structures. Comprehensive school reform involves an encompassing review of the whole school's organization and methods. Because of this, schools and districts must look closely at how existing resources—time, staff, and dollars—might better support new comprehensive school designs, improved teaching practice, and chosen academic priorities.

District leaders typically need to (1) realign district spending levels and patterns to better support comprehensive school designs and academic priorities; (2) support and motivate schools in reforming their application of resources to boost their comprehensive school-reform plans and important academic programs; and (3) redesign district practices to give schools and their principals more control over the use and organization of their resources.

When estimating levels of expenditure and trends, districts need to address three questions: Is there enough money to support high-quality education? Does each school get its fair share according to the district's strategy? Does spending on district-level activities focus on instruction and align with a comprehensive school reform/standards-based reform strategy?

First, district leaders need to articulate priorities and direct spending without concern over overall spending levels, but they must ensure that the community has sufficient funds in order to begin the task. It is difficult to ascertain how much money is enough, but there are some questions for the district to consider. These include: How does spending per pupil compare to other districts with similar student populations? How do teacher salary levels compare? How does the community's tax rate compare to other similar districts? Second, districts must be sure that each school has received its fair allocation of dollars to begin its redesign work (Roza, Guin & Davis, 2008).

As schools begin to realign their resources to better fit their designs and goals, they often request changes in staff or budget. The changes required are initially small, but districts must be aware of each school's requirements. Districts must ensure that transparent guidelines are established for school-level resources that enable them to address issues by fair and flexible means in each school. If there is any uncertainty about how much of the district's total budget is required to be allocated to each school, district leaders are in peril of confusing budget cutting with decentralization, and frittering away a school's energy developing projects based on money that does not exist (Roza, Guin & Davis, 2008).

As a preventive measure, a district might therefore address: What is the total amount, including the whole funding, allocated by the district for the elementary grades in comparison to middle and high school? And has the district distributed dollars equitably? In other words, are the same resources given to schools at the same grade level, with the same number and mix of students?

Districts typically allocate staff positions rather than dollar amounts to schools. Each type of staff position may often be assigned separately, altering allocated positions in line with annual budget status. Moreover, a change in allocation rules may be utilized according to the source of funding. The result is that districts may not have a clear sense of total spending for each level of school and type of pupil (Title I, bilingual, or special education for example).

Thus, despite apparently objective formulas, schools can end up with very different levels of resources. At the beginning of the process of implementing comprehensive school reform, it helps to see the bottom line in terms of dollars allocated as well as total staff. With the "how much" questions answered, the district can look at how the dollars are spent to aid the improved learning establishments. Adjusting district spending to meet a total school-reform project is a two-stage process.

During the first stage, it is necessary for districts to find or free up funds to jump-start the introduction of a comprehensive school-reform design. These funds support the purchase of new materials and hiring outside experts to work with teachers and principals as they learn the new practices. In the second stage, districts must objectively review their organization of support to schools and teaching staff in upholding their work to reform practice. They should also examine whether resources match their stated strategy and academic priorities (Roza, Guin & Davis, 2008).

IMPEDIMENTS TO EFFICIENT RESOURCE ALLOCATIONS

Critics of greater financing demands routinely highlight nationwide cases wherein major increases in spending were misspent and provided little or no positive outcomes for student learning. As no one would seriously argue that extra spending could never achieve school improvement, strong evidence exists that without adjustments in the distribution of resources, their use, and accountability, it may prove that Americans finally get a more expensive, though not necessarily more efficient, public education system.

While many district leaders do indeed worry about the role that resource allocation plays in improving student-learning outcomes, crafting district strategy for reform and managing an urban district's megabudget are, in fact, treated as separate, albeit important, activities in practice. Whether recognized by public officials or not, the system of resource allocation is the very method by which organizations illustrate options about means and ends.

District leaders do not appear to fully recognize the means they employ to assign resources or their available alternatives. Thus, while it is apparent that many district leaders have become quite clever at articulating the objectives and protocol vision for enhancing student performance, such verbal descriptions often bear limited resemblance to the actual strategy decreed in resource allocations.

District leaders may think their allocation strategies are straightforward, but most don't recognize the many different forces at play, and just how far beneath the surface of the regularly published district budgets the allocation policies, patterns, and decisions that crucially influence the sharing out of resources in a school district are. Public education, similar to other public sectors, is a multilevel operation where funds are allocated to districts by the federal government and states.

In combination with other local incomes, these resources are rebudgeted and then separated into broad categories, such as education and administration, or possibly into broad program types such as special-education needs. A more helpful way of looking at district strategy is the next rung in the allocation process of dividing these large sums and then converting them into services, programs, and staff, and finally distributing them to determined schools and students (Roza, Guin & Davis, 2008).

Allocating Resources to Targeted Needs

Leaders in many districts have begun to adopt new strategies that will have real implications for the use of resources in districts, including targeted resources in order to narrow the achievement gap. In this particular approach, district leaders work in order to concentrate resources and efforts on students who are at the greatest risk of poor performance. The expectation is that by decentralizing the decisions about how to meet student needs, as well as locating accountability for student performance with schools and school leaders, schools will then become more effective and efficient at meeting their students' needs.

Centralized reform (sometimes referred to as "managed curriculum") reflects a more centralized, systemic reform where district leaders create an aligned curriculum and seek to build capacity throughout the district. Some districts use a small-schools concept to look at challenges with performance at high school level. The theory being that in smaller, more personalized settings the students will interact with a set number of adults who are familiar with them and who work in a more integrated style to fulfill their needs.

Unraveling the Budget Conundrum

School budgeting systems are particularly complex and involve a great deal more than line items in budget binders. Some budgeting methods use protocols or formulas that determine the allocation of funds and resources and their amount; this includes student-to-teacher ratios and per-pupil protocols.

Also, budgeting methods assign set amounts, either to central departments that provide a certain service to schools, their staff, or students; or directly assign an amount to the schools. School-finance staff members proceed to utilize these budgets and accounting practices over the fiscal year to ensure actual district expenditures are captured, observing financial patterns in the same typical budget categories: fund source, object, and activities.

Typical budget categories will illustrate district leaders' overall approaches to dividing up a large amount of money into separate resource areas. Financial documents of a district do not integrate many of the crucial details that will eventually sway the process of resource allocation among schools or students. There is no tracking or understanding of the sort of decisions that will ultimately decide the fund's flow and many people involved are not sufficiently able to determine their own part in the patterns of resource allocation thus created (Roza, Guin & Davis, 2008).

To understand the budget system, it is crucial to understand how tiers of policies order the resources to flow through the levels and eventually to the schools (Miller, 1965). Even though district leaders create the budgets, individuals implement them in the districts and schools. These individuals decree not only the expenditure and which category will benefit from it, but also serve as managers of the funds (Wildavsky & Caiden, 2004; Lee, Johnson & Joyce, 2004). Even though the same goal may be shared by different district departments, it is possible that individual groups will elect to use their own methods of allocation (Trinkl, 1973).

Therefore, it is essential to determine not only the source of resource management but also which individual is responsible in the allocation of said resources. Budgeting formulation is complex, and is frequently swayed by politics, control struggles, and the processes of human thought. Therefore, we should anticipate a disconnect between what top leaders comprehend is a district's policy of the flow of resources and how that is manifested at school level (Deeming, 2004). Hunter (1979) suggested that a definition of each resource allocation can be determined by which policy stimulants are present in resource use and shared among subunits. Some label this method "apportionment" and find that practices with the ability to create "multiforms" direct resource flow across subunits.

Understanding the restrictions that accompany public funding is fundamental to understanding the allocation patterns of resources. Different funds have different restrictions imposed by state, federal, and local agents as to the purpose of resource use or distribution. For example, resources may be restricted for use in the reduction in class size, or compensatory education like Title I grants matching, or services for special education. These restrictions apply to all levels of individuals, often by statutory means, and can have implications for the deployment of resources.

NEW MODELS AND TRENDS IN RESOURCE ALLOCATION

Many investigators have requested new methods to determine expenditures as a means for better understanding priorities, organizational investments, proposed strategies, and as a tool to quantify the deployment of resources across subunits. Completely new expenditure models have been pioneered by manufacturing theorists that include costs that are activity and program based, and which assist in forming fiscal data to further broaden its comparability to strategic decision-making.

In education, several reports have demanded new methods of expenditure recordkeeping as a means to modify district strategy, mostly toward ensuring the real expenditure involved in individual schools, programs, or services is duly identified (Odden et al., 2003; National Forum on Education Statistics, 2003; Miller, Roza & Schwartz, 2005; Coopers & Lybrand L.L.P., 1994).

Though the models demonstrate some differences regarding the terms of the categories used, all of them propose assigning a larger percentage of costs two specific types of students and schools. For those having interest in resource data in relation to the context of educating students, it makes sense to review central and indirect costs that are associated with joint district resources, as well as resources that are typically school based. Costs that have less relevance are associated with district leadership, other operations, and services of a noneducational category: e.g., transportation, food services, school facilities, and maintenance systems.

Reforms relating to accountability have placed a focus not only on performance inequalities between white students and students from minority backgrounds, but also between students having differing determinable needs that result from disability, poverty, or limitation in English proficiency. Many policymakers stress that the first stage in tackling these performance gaps is to align fiscal policy with student needs. But as policymakers refurbish their established funding formulas to fulfill the needs of different students, they do so without evidence. In the first instance, there is little explanation of the way resources are currently aligned to different subgroups.

Basically, for a state policymaker attempting to assign an allocation to particular student types, no baseline data exist on current expenditure in regard to each type of student within their own districts or other schools within other districts. School districts in most states do not fully track costs by student type or the school level.

Even where these data are tracked, they are not accessible from published works for policymakers attempting to pin answers down (Roza, Guin & Davis, 2008). Equally challenging is the difficulty in accessing comparisons from other states regarding spending. Accurate ways of defining or reporting expenditures influenced by student needs are not available, which makes it impossible to compare data between states.

Furthermore, policymakers have not yet determined how to flow funds from one level of government to the next, so that funds finally reach students. For example, funds may be designated by the federal government for students living in poverty, with the goal of enhancing expenditures at schools having high concentrations of poverty. However, by the time funds are dispersed through state and local allocation streams, they may not reach their intended target.

Finally, only limited documentation exists on different decisions for structuring assigned allocations and the way those decisions relate to policy aims. Put in other terms, allocations meant for students having limited English proficiency (LEP) might be realized as a fixed dollar amount per LEP student, reimbursements for the spending on bilingual education services, apportionment of staff full-time equivalents (FTEs) to high-needs schools, or as funds for other areas. Research has not yet delineated ways these different decisions influence either what is finally spent per pupil or how efficiently that funding reaches the intended students.

For districts wishing to commence anew with student-weighted allocation systems (whereby funds are allocated on the basis of student types), offering clear-cut guidance on what increments should be assigned to each student type is a crucial first step. However, a definitive response plainly cannot exist in the current state of fiscal allocation policy. The difficulty here is that currently there is no efficient resource allocation system whereby an answer can be reliably extrapolated.

Policymakers are consequently forced into determining fiscal policy without information relating to expenditure on student types. They are forced to do so with no understanding of the workings of allocation policies at different levels (federal, state, and local) either together or in conflict. Policymakers have little clarity on expenditure for different student types at the school level, nor awareness of the types of policies that would be more effective at guaranteeing that dollars reach students in the proposed ways.

School finance today works in opposition to the focused and effective utilization of resources that promote improved education of students. Just as an archaic computer can no longer function properly in a technological environment inundated with the latest software, this nation's school finance system frozen by a combination of unrelated expenditure policies and administrative plans can no longer serve the needs of an educational system calling for reform. A new model is required to do one thing—ensure that every child receives instruction for his or her needs in order to become an involved citizen having total participation in this modern economy.

Current school finance systems fund programs, uphold institutions, and offer resources and staff employment so the school and district administrators can fully execute the multitude of laws and regulations that have become part of public education. However, the methods employed by today's school finance systems—deploying expenditure levels based on habit and not need, covering up funds' actual allocations, supporting institutions whether they are viable or not, hypocritically addressing equity, spending resources flippantly, attempting to make adults accountable by compliance and not by results—confuses the links between resources and academic aims that make finance relevant to student performance.

The school finance system evolved in a previous era in which programs were funded, and students passed or failed without much regard paid to the role of funding in student performance. This pattern was sustainable then, as jobs were available for people with low skills, and the vast majority of workers were not required to be well educated in order to maintain a healthy economy. Unfortunately, that legacy has proven unworkable in today's highly technological, information-based economy, where low-skilled workers cannot rise above poverty level and overseas workers are able to compete effectively in the market for skilled jobs, once available solely to Americans.

The current finance system focuses on maintaining programs and paying adults, not on seeking the ultimate way to educate our children. It is essential that schools adapt within a fast-changing economy, but our system arranges funding for the very same courses and teaching methods developed by previous generations. Experiments by schools must be deployed with technologies that might alter teacher and student work, but the current financing system dictates that their money be spent on a predetermined set of factors, including organizations, programs, and people. Those realities severely limit our nation's ability to effectively and accountably use resources in planned ways.

Our children require and deserve a proper education, and we must strive to provide them with the type of education that befits the stature of this country. It does not matter how much concern Americans take with regard to education; in reality, spending will always be finite, and schools will never achieve the luxury of affording absolutely every item that some educators might discover to use effectively.

Increasing costs and competition by way of other sectors, such as health care and public safety, will inevitably squeeze funds available for education. Even if we doubled or tripled expenditures on public education, it would still be crucial to ensure that every dollar counted or it would be forever true that Americans—including parents, taxpayers, and educators—would be offering less for our children than we could with the money available. Therefore, whatever money is available for schools it must be utilized in the greatest, most effective manner possible.

Chapter 11

Sustaining School Reform: The Race Is Won by Those Who Endure

TODAY'S SCHOOLS

The structure of schools in the United States is no longer suitable for the educational needs of children today. No longer are the poor restricted to manual labor or blue-collar jobs. Nor are the benefits of education confined to the elite in society. Times have changed and it would be only natural to expect that the demands on our education system have changed as well. No longer can we rest assured that the best and brightest members of our society will educate our children.

A number of alternative occupations may prove to be more attractive than the teaching profession. Many of the most talented among our citizenry could be exceptional teachers—however, they are free to become astronauts, attorneys, accountants, and aerospace engineers, for example. This leads to massively increased competition among teacher education programs to recruit the best potential teaching talent and lure them away from jobs with salaries, benefits, and work conditions perceived to be far more attractive that those in the teaching profession.

Our schools are replete with educators who have become experts at gathering data but have yet to channel their newly gained knowledge into constructive actions that benefit America's students. It is one thing to obtain data and identify a problem, but unless this information is used to solve problems, nothing has been gained. It is also possible for data to leave as many questions as it does answers, particularly when there are questions about the source of the data.

A case in point is the Maryland School Performance Assessment Program (MSPAP). The MSPAP was meant to be an innovative statewide assessment program to support school reform in the mid-1990s. Measuring student progress at the school, district, and state levels, along with the collection of data to inform changes in instruction, were among the goals of the program. Findings based on a survey conducted by Koretz et al. (1996) suggested general support among teachers and principals for the program.

Forty percent of teachers surveyed believed the MSPAP included tasks that were developmentally inappropriate for their students. Further, half of the teachers surveyed felt an accurate measure of math skills would not be possible for students who had poor writing skills, given the structure of the assessment. Hence data collected would not be able support at least two of the goals of the assessment program. Data collection did not result in information that could be used to make needed changes.

It is more difficult to focus on whether or not students are learning than to focus on teaching strategies. There must always be attention to what, or if, students are learning, and not just what teachers are teaching. It is the job of teachers to facilitate learning, and not teach children how to memorize a predetermined material. Consider a scenario where two people who speak different languages attempt to communicate. It is likely they will not be able to understand each other.

When this happens, the common response is not to try to make things simpler, but to speak louder. When this doesn't work, one or both communicators will speak louder still, and this time place more emphasis on diction. Teachers sometimes fall into the same trap when dealing with children —if they try a learning strategy and it fails to take, instead of changing their approach, they simply try the same thing again, over and over.

The solution is not just to give teachers information on what to do, but to train them in how to deliver instruction through alternative means if their strategy doesn't work. They will be much more successful if they have a range of options and strategies from which to choose. More importantly, however, they develop the disposition that learning must take place—giving up is not an option.

Testimonials are easy—conducting thorough evaluation can be challenging. Evaluations involve detail and in-depth reviews of program, policies, and practices to determine whether they are working or not. We may not always like the responses we get regarding favored practices. While we may be able to state that everyone involved in a popular program loved it, anecdotal information alone cannot take the place of a solid, detailed evaluation process.

It's a universally acknowledged fact that elementary school children love the volcano experiment—the one that involves lots of papier-mâché and mess—and teachers will spend days putting it together. That does not mean the experiment contributes in any meaningful way to addressing school learning outcomes. This can best be derived from an adequate evaluation, which would very quickly establish which activities contribute to learning and which ones are more of an exercise in enjoyment.

Collecting data and information for evaluation is the first step toward problem solving. It frees us from engaging in the blame game, which has been a tendency when we finally pay attention to problems existing in our schools. Society blames teachers, teachers blame parents, and parents in turn blame teachers. Life, and indeed the reasons for our deteriorating educational system, are very complicated. Singling out one group as the cause for problems that are burdening our educational system will not ameliorate the situation.

Lasting and beneficial change in our schools will require hard work from a committed group of stakeholders—teachers, administrators, parents, policymakers, and community members alike. Ultimately, it is all about the children we should care deeply about in this nation. At the end of the day, they are the reasons we must champion the work of public education.

IMPLEMENTING AND SUSTAINING SCHOOL REFORM

It is obviously hard to institute sustainable school reform when much of the reform undertaken in schools is the result of constant policymaking and changes mandated by incoming district administrations or temporary popular measures. Sustainability does, though, require change to happen, as a "lack of change" speaks more of conservatism than reform. Essentially, sustainability means that improvements should be ongoing.

The evolution of transportation provides an instructive example. Transportation did not stop with the invention of the wheel. In the intervening centuries, transportation mediums were being developed, refined, and improved upon until they evolved into the industry we know today. The process has not stopped, nor should it. Innovation is always taking place, which means improvements are occurring. Our schools should emulate this type of process—school improvement should never end.

Let us consider five key points to sustaining school reform. The first of these is a substantial level of commitment, which stems from the belief that change is possible. There is, in fact, a great deal of power to be found in belief. Belief is what gives disadvantaged people the will to try to succeed and minorities the will to prosper. Conversely, the lack of belief can impede the success of reform efforts, regardless of how promising the proposed content of the reform may be.

If the will is not there, reform will not happen. Belief is just as important in school reform as in any other areas of life. If support, belief, and commitment are missing, then schools can paper over the gaps in the short term, but without the commitment of staff and faculty, the reforms lack stability. The likelihood of successful reform is, therefore, dependent on faculty and staff members embracing the implementation process of reform and sticking to it.

Reforms that originate outside of schools (e.g., reforms initiated at the district level) are by no means doomed to fail. Even so, district or other administrators need to make special efforts to assist teachers and other school staff in developing a feeling of ownership of the project in order to foster commitment and a belief in the efficacy of the reform.

Sustainable reform depends on the development of capacity. As our knowledge of cognitive science grows, we learn more about the ways individuals take in and process information. This knowledge has led to greater focus on how effective learning environments are built. Schools and districts are somewhat restricted in how they operate due to political, financial, and practical concerns, but they can still use their increasing knowledge to develop practices relevant to student learning needs and to structure learning environments to more effectively support these needs.

One absolutely vital aspect needed to sustain school reform is the time to accomplish it. It is a commonly reported issue that one of the most challenging issues schools and districts face is the need for time to plan and implement reform that would lead to improvements. No matter how successful the leadership of a school happens to be, leaders only have the same number of hours in a day as everyone else. Nonetheless, they likely have more demands on their time, which places them under pressure to maximize how their overcommitted time is used.

This issue often separates effective from ineffective leaders: the best ones will make much better use of their time, and have more control over it. Naturally, they will still come up against obstacles they can't change, but they also have strict time-management processes and will constantly evaluate how effective they have been in their use of time.

Sometimes the result of leader's evaluation of time use will help them realize they stretched too thinly. Effective leaders are able to delegate some of their leadership responsibilities to other staff members who can perform those functions with support. They also make sure that all the activities they undertake—particularly those relating to reform—will be structured around teaching and learning. Effective leaders will also make sure that their processes are efficient and that their actions will always work to further the goals of the school.

The actions of effective leaders may leave some staff or stakeholders feeling a little neglected or angry that they have not been given sufficient time with their leader. Ultimately, however, nothing comes without a cost, and it's a case of weighing the benefits of spending time on reform against the costs of not focusing on other duties. The aim is to minimize the cost of actions while maximizing their benefit. This means that good planning and implementation are vital in order to manage time effectively.

Also vital to sustaining school reform is retaining staff to implement reforms and improvements, as the success of any given reform often depends on the consistency of its implementation. Of course, the implementation of reforms can withstand a certain level of leadership or staff turnover, but it is more difficult to sustain reforms when new faces are being introduced all the time.

A shared vision is challenging to create and maintain without stable leadership and a supportive culture from the staff. It is a simple fact of life that high staff turnover can create instability and have a negative impact on efforts to establish a consistent learning environment for students. High staff turnover is also quite costly, particularly when the recruitment of teachers, and then the training of new teachers in the intricacies of the reform effort, are considered.

More effort and support needs to be given to the recruitment process for teachers at the outset as schools and districts initiate reform efforts. Hiring teachers who "fit" reform goals will likely reduce teacher attrition. Still, more support needs to be available for new teachers. Even teachers who ostensibly have the skills and attitudes that align with reform goals will need mentoring and other supports as they begin their jobs. Every attempt must be made to reduce the debilitating rate of turnover.

Inevitably, a major factor for sustaining reform is having the money to do so. Most efforts now are centered on how to make the most of current funding and utilizing money effectively in order to maximize the positive impact of reforms, rather than how to access untapped resources. Despite the dearth of new money, it is possible to free up cash through alternative means of spending.

An extreme proposal to accomplish this is to reduce staffing to the absolute minimum. For example, a school with five hundred students would have twenty teachers and one principal. Approximately one million dollars could become available, depending on how many education specialists (regular and categorical) and instructional aides worked within the school. This is radical option, and there are other, less extreme ways to change the way money is spent, to include increasing class sizes, spending less on upgrading technology, and eliminating some programs.

The key however is to look in detail at all financial outlays, measure them according to the extent to which they contribute to the goals of the school reform, and rank them according to how well they do this. This will enable schools to break down spending into its core components and work out what is necessary and what can be cut during the process of change in order to better implement their improvement strategy. This is particularly important in times of austerity, when elements that are not essential may have to be reduced or cut in order to help drive reform, no matter how popular or long-standing they may be.

Spending money on nonessential areas does support school-reform efforts. It is important to keep the focus on the school's key goals, whether they are academic or extracurricular, which contribute to students' overall development. (e.g., music education or leadership training). Prioritizing where money is spent does not automatically mean cutting all nonacademic projects. What gets cut will depend on the goals of individual schools. This should be a workable situation, as long as the school is still accountable to the state and the district for shifts in expenditures.

BARRIERS TO IMPLEMENTING AND SUSTAINING SCHOOL REFORM

Over the past few decades, districts have partnered with or otherwise watched the efforts of private, local, state, and federal bodies to radically alter schools. These efforts have included changing the structure of the school day, imposing accountability for performance on teachers and students, coming up with new curricula and different instructional approaches, offering more training and development for educators, and decentralizing the work of districts.

Attempts to alter the way schools work require districts to develop agendas and strategies for change (McLaughlin & Talbert, 2003). Despite all the hyperactivity, many reports from external analysts suggest that—particularly in urban areas—district reform agendas have not resulted in many changes. Even in areas where success has been realized, it has most often been on a small, local scale that would be extremely hard to replicate (Bodilly, 1998; Cuban, 1990; Elmore, 1996; Fullan, 2001; Hess, 1999; Hill, 1995; Ladd, 1996; Sarason, 1996; Tyack & Cuban, 1995).

Districts have a lackluster school-reform record. Policymakers and reformers see districts as part of the problem, not the solution. Major school-reform projects have shut districts out of the process. Coalition of Essential Schools, Goals 2000, and the Annenberg Challenge, believed central offices were inherently incompetent, and unlikely to improve, thus any school reforms involving districts would likely fail. For example, district incompetence and corruption in Chicago during the late 1990s interfered with reform initiatives at the school level (McLaughlin & Talbert, 2003).

A growing number of researchers and analysts have come to the conclusion that without the school district to act as a mediator between the educators and the state, our education system would be in limbo. Without their effective engagement within schools, any potential reform is a losing battle and will only result in disappointment.

Research on the integral role school districts play in the management of the standards of instruction and their potential to lead education reform throughout the district supports this view (Elmore & Burney, 1998, 1999; Massell & Goertz, 1999; Spillane & Thompson, 1997; McLaughlin & Talbert, 2003; Togneri & Anderson, 2003). Eventually, this will lead to effective and sustained reform of schools by essentially targeting the root of the problem (House, 2000; Lewis, 1995). The challenge of reforming districts is difficult but necessary to sustaining school reform.

Over the past twenty years, many reforms of some sort have taken place throughout the United States on a continuing basis. Despite the constant need for change, very few, if any, of these reforms really made their way to the school level. Rothman (2005) believes this lack of implementation and sustainability to be a result of several factors.

Most of the initiatives that led to reform originated from dynamic leaders who were capable of implementing these changes in extraordinary fashion, despite the presence of various radicals in strong opposition to these changes. However, as soon as the leaders moved on to their next challenge, these radical individuals returned to their old ways. The reform was diminished, and eventually there remained no trace of it. A reform rarely became set in stone without any opposition. Therefore, unless the leader kept a vigilant eye, it would fade away like all its predecessors.

MUTUAL ACCOUNTABILITY

Gering (2005) discusses lessons learned in the Kansas City school district's successful efforts to sustain reform. In 1996, Associate Superintendent Bonnie Lesley made an influential presentation to the Kansas City School Board in which she revealed the dismal state of its education system. Her presentation was well received, and the school board responded favorably by demanding that immediate action be taken.

District-wide reform was initiated based on Lesley's presentation—reform that could not have been achieved without a certain amount of risk. Lesley revealed a number of facts that had the potential to cause irreparable damage to the various parties involved. Naturally, the district leaders confronted the data as soon as it emerged, and the school board demanded immediate action.

The Kaufman Foundation, a Kansas City-based philanthropic organization, took an interest in the Kansas City schools reform efforts, and decided to contact Dr. James Connell, president of the Institute for Research and Reform in Education (IRRE) , for a consultation. Although Connell's background was not in education itself but in youth development, he was convinced that his theories supporting youth development would apply within the school system as well.

The Kauffman Foundation commissioned Dr. Connell to write a "white paper" applying his ideas to schools. This white paper was the beginning of the First Things First reform, and a starting point for a triangular relationship between Kansas City, Kansas Public Schools (KCKPS), the Kauffman Foundation, and IRRE. These three organizations became mutually accountable partners in a reform process. They created yearly "mutual accountability" plans to ensure a continuous supportive structure for reform.

The relationship among the three organizations was unique in that it did not limit them to the traditional roles of philanthropist, technical-assistance provider, and school district. This relationship was a partnership in which all three organizations held each other accountable for the work and engaged in rigorous conversations around the goals, strategies, and interim outcomes. These collaborative conversations resulted in flexing the reform to meet the changing needs of the district (Gering, 2005).

KCKPS's approach to reform was based on the premise that the entire school district needed improvement. To realize this, all schools, pre-K through grade twelve, participated in the reform, along with central office. Staff members across the system, across grade levels, and across sites were able to discuss reform principles using a common language, resulting in a sense of collective responsibility for all students. Districts are by nature large, bureaucratic organizations that resist change. In many reform models, the district is ignored or seen as something to work around.

Some reform models proclaim the district obsolete, allowing schools to be independent entities. In KCKPS, the role of the district was clear: to lead and support the First Things First reform framework in all schools. There was a single reform for the entire school district, with a common set of principles, a common vocabulary, and common outcomes. This singular focus meant that the district had to get involved with the process of reform, as opposed to being on the sidelines or, even worse, a saboteur (Gering, 2005).

The reform work in KCKPS became the work of everyone in the system: teachers, support staff, central office staff, and the board of education. In the early stages of reform, the board agreed to a district-wide, two-hour early dismissal every Wednesday afternoon for staff development. Although this difficult decision was met with some resistance in the community,

Wednesday afternoon early releases became symbolic, both to district staff and community members, as an action that solidified the board's commitment to the First Things First reform (Gering, 2005).

As KCKPS faced the reality of its student-achievement data, it also had to share the data with the community. If a district honestly shares student data that is unacceptable, the district needs to have a response to that data. The key is to move the sense of investment individual parents may have in their children's education to a collective sense of responsibility for the education of children in the total community.

As the superintendent shared the data with the community, his stump speech went something like this, "We have done good work with many of our students over the past many years, but for a large number of our students we have not been as successful. As you can see in our results, too many of our children are not graduating from high school, and too many are not achieving at high levels. We can do better, we have to do better, and we plan to do better" (Gering, 2005).

The community responded positively to the general outline of the reform plan, although staff members would naturally require a thorough briefing on the responsibilities of the various players and the estimated timeline of implementing the various changes to the current system. In 1997, the reform plan was initiated in KCKPS, initially targeting one quarter of the district, the Wyandotte cluster, with the inclusion of all pre-K through grade twelve schools.

All involved individuals, including community stakeholders, were thoroughly briefed on the various elements of the reform and how the reform plan was to be implemented on a step-by-step basis. The implementation process was set over a period of four years and the aim was to have all schools in the district engaged in the reform work by 2001 (Gering, 2005).

The definitive nature of the reform plan and the presence of a timeline made it more impressionable and gave it an aura of permanence. It was simply a matter of time until all the schools within the district were consumed with the elements of the reform. This sense of inevitability had not been experienced before and certainly came as a shock to the authorities based in KCKPS. Indeed this level of synergy was so unprecedented that it captured the attention of educators and policymakers throughout the country (Gering, 2005).

First Things First was not without its problems however. One of the factors that counted against the reform plan was the way in which it was executed. Contrary to the general notion that school districts were to be sidestepped rather than consulted on plans for reform, it was expected that the KCKPS district would support the reform effort.

As it turned out, the district was fully involved with the selection and implementation of the reform plan. They were not, however, collaborative in their efforts, as decisions were made solely by the district leadership. Since neither the community nor the local NEA unit were consulted about implementation plans, the district staff initially disapproved of the reform plan. The district had not followed the "buy-in" process that had become the norm with reform over the years.

Many people believe that the success of a reform plan relies, to some extent, on a highly collaborative reform selection process that would lead to buy-in from all stakeholders. In the end, the plan did not receive 100 percent support from all parties, as many of the staff members retired earlier than they initially would have because of the reform plan, while other staff simply left the district because of the plan. This could have had disastrous effects if it had escalated.

Problems associated with the exodus of staff were compounded by the fact the exodus occurred in the midst of a teacher shortage in the Midwest. In fact, in 2000, the district started the year with over a hundred long-term substitutes, due to the departure of more teachers than normal and the shortage of teaching candidates. This led to a chorus of naysayers saying, "We told you the reform would drive good people from the system." However, even with these departures, the system was seeing improvements in attendance, graduation rates, and suspension rates (Gering, 2005).

Districts wait to implement significant reforms, believing everyone should "buy in" before reforms commence. The buy-in process is usually complete before any significant work of the reform is implemented. This can lead to reform burnout, due to the buy-in process being stretched out over an extended period.

The end product is often not optimum and the impact is greatly reduced. In addition, stretching out the buy-in period allows resisters to rally and possibly sabotage reform efforts. Many well-intentioned reformers never get significant reforms off the ground, due to an ill-fated belief that they must secure buy-in before they begin.

District leadership sought ways to embed reform into multiple external documents, grants, and outside service providers. For example, First Things First was written into the request for release from a twenty-year-old desegregation order. When the courts finally approved the desegregation plan, it was released along with the roll out of the First Things First reform plan.

The district's work with NEA, while not beginning until after the selection of First Things First, was essential to providing outside support and pressure (Gering, 2005). In 2001, Dr. Ray Daniels, superintendent of schools, declared that the school district was no longer in a reform but, rather, the reform was now the "work" of the district. This sent a clear message to the staff, telling them that just because the end of the initial implementation had been reached, that didn't mean that the reforms were finished.

KCKPS has invested significant resources in developing leadership within the system. Leadership development has focused on the reform work and not on generalized leadership activities. Also, the district accepts responsibility for generating the next wave of leaders in the school system, highlighting the ongoing nature of the work (Gering, 2005).

SUSTAINING SCHOOL REFORM INDEFINITELY

People involved in the piloting stage of school reform often see what they are doing as something limited by time. Other stakeholders likely share this view, or are of the opinion that the work will stop when the reform money runs out, or that the new reforms won't take hold. This generally leads to fragmentation or a lack of a coherent approach to reform, and as a result, reform efforts often end up sidelined (Adelman, 1995; Adelman &Taylor, 1997a, 1997b, 1997c, 2003). Unfortunately, this circumstance runs contrary to the realization of in-depth, sustained school reforms.

The cyclical turnover of superintendents and school board members makes it difficult to ensure that others will continue effective systemic reforms begun by one board and superintendent. New superintendents and new school boards often want to make their mark by initiating changes rather than sustaining the strategies created by their predecessors.

This is often the case even when evidence suggests that existing programs are the ones that need to be sustained to meet long-term goals, such as closing the achievement gap or getting all students to proficiency. The new leadership appears to forget that there are no quick fixes or short-term reforms that guarantee continuous improvement in student achievement, as they jump to exchange existing efforts for improvement with new ones.

The process of school reform can become very lengthy, and on the whole it is expected to stretch across a period of several years. Ironically, school districts are placed under tremendous pressure to turn a new page each year, allowing for only a fraction of the time required for any reform plan to produce results. This is sometimes part of a government ploy when budget cuts are enforced with little notice, or a result of resentful parents streaming to the authorities in opposition to some aspect of the an existing plan.

The process of annual makeovers comes at substantial costs to the states that are likely already operating on limited funds. Cost is not the only issue however. By reinventing the system each year, educators, teachers, and principals alike have no chance to come to terms with the details of any particular plan before it's time to implement the next one. As a result, educators are never fully versed on any plan, in effect making the process of reform fruitless.

The role of the school district is to take a long-term approach, define, and articulate the school-reform agenda for the district, as they are a crucial source of leadership in implementing and sustaining reform. Their role should be to develop a framework by which sustainable reforms can be measured even if there is a turnover of staff.

Framework should include three key points: improving student achievement; fiscal accountability and increasing organizational effectiveness; and building and improving relationships with staff and the broader community. This framework provides an agenda that the school board and staff can work from and use as a checklist to measure the success of reforms. It also means that when recruiting new staff you should look to hire people whose vision matches the already defined vision of the district, an important factor when it comes to sustaining change over time.

Chapter 12

Turning Theory into Practice: Implementing and Sustaining Successful School Reform

THE CURRENT STATE OF AMERICAN EDUCATION REFORM

Educational change will never occur if school systems are expected to implement change on their own. State and federal governments need to oversee changes to ensure that local school districts are held accountable for needed changes. School administrators often seem to buy in when educational reform is suggested, but somehow genuine change in education is rarely implemented. Americans cannot continue to allow the educational system to operate in its current state. While there is no magic formula or configuration to solve the problems our schools face, we must engender change, and we must do it now!

On the surface, the concept of sustaining school reform is an oxymoron, simply because change is inevitable. In many ways, what is needed is sustainable change! In other words, schools must change to meet the current needs of children and youth in order to support their development into contributing and productive adults. As the needs of society shift, our education system must adapt to ensure an educated populous for society's needs.

Continuous evaluation can be used to measure the impact of the reform, its progress, and sustainability. Although evaluation is based on data, it should also reflect and examine policies and practices, which can either engender success or doom the reform efforts. American educators are supported in their efforts to sustain school reform by the availability of research-based practices. Our youngsters are the future of this great country, and our educators must do their part to help put America back on the top as a major world power in both economics and education.

EDUCATIONAL POLICY AND RESEARCH

Educational policy is a major component of sustaining education reform. It is incumbent upon reformers to ensure that policy is backed up by research. Reformers and policymakers alike must be able to distinguish between reliable and unreliable research. Many empirical and case studies delineate the correct way to implement needed educational change. Researchers and educators can use search engines and databases such as Google Scholar and ERIC database to find peer-reviewed articles on educational practices.

In order for school reform to be successful, the person creating the changes needs to know the inner workings of each school. Having an abundance of theoretical knowledge is not enough. Although theory and research are at the roots of education reform, that knowledge should be coupled with tacit knowledge derived from being a practitioner. School reform must be evaluated by the data collected from student assessments, but statistics and data are not a replacement for intuition or practical knowledge.

Based on the combination of practical and theoretical knowledge, administrators who suggest systematic change should be able to answer four essential questions before initiating plans for change. They must be able to respond to the question of: why change? In the process of responding to this question, leaders will need to analyze the cultures and beliefs of all participants in the organization and decide if reform or change needs to take place.

The second question they respond to is: what is the nature of the change being implemented? Administrators will need to clearly articulate their vision for reform. They must also prioritize the changes and implement them based upon importance. The third question that requires a response is: is change feasible? Administrators need to decide if the recommended changes will produce tangible results. Finally, the fourth question in need of a response is: how will the school implement the changes? An assessment of the organization's resources and capacity is recommended when considering implementing systematic change.

The key to sustainable reform is the country's ability to support educational change at the school level, and to ensure that administrators have access to the multiple resources (i.e., information, human, and financial) necessary to make and maintain changes. Administrators facilitating procedural change should not be shocked when cultural and structural change is resisted by the educators and staff of the school. It is a psychological fact that people do not like change (Moerschell, 2009). For this reason, structural and cultural change should not be taken lightly.

In the end, the purpose of school reform is to make sure schools are meeting the needs of their students. With a changing population, schools must also change. American school systems were created based on middle-class needs, values, and expectations. With the current economic crisis, many families who were once middle class are now living at the poverty level.

The gap between the rich and the poor is steadily widening. Also the minority population is now becoming the majority. According to the 2008 census, the Hispanic population will become the majority by the year 2050 (CNN, 2008). American children need schools that understand their diverse needs, and schools that are able to provide all with a quality education.

TYPES OF REFORM

Based on many empirical studies, there are three types of change a school can make when creating school reform. These include, but are not limited to, procedural change, technological change, and systemic change. Procedural change requires amendments of the procedures already in place. This type of change usually concerns the sequencing of events and altering the speed at which they occur.

Technological change deals with the everyday practices of the faculty and staff. The job remains the same, but the method used to complete it has changed. Systemic change concerns changes in the tasks of a normal day in the school. It requires amendments to rules, attitudes, and beliefs, all while recreating the culture of the organization.

Procedural change is a commonplace occurrence in organizations like schools. This type of change is usually a matter of assessment and the correct conveyance of information. The new procedures need to be correctly conveyed to the faculty and staff who are directly and indirectly involved in implementing the reform. If at all possible, the changes should be communicated face-to-face, but written communication is also acceptable.

Incentives for change may need to be given if the old procedures are deeply rooted in the organization. Once the change has been conveyed, a system of checks and balances must be implemented to ensure the old procedures are not revisited. Lastly, an evaluation has to be performed to ensure the new procedure is serving its intended purpose and is benefiting the school more than the original procedure(s).

Technological change requires constant assessment and communication. In addition, it requires continuous staff development for those directly and indirectly involved in the process. It is likely that all faculty and staff will need to attend a specified number of professional development sessions in order to obtain the skills necessary to incorporate technological change.

Administrators should anticipate staff resistance to technological change and should prepare ways to help staff combat their uneasiness with technology (Moerschell, 2009).

When school districts meet resistance from certain sectors of the community and within the district, they generally interpret these signs as a warning that reform will not be effective. The signs of resistance could mean that the initiative or reform is actually working. It is human nature to fear the unknown. However, the fear of the change does not speak to the quality of the reform. Members of a school community are used to the status quo, and when they are faced with something unfamiliar, their skepticism is their way of holding on to the past instead of moving forward (Moerschell, 2009).

Fear of the unknown accompanies educational change. People tend to revert to the familiar when faced with the unknown and the possibility of failure. This thought process is counterproductive to school growth and improvement, and precludes the possibility of genuine reform. Administrators in this predicament always find ways to rationalize why the existing plan is the best course of action. They need foresight to address the rebellion before the movement can gain support. If the administrator is able to foresee problems or rebellion, he or she might be able to turn the negative energy into positive energy.

As with all organizations, it is not enough to provide professional development when implementing technological change. Leaders and teachers making the change also need the opportunity to practice new skills within a specific school context. In some cases, it may be necessary to receive mentoring from qualified persons. When technological change falls short of expectations, administrators might not have developed well-crafted training opportunities or did not give the educator enough practice carrying out the new skill or skills.

Another reason for failure of implementation could be that the change was not gradual enough nor sufficiently scaffolded for those trying to make the transitions necessary for successful reform. Teachers will often scaffold instruction to allow students to build upon previous knowledge (Gijlers et al., 2009)—the same strategy can work for teachers and administrators as learners.

When implementing systemic change, the same dynamic applies. Systemic change usually needs to combine the steps of procedural and technological change in order to be successful. Above all else, in order for systemic change to be successful, administrators have to be strategic and demanding, but also respectful and supportive. If the administration understands their staff, they will be better prepared to facilitate understanding and a more successful reform of the school's policies and procedures.

CORRUPTION ON SCHOOL BOARDS

A major cause of obstruction of school reform is the presence of school board politics. School board members are voted in at local elections. Nominees may campaign on the promise of change to gain the popular vote with no intention to actually make the promised changes (Berry & Howell, 2008).

Once the members are voted onto the board, political bickering and infighting greatly diminish the effectiveness of the board. Schools and their boards were created to protect the average student and to ensure all school-age children are given a free and public education. School boards were not created to benefit the members' selfish needs for petty power trips or to endorse a certain brand of textbook.

Like all divisions of government, corruption can occur on school boards. For example, in choosing a textbook, the board might select one that is not as beneficial as another but saves the school system money which they surreptitiously intend to recommend be used for a personal agenda at a later point in time. When adults allow politics, as opposed to what is the best interest of the children, to drive their actions, essentially they are abusing their power. Federal, state, and local governments preach reform and promise to do everything in their power to ensure that every child in America receives a quality education.

Unfortunately, American youth rarely reap the benefits of the new quality education or witness the promised changes. Only about 70 percent of school-aged children graduate from American schools (Kiley & Racusen, 2007). The statistics are both alarming and heartbreaking. There should be no room for self-serving politics when it comes to the education of our children.

BEWARE OF MODEL SCHOOLS

Model schools can be found in every major city, but when trying to recreate their success, many schools fail to achieve the same results. Trying to recreate another school's success is potentially dangerous, even when schools share similar characteristics. This is because, regardless of the similarities, every district is unique. Often, after a large amount of time, energy, and money has been spent, the school declares the plan a failure and has nothing to show for the efforts.

Even model schools have problems sustaining school reform over long periods of time. A school can develop a record of excellence for implementing a particular type of reform, but soon after, the school will abandon the previous plan and institute a new reform by the time word of the success of the first initiative has convinced others to try the same reform. The quick turnover can be caused by a large number of educators leaving the district for new opportunities.

Many ask why the management of educational change is contingent upon the presence of certain individuals. The answer resides in the fact that educational change requires change in school culture. Educational change requires that traditions and procedures be reevaluated and amended. If change is resisted by the faculty and staff, then the school system must implement strategies to combat it. When the initial excitement starts to fade, strategies must be implemented to revitalize the excitement felt at the beginning of the reform.

Strategic planning, which is widely used in the educational arena, closely examines the goals and visions of specific school reforms. Many researchers will be hard pressed to find a school district that does not have one or more strategic plans awaiting execution. Some schools will successfully execute a strategic plan, but will fail to share the secret to their success. In order for the plan to be effective, it is important that school districts show fidelity to their plan.

Too many plans to change can be as dangerous as not having a plan at all. Strategic plans are a district's consistent road map, even in the fact of overturning staff or administration. The plan will also serve as documentation when the federal government looks into accountability. In this way, schools should glean what they can from the efforts of other schools to implement and sustain change. In the end, a strategic plan that reflects the culture and needs of the individual school is likely a better route than attempts to replicate the efforts at another school.

BEWARE OF QUICK CHANGES

When initiating reform, an action plan must be developed before the school can determine how the reform implementation will be carried out. Too often, administrators become anxious and feel the need to change the implementation processes before any data has been collected. More patience is warranted because if a plan is not working, it can be amended.

The school team, which consists of educators, administrators, and all others who work in the school, must make the necessary amendments without hindering the efforts to create or sustain school reform. Creating too many changes within one reform plan would be counterproductive, however, and frustrating for all parties involved. For instance, when a new principal is hired, he or she sometimes finds it necessary to shape the school in his or her own image, causing the reform efforts to be put on the back burner. The same concept applies to new school board members and superintendents.

Many administrators enter the field hell-bent on making a name for themselves and refusing to live in the shadows of their predecessor. Often, they feel as though their only choice is to go in a totally different direction, making the previous reform null and void. This situation creates frustration among the surviving faculty and staff. The changes of the new administrators often happen before they fully think about the consequences or repercussions of their actions. Perfectly competent adults massage their egos instead of thinking about what is in the best interests of the school and the children.

It is counterproductive to start one reform and then decide to start another several months later. In rare cases, school districts have been known to revert to a model proven to be ineffective due to impatience and the desire for quick results. Once reform has been implemented, all parties involved must show fidelity to one reform until there is concrete data or evidence that indicates the reform is effective or ineffective. Reform is about creating an environment in which students are the priority and we as their teachers assist them in starting and finishing their journey to becoming educated citizens.

It is hard for many administrators and educators to grasp the fact that frustrations may worsen as the process for change is being implemented. Often, issues arise because people do not welcome change. Some educators need to see the change is for the better before they completely support the reform. Once the rebellion to change has subsided and reform has been implemented correctly, the waiting game begins.

During this time, educators and administrators must go about the business of collecting data for analysis. The findings will give them a clear indication of whether or not the reform has served its intended purpose. If students are not progressing under the implemented reform, then the reform may not be well suited for the needs of the students or faculty.

Strategic planning and the implementation of school reform sometimes require schools to absorb temporary setbacks in order to reap the benefits of long-term gains. Student progress might dip for a month or two before teachers and administration see a significant gain in learning and performance. Teachers and administrators need to allow change to take place and not panic when instant, significant progress is not apparent.

In many school-reform efforts, educators and administrators must understand that policies and practices that met the needs of the past, do not necessarily address current needs or the needs of the future. They must realize that in order to obtain a great future you must let go of a great past. When teachers are forced to change the curriculum, they are forced to look at more recent studies, thus benefiting the ever-changing student population.

CREATING AND SUSTAINING SCHOOL REFORM

When considering school reform based on NCLB, it may be advantageous for administrators to think of their schools as businesses. If the structure of the school were to reflect the business model, we would work from the assumption that students in the school system are customers, schools are the businesses, teachers are the employees/supervisors, and the administrators are the CEOs. This notion is not too farfetched given that NCLB was created by a group of politicians and businessmen. With this in mind, one would assume the plans were created based on a business model.

In any business, customers' needs always come first. The reputation for customer service is the best advertising a business can receive. Keeping this savvy business strategy in mind, the business of the school should be to create learning opportunities that lead to greater academic achievement. If educators make lessons fun while adhering to the curriculum, the graduation rate will increase dramatically. If children feel safe and entertained, they will want to come to school. It is the educator's task to make sure students develop a love for learning, while it is the administration's task to support their efforts.

The most critical question administrators must confront is: where do we begin? Beginning reform by tackling several goals at once is noble, but not recommended. When trying to start reform in a complex environment such as a school, administrators need to focus on one task at a time. When making decisions, the administration needs to be sure to complete all steps of the reform in sequential order, using a strategic way of thinking. In some cases goals can be independently accomplished. Departments will be able to achieve short-term goals while accomplishing the larger goals. In education, the improvements that matter the most are those that directly concern children. In order to create the necessary improvements, school districts must be reformed in ways that will sustain the changes. The ability of a school district to sustain reform should be of the utmost importance to the superintendent and the board of education.

Three conditions must be present in order to sustain reform. First, administrators must come to an agreement concerning the issues that have made it necessary for school reform to take place. They must be open and honest and refrain from blaming others for the issues faculty and staff have agreed upon. All individuals directly and indirectly involved in the school reform must share a common vision.

Administrators should try to come to a consensus regarding the purpose of education and the roles of the faculty and staff. They also need to agree on the rules and guidelines that will support the implementation of the reform, while respecting cultural beliefs of the faculty, staff, and students. Finally, administrators must communicate the current issues of the school and the vision for the future to stakeholders. Those who support and participate in reform need a clear vision of the common goal. Administrators must paint a reform picture that alleviates fears, and entice all to buy into the vision.

Communication is the key to running and sustaining a successful school when creating concrete reform. All participants and key administrators must agree to communicate with each other their understanding of the school reform, including their concerns. The administrators and participants must have a shared understanding of the issues the district faces, as they must learn to articulate, analyze, and explain the issues in a similar way.

There needs to be a common vision concerning students, schools, and the allocation of resources. Administrators must also anticipate new trends and issues preventing reform. Once the obstacles have been identified, it is the duty of the administrator to articulate these trends and issues to the powers that be, i.e., superintendents and school board members. Finally, the most important communication between administrators and staff is how to create the reform to provide quality education for all students.

Communication must also take place among school districts, superintendents, and the board of education in an intentional and ongoing manner. They must continuously reflect in an open and honest way on the effectiveness of the reform, and successfully communicate between departments in the case of promotions, retirements, or sudden resignation.

When creating school reform, administrators should consider communicating with community members. Community members and parents have a lot to contribute when it comes to school reform and they should be encouraged and allowed to do so. Parents and educators undoubtedly have a genuine concern for the needs of students. Why not place the important decisions concerning our students in the hands of the people that have the children's best interests at heart?

Administrators should also consider teachers a major part of school reform. Reform is considered a success or a failure based on the students' performance, but teacher performance is inextricably linked to student performance. Through positive teacher-student relationships, genuine learning can take place in the classroom. Teachers know their students and the educational practices that work best in their classroom. In schools across the nation, the people in the best positions to create positive outcomes have little to no control over changes that are made and how they are implemented. Too often, the most critical decisions concerning the educational system are made by people without the capacity to understand the inner workings of the individual school and what it takes to ensure no child is left behind.

THE KEY TO STUDENT SUCCESS

To sustain school reform, there needs to be collaboration among schools within the same district. Sometimes schools within the same district see each other as competitors and have a tendency to keep information concerning best practices to themselves. Most schools within the same district have a similar student population. If the schools have similar types of students, the odds are that the working reforms made to one school will help another, though details may need to be modified to address the idiosyncrasies specific to a certain school.

Successful school reform requires having the right resources. Schools cannot succeed unless they have the resources to pay for the various components of the reform. Some students from low-income homes do not have access to basic resources or supplies. In this case, it will be important for schools to have working relationships with social service agencies. It is difficult for schools in low socioeconomic areas to receive the aid necessary to allow students to be comfortable in school. When parents are unable to provide for their children, the onus then falls on the schools and the community.

According to Maslow's hierarchy of needs, students need to have physiological needs met before they are able to learn. If a child is hungry, he or she will focus on that fact and not on the schoolwork. Federal law allows schools to provide breakfast and lunch for students whose families meet federal poverty guidelines. The law was created in an effort to meet the biological needs of students if parents are unable or unwilling to do this. If children have all of their physical needs met, they will be more likely to succeed in school (Huitt, 1987).

Another need that must be met is the safety of the child. Students need to feel comfortable and safe in order to learn. They will not be able to focus unless they feel safe both at home and in school. When teachers become certified to teach, they become mandated reporters of child abuse. This means that a teacher who suspects abuse in the home of a student is compelled by law to report this information, using protocols established by the school or the district.

When a parent is unable or unwilling to meet their child's physical/ biological needs or ensure their safety and security, teachers have the means to support the child's well-being through the use of a number of resources, including federal and state laws (Simons, Irwin & Drinnien, 1987). Teachers must perceive these actions of advocacy as professional responsibilities that serve not only to support the child's well-being but also help the child learn at school.

The main job of schools is to deliver effective instruction for student learning. If the school needs to provide some or all of the necessary physical/biological needs, it should do so. Schools should be concerned about the welfare and the safety of the children they serve. The school's purpose in the community is to ensure that students have the support and resources they need to be successful.

It is important to realize that the schools are not required to provide said support. Schools not operating as full-service organizations should advocate for the students whenever necessary. Ruby K. Payne (2005) discusses support systems in her book *A Framework for Understanding Poverty*. Payne posits that students from poverty need support systems to succeed. She believes that students with the right resources and support systems can succeed even if they are living in poverty.

Local schools are the only community-service organizations that come in contact with virtually all school-aged children in a given area. Many would assume that educators and administrators are in a unique position to understand the needs of children and the communities in which they live. Teachers are among the few people who understand children's hopes, aspirations, and impediments; however, only a small percentage of teachers take advantage of this awareness.

With all the problems and the issues that our children face, we can ill afford to miss opportunities to connect with them. A strong student-teacher relationship will in turn help the teachers better educate their students. One of the keys to the teacher-student relationship is the creation of mutual trust and respect. Once students understand that their teacher trusts and respects them, they will do everything in their power to live up to the teacher's expectations.

James P. Comer, a child psychiatrist who studied students from low-income neighborhoods in New Haven, Connecticut, developed the Comer Process which focuses on child development in urban schools. The Comer Process is based on six interconnected pathways that lead to healthy child development and academic achievement. The pathways are physical, cognitive, psychological, language, social, and ethical.

Comer believes that the pathways should be considered a road map to a child's successful development into adulthood. If a child's needs are not met in one of the pathways, there will likely be difficulties in the child's ability to achieve. Comer explains that a child could be smart, but unable to be socially successful. He wants teachers to be aware that they should not teach for the sake of teaching, but rather help the child learn how to negotiate life both inside and outside of the classroom.

According to Comer, if a child is intelligent but cannot socially interact, then the school system did not do its job of preparing the child for the world. The theory pushes teachers to make sure that children are developing emotionally, physically, and socially before the child can learn the school-related topics. Comer believes that children will not be functioning members of society if they are only successful in academic skills such as math and reading (Ben-Avie, Comer & Joyner, 2004).

Comer proposes that children need a primary social network—one that includes parents and people from the child's school and community. Comer emphasizes that the people in this network are concerns all needs that are part of the developmental pathways. Children who have this level of support will likely be more successful in school. This is the main premise behind Comer's idea of sending letters home to the parent or caregiver. He wants to make sure that the parents and caregivers are aware of what is happening in their child's school life so they are able to share in creating a positive experience at school.

Comer's notion of developmental pathways is now practiced in many schools across America. In fact, there is such interest in his theory that a field guide is now available for creating schoolwide interventions to help students achieve academic success. Comer's theory is concerned with the ways in which the world is changing. He predicts children needing to have more skills and more "book smarts" than previous generations. The future adults of this society will need to be socially accepted while also being "book smart tech savvy" and multitaskers (Ben-Avie, Comer & Joyner, 2004).

Educators today should understand that when they become teachers, their duty is to advocate for not only the children in their class, but also the students in the entire school. Teachers are often the creators of grassroots advocacy organizations and coalitions. Advocacy is an essential part of a teacher's profession. When teachers advocate for a student, their action conveys to children a message that the teacher cares about their well-being and creates a positive bond between teacher and student.

Many Americans feel that the sole responsibility for a child's learning rests on the shoulders of teachers. Yet there is an abundance of research indicating that the task of educating American youth lies on all staff, including counselors and nutritionists. Recent research highlights the importance of counselors and nutritionists in the American education system and how their roles affect the student's ability to learn (Edwards, Thornton & Holiday-Driver, 2010; Shor & Friedman, 2009).

SCHOOL SYSTEMS AND BUSINESS MODELS

Schools must decide expectation for teachers with respect to student performance, and the repercussions if students fall below expected proficiency levels. However, in most schools throughout the United States, the focus is not on established goals for, but rather on who is to blame for, failing students and the recent dropout crisis. There is too much focus on requiring students to learn to work within the confines of the school structure, rather than being accepting of all differences and working with the students in their own comfort zones.

Education could be changed for the better if schools were to think of themselves as businesses and the students as the customers. In a business model, students might receive more one-on-one attention, making them feel more satisfied with the education they are receiving. If a child acquires the love of learning at a young age, he or she is more likely to reach higher levels of educational attainment. According to the National Center for Education Statistics (2008), a person with a college degree will make a million dollars more in a lifetime than someone without a degree.

In all good businesses, employees create and produce products based on the general needs and wants of the customer/consumer. If students are the customers, then school reform should be created to meet their needs. The task of the employee is to manage and motivate the people they are supervising. Teachers will implement change in their classrooms by individualizing the reform to the general needs of their students.

The idea that educators are transmitters of knowledge and students are passive vessels receiving the knowledge is an antiquated notion that has long since been dismissed as fallacy. A student should be an active participant in the educational process. If schools adopt student-centered lessons and reform, administrators can then move their schools onto a productive path (Fluellen, 2010).

More often than not, students learn best when working with their hands and having visual aids to enhance their understanding. Research shows that when teachers used a plethora of visual aids, the students were better able to remember and comprehend the concepts being taught (Eilam & Poyas, 2010). One of the ways in which teachers evaluate a student's comprehension of a lesson is by evaluating if he or she can relate the material to their own lives.

Students learn from their own interpretations of what is being presented to them. Teachers should be sure to create authentic lessons using visual aids, allowing students to use their deductive reasoning skills and ability to connect the activity to their lives or the lives of others. The skills described are skills most employers look for when hiring respectable and hard-working employees.

TEACHERS' ROLES IN THE CLASSROOM

Although schools were created to meet the needs of students, and the teachers were hired to meet those needs, students have to be held responsible for their actions. Teachers will need to find an instructional strategy to promote learning that meets the needs of the students, while also teaching life skills and holding students accountable for their actions and choices.

Teachers are often considered jugglers, because they must gain the trust of their students, but also play the part of the students' instructor and disciplinarian. If a teacher lacks the ability to control his or her classroom, learning cannot take place. Teachers need to demand the attention and the respect of their students (McGhan, 1978).

Schools operate on the notion that students have no choice but to attend school and do what is asked of them. This cannot be further from the truth. Some students choose whether or not to attend school on a given day. Even students who attend school regularly choose whether or not they want to comply with their teachers' directives, or whether they want to participate in the learning process. Some students comply with teacher directions, even if they find the activity uninteresting. Too many students do not give teachers what they need most: undivided attention and engagement.

Many educators today are concerned with the lack of respect for authority many of our young adults and children display. The lack of respect for teachers can be traced to the growing mistrust of parents towards teachers. In today's society, it is not uncommon for parents to sue teachers for educational malpractice or some form of mistreatment of their child.

The increasing distrust of teachers could be brought on by the increasing number of teachers who have inappropriate relationships with their students (Sexual Harassment Support, 2009). Parents need to realize that the majority of teachers have their student's best interest at heart. Educators earned their degrees to help the children and youth of America, not to cause them harm.

Sometimes, parents feel the teacher is trying to parent their children and that certain disciplinary actions should only be carried out by themselves. The reason for this misunderstanding is the lack of communication between the parent and the school. With the increasing numbers of children per teacher, teachers have less time to ask the parents what they feel their child needs, and to discuss with parents what the teacher believes is the best way to accomplish the set goals.

Ruby Payne (2005) mentions a term called "mama law." This law goes into effect when a teacher or administrator tries to explain why a behavior is not acceptable in school, and the child responds, "Well, my mama said it is okay." Teachers and administrators need to understand that students may come from different environments than the teacher or administrator, and that there is a discrepancy in the way the teacher/administrator was brought up compared to that of the student.

Often, when students come from a rough neighborhood, their mothers tell them it is okay to defend themselves in any way possible. Students feel they have been given permission to engage in behaviors supported by the home, even though these behaviors may interfere with teaching and learning in the school environment. It is up to the teachers and the administration to explain to the student how his/her actions are wrong in ways they will understand and respect (Payne, 2005.)

There are two positions teachers might take when combating negative feelings students display toward them or other teachers. They can spend their time complaining about the lack of respect children have for authority or they can accept the fact the students are the customers and, like all customers, teachers have to accommodate their needs.

Thinking of the students as customers reinforces the idea that the student is in full control of whether or not they pay attention or engage themselves in academic activities. Certainly, state laws require the majority of American students to attend school until they are sixteen (Oreopoulos, 2003). Sooner or later, truant students will be tracked down by the school attendance officer, who will inform parents that their child's lack of attendance is against the law. However, once the student is at school, there is absolutely no way for teachers to force the child to pay attention and fully engage into schoolwork. Part of the teacher's profession is to find ways to motivate children by providing them with appealing learning activities. Also, schools have to accept the fact that in order to engage students and keep their attention, their respect and trust must be earned. Student learning is comparable to profits in a business. Student learning is what happens when the business of schooling is managed correctly.

In keeping with the business model, successful schools must realize that quality education is paramount. Administrators and school boards need to understand that students are not products and schools are not businesses, but rather schools are places to foster a love for learning and to create productive futures for American children and the country itself.

THE STRESS OF STUDENT ASSESSMENT

When attempting to sustain reform efforts, it is important to focus on student assessment. However, American schools will also have to report other student data such as dropout rates, information on special-need students, number of ELL learners, etc. Schools' federal aid is dependent on report of these types of data. Administrators and educators have to be prepared to assess different aspects of learning in different ways (Schlechty, 1997) as they gear up to submit required federal reports.

Still, when children are forced to take standardized tests, they can suffer huge amounts of anxiety before these tests begin (Osburn et al., 2004). Politicians and school board members may view an improvement in test scores as positive, but they have no perception of the level of anxiety that students face as a result of having to take tests.

Teachers are often anxiety ridden as well, when preparing their students for standardized tests. Since teachers are held responsible for their students' test scores, they often find themselves teaching to the test, and teaching students how to take the test. Teaching should not have come down to test scores. Evidence shows students learn best when they are exposed to inquiry-based and authentic learning experiences (Purcell-Gates, Duke & Martineau, 2007).

Test scores have become the focal point when assessing schools' ability to effectively teach their students. School budgets are affected, along with parent and community perceptions of administrators and educators. Public organizations obtain their power and authority from their surrounding community, which means community opinions are essential for the success of school-reform efforts. If test scores consistently remain low over a period of time, the school is subject to a range of government-approved sanctions, including the removal of all staff and administration.

SUPPORTING INTRINSIC MOTIVATION

What students desire from their school experience is not necessarily what their parents and members of the larger community want them to learn or experience. Only a small percentage of students come to school with an overwhelming desire to learn. Many attend school on a daily basis because their parents and other members of their support system force them to do so.

It is very difficult to motivate a student who is not intrinsically motivated. With authentic lessons and inquiry learning, educators can start to make learning enjoyable. To assist in motivating students, schools could put out a survey asking them what they want to learn, what they have already learned, and what the teacher could do to make learning more exciting. With the stress of standardized tests, it might be difficult to take time out of the day to distribute the survey, but every effort should be made to do so.

Students are more prone to become engaged in assignments when the teacher has created a safe and inviting learning environment. Students want to work in an educational environment where a teacher's expectations are explicitly outlined. In order to be successful, students must be given the opportunity to engage in activities just above their abilities.

The teacher also has an obligation to create a teaching environment that promotes learning. This means, for example, that teachers should not embarrass students for a wrong answer or a below-standard test score—nor should they allow other students to make fun of wrong answers and below-standard test scores. We need to make sure that the debate on the quality of American schools focuses on the academic practices directly affecting student learning.

Schools are concerned not only with test scores but also with equality. All students should be considered equal, regardless of their age, race, religious beliefs, sexual orientation, cultural beliefs, and ability levels. If all students feel they are being treated equally, then they will be more motivated to work. Students will feel intrinsically motivated to learn when they feel respected by teachers and the staff, and will work harder to achieve the goals the teachers and schools have outlined (Ben-Avie, Comer & Joyner, 2004).

Student-teacher and family-student relationships also influence intrinsic motivation. In order for students to perform well in school, they will need to have the proper support system both in school and at home. Most students are only interested in performing for the people that matter most to them. If these people do not hold education in high regard, then the student will not hold education in high regard either (Payne, 2005).

When students are in the elementary grades, they will usually perform for their parents and for their teachers with little to no resistance. Once students develop social networks, parents and teachers are quickly replaced by peers. Adolescents are prone to peer pressure and succumb easily to their peers' suggestions and viewpoints. It is important for high school teachers to create strong student-teacher relationships, in order to more effectively motivate students to remain engaged in behaviors that lead to positive academic achievement and outcomes (McClure, Yonezawa & Jones, 2010).

It is also important for teachers to create and support opportunities for students to collaborate with others. Schools and teachers that create high levels of student engagement understand the possibilities that collaboration affords. Teachers can also provide opportunities for students to collaborate with students in other countries. Collaboration among students in and outside the classroom will have to be closely facilitated by the teacher. If carried out appropriately, outcomes for this strategy can be very positive for all students concerned (Diziol et al., 2010).

Student engagement is one of the potential indicators of the effectiveness of a school. Educators and administrators have to concentrate their efforts on activities that engage students in order to foster academic achievement. If they do not, they will have a room full of students who are either academically disengaged or who are merely giving the impression that they are academically engaged. Students are less likely to pay attention when they are on board with what is being taught.

If students complete a task they feel is boring, then they do so to comply with the teacher's directions and not because they are intrinsically motivated to do so. In too many instances, students operate from a point of extrinsic motivation, sadly including the motivation to avoid being singled out or incurring the teacher's wrath. If the classroom is devoid of fun and excitement, students will not acquire the love of learning, leaving them less likely to move on to higher education (Guay et al., 2010).

SCHOOL RESTRUCTURING AND REFORM

Successful school systems share a number of common traits. These include: effective administrative leadership; safe learning environments; strong family and community partnerships; opportunities for increased time on task; incorporation of instructional best practices; interventions for underperforming students; continuous assessment of student achievement; and lofty expectations for all students. These successful schools exist in a number of different school environments.

Schools should keep these traits in mind as they begin the school-reform process. When attempting school reform, the school must first assemble the district restructuring team. Groups no larger than seven usually work best. The team can be made up of a variety of district personnel and staff. Restructuring teams normally consist of a school board member, the superintendent and assistant superintendents, principals, teachers, and other pertinent individuals.

Once the team is created, efforts must be made to assess the district's capacity for implementing and sustaining school reform. The team must ask itself whether the district has all of the resources needed to implement and sustain a successful school reform. In extreme cases, when the district feels it is unable to coordinate its own reform effort, the team might want to consider allowing the state department of education to oversee the reform process.

Another option for schools that feel they are lacking in the area of certified and experienced reform personnel is to hire an educational consulting firm. There are many well-qualified firms that will be able to either work in conjunction with a restructuring team or oversee the process themselves. Note, however, that this can turn into an enormous job with an enormous price tag. It will require resisting the urge to compromise on any phase of the restructuring process.

The consulting team or team leader must be committed to finding and implementing innovative strategies that have the potential to effectively produce educational change. Assembling a top-notch team is simply not enough however. All of the major administrators, including the superintendent and school board, must fully support the decisions of the district restructuring team.

Remember that parents, community leaders, and policymakers must be included in the school-reform process. Many parents are involved in their students' educational plans and simply want to be informed of any changes. The reform task force will need to decide if parents and community leaders should be included as formal members of the district's restructuring team, or to simply elicit their advice and expertise as needed. When making decisions concerning which individuals will populate the task force, members who have the expertise to be taken seriously within the district should be included.

Involving parents and community members in the restructuring process might provide the restructuring team with a way to engage other members of the community, such as grassroots organizations, local business leaders, and area politicians. Community members can also assist the school in choosing the correct restructuring plan. It is vital for the task force to understand the culture of the community, its needs and wants, and the life skills young people need to fit in and survive in the community.

If the school would like to create fundraisers to assist in the efforts to restructure the school, it is important that the community members understand why the school wants extra money and why the community member should give the extra money. If the community members disagree with the changes being made, they will be less likely to participate or contribute to the cause.

Having an effective restructuring team is an important component in a successful school reform. The task of choosing the leader and deciding on roles within the task force should not be taken lightly. Once the leader has been voted in, other members of the team and their roles will need to be decided. In many instances, the leader of the restructuring team will be the superintendent or someone he or she appoints.

The leader does not necessarily need to be the superintendent, unless the reform is district-wide or the school has performed below standards for a lengthy amount of time. The leader must assume the responsibility of being held accountable for ensuring the success of the entire team as it moves to implement and sustain school reform. The leader's roles might include, but are not restricted to, determining the areas of expertise the team members bring to the table and how he or she can utilize their expertise. The leader must also keep the processes on task.

To ensure the minimum amount of time needed to implement the reform, the leader will need to establish a standing meeting time and develop an agenda to utilize time to the fullest extent possible. The leader must decide if the team should have mandatory or optional meetings. If the meetings are optional, how information is disseminated to members who do not attend meetings will need to be decided by the leader.

Prepared agendas are essential for smooth meetings and excellent communication among the team. Preparing agendas are team leaders' responsibilities. The leader of the task force must remain patient, but a sense of urgency must be the catalyst of all meetings. Outside consultants could be considered, but are not necessary for the success of the reform. Since the team will be made up primarily of school district personnel and various other community members and parents, having an outsider on the team will give the team valuable expertise, in addition to an objective lens through which to gauge progress.

It will be helpful to determine what viable options of reform the team is able to utilize. If the reform is district-wide, each school will need to analyze its individual needs and the options available. A district-wide plan must be developed, while bearing in mind that each school will need to modify the plan based on the needs of the students. Once the system of reform is created and approved by all team members, the plan will need to be approved by the superintendent before it is presented to the school board. The same rules apply whether reform is needed by one school or by all the schools in the district.

The leader of the task force must determine the approach the team will take when implementing changes that have previously been decided upon. Finding the right restructuring strategy is the key to success. The task force's available choices include, but are not limited to:

- School turnaround
- School transformation
- School restart
- School closure
- State takeover

A concern, alluded to in the above comments, is the need to assess the district's capacity for implementing and sustaining educational reform. To appropriately assess the abilities of the district or school, the leader will need to complete an inventory of the qualifications and areas of expertise the team members have. If the inventory concludes that the district or school does not have the capacity to implement or sustain the plan for reform, state takeover may be the only option.

Another concern might be that the volunteer team members do not understand the dedication and length of time it will take to carry out the reform. Before the team starts to implement the necessary changes, the leader will need to stress to all team members the enormity of the task, the number of hours the members will need to dedicate to the project, and what is truly at stake.

Once the team's reform plan has been approved, it is time to implement the approved plan. The task force will discuss possible impediments to the approved plan and ensure the team has a contingency plan to deal with these issues as they arise. Next, they will implement their target goals and timelines. The leader appoints a task force member to be responsible for collecting, reporting, and evaluating any data collected. The leader will then use the data collected to continuously revise and refine the team's restructuring efforts, as well as report their findings/data to the superintendent and the school board.

POSSIBLE PROBLEMS

Some school turnaround models lead to the removal of administrators and teachers. Reform initiatives in place at the time of school turnaround efforts may be completely eliminated. The most important component in facilitating a school or district turnaround is choosing the right leader. In order for this leader or leaders (depending on district need) to be successful, he or she has to obtain autonomy to facilitate his or her plan.

During the school turnaround process, the leader will still be held accountable for the necessary changes while the new team is being formed. The presence of parental and community support has a lot of influence on the success of the reform when a school turnaround occurs. The parents and community members involved in the school reform can help train or educate the new task force team members.

In order for restructuring efforts to be successful, they must include all active participants. As stated earlier, the leader of the turnaround efforts is a key ingredient. He or she must be able to articulate an encouraging view of possible results in order to motivate the new team. One of the leader's many skills will need to be diplomacy, because he or she will be charged with ensuring that all the participants buy into the plan of action.

SCHOOL REFORM IN A CHARTER SCHOOL

Charter school reform is a rare occurrence. When it becomes evident that a charter school needs reform, it might be best to close the school. When a charter school is closed, students are reassigned to their local public schools. When making the decision to close a charter school, districts should look at the situation holistically. They should think about how closing the school will affect the district's school-reform efforts, if the district is reforming its schools.

All the pros and cons should be considered before making the final decision to close or reform the struggling charter school. If the district decides to close the charter school, the criteria for distributing the charter school students among the public schools should be uniform and schools in the district should understand that they may receive students.

It is important for details concerning student dispersal to be quickly and thoroughly explained to parents and the community, so that misconceptions are not allowed to develop and fester. School leaders should take care to articulate, in layman's terms, the rationale for closing the charter school and reassigning students, to ensure all listeners understand.

All of the adults affected by the school's closure will need to be immediately briefed on issues such as student placement, transportation, and safety. Faculty and administrators from the school will also have questions concerning reassignment and termination. These questions and anxieties should be answered immediately to ensure a successful and relatively pain-free transition for everyone involved.

STATE TAKEOVER

NCLB requires that schools falling below the standards outlined in its guidelines will be evaluated and corrective action be implemented. In rare cases, when schools are unable to adhere to the government's standards, the school is taken over by the state and reformed, using the state's administrators. The worst-case scenario happens when the state itself facilitates the takeover against the wishes of the school district.

When the state decides to take over a school, the state government essentially creates a restructuring plan suited for that particular district or school. The welfare of students attending underperforming schools is the overriding concern of both parents and state officials. If the school continues to underperform, the students' parents have the right to place their student in a better-performing district or school.

When schools are taken over, the state develops a board of directors charged with overseeing the restructuring effort. The board represents community members, as well as individuals with expertise in the area of school reform. The state department of education usually has a section responsible for school takeovers and restructuring. Department of education affiliates coordinate day-to-day management related to the school takeover process with the school personnel and appointed administration. The board of directors is also responsible for hiring administrators to lead a school's reform effort.

After the department of education has given the school the plan for reform, it is up to the team to implement the necessary changes and collect the data required by the reform. The appointed administrator will need to appropriately and periodically report on the data collected. The department of education will then need to decide if the reform plan is effective or if a new plan needs to be implemented. In rare cases, if a school is unable to make the necessary improvements, the state may make the decision to close the school and disperse the school's students among the other schools in the district.

EVALUATION OF SCHOOL REFORM

In order to complete the process of school reform, the leader of the task force will monitor and evaluate restructuring efforts. The process of evaluation can be completed in-house, or the leader can hire outside consultants to perform the task. If the task force is willing to evaluate the success of the school's reform, they must first develop a plan for evaluation.

The team's evaluation plan should be developed before the reform is implemented. Performance goals that are created at the beginning of the restructuring process should be used to guide the evaluation process. The team will need to decide who will collect, analyze, and interpret the data. In order to avoid biased results, it may be in the best interest of the school to hire an outside consultant, who may provide a more objective assessment of the reform efforts. The team will also use the results to determine whether or not the reform efforts were effective.

The results may indicate that the reform was not a success. In this case, the best solution is to build upon the small successes and learn from mistakes. Another reform could then be implemented or the unsuccessful reform amended to better suit the needs of the school. School restructuring is a long-term process. Reform occurs on a continuous cycle that must be sustained in order for improvements to be maintained and furthered. Keep in mind that not every restructuring effort bears fruit. Even the best schools have to continue to work in the restructuring process.

IMPROVING EFFECTIVENESS

Student performance is contingent upon the existence of an innovative, organized system at district level. Any model with the goal of increasing the academic performance of students must involve every segment of the district, from the custodians to the school board. Most districts know exactly what their students need, and their district-wide curriculum and reform should reflect those needs. The district will need to make sure the developed curriculum aligns with the standards set by national and state entities.

Districts that demonstrate continuous positive results often base their decisions on data alone, as opposed to relying on observations and data together. Schools should regularly evaluate the pros and cons of instructional programs and realize that standardized tests should constitute only a piece of the assessment puzzle rather than the entirety. Continuously monitoring the progress the school's student body makes will allow the task force to amend the reform plan as needed.

Successful schools also take measures to institute checks and balances, to ensure the decision-making process is distributed among a variety of reform participants. Superintendents are charged with the duty of ensuring that the implementation and maintenance of improvement efforts are done in a positive manner and meet the needs of the students. The team leader's job is to ensure teachers and staff have all of the tools needed to foster the academic performance of students.

Districts all over the country recognize accountability as the key to schools' improvement process. Everyone is expected to perform at optimal levels, or must face the consequences. To ensure that staff and faculty members are able to perform at optimal levels, the school district must provide them with high-quality professional development. Successfully implementing and sustaining school reform is possible.

It may not be easy, but with a tremendous effort, the utilization of all resources, and the expertise of professionals, school reform can be successful. The level of success the school is able to achieve will be based on the school's predicament. Whatever the obstacles, the leaders' decisions need to be resolute to foster academic achievement (Center for Comprehensive School Improvement and Reform, 2006)

References

Accountability. (September 10, 2004). *Education Week*. Retrieved from http://www.edweek.org/ew/issues/accountability/.

Achieve, Inc. (2010). *About achieve: The American diploma project*. Retrieved fromhttp://www.achieve.org/node/604.

Adams, C. M., & Forsyth, P. B. (2006). *Promoting a culture of parent collaboration and trust: An empirical study*. Washington, DC: American Educational Research Association.

Adams, K. S., & Christenson, S. L. (1998). Differences in parent and teacher trust levels: Implications for creating collaborative family-school relationships. *Special Services in the Schools* 14(1/2), 1–22.

Addonizio, M. F. (2000). Private funds for public schools. *The Clearing House* 74(2), 70–74.

Adelman, H. S. (1995). Education reform: Broadening the focus. *Psychological Science* 6, 61–62.

Adelman, H. S., & Taylor, L. (1997a). Addressing barriers to learning: Beyond school-linked services and full service schools. *American Journal of Orthopsychiatry* 67, 408–421.

Adelman, H. S., & Taylor, L. (1997b). Restructuring education support services and integrating community resources: Beyond the full service school model. *School Psychology Review* 25, 431–445.

Adelman, H. S., & Taylor, L. (1997c). Toward a scale up model for replicating new approaches to schooling. *Journal of Educational and Psychological Consultation* 8, 197–230.

Adelman, H. S., & Taylor, L. (2003). On sustainability of project innovations as systemic change. *Journal of Educational and Psychological Consultation* 14, 1–26.

Alexander, K., Entwisle, D., Steffel Olson, L. (2007). Lasting consequences of the summer learning gap. *American Sociological Review* 72, 167–180.

Allensworth, E., Ponisciak, S., & Mazzeo, C. (2009). *The schools teachers leave: Teacher mobility in Chicago Public Schools*. Chicago, IL: Consortium on Chicago School Research. Retrieved October 1, 2009, fromhttp://ccsr.uchicago.edu/publications/CCSR_Teacher_Mobility.pdf.

Alspaugh, J. W. (1998). The relationship of school and community characteristics to high school drop-out rates. *The Clearing House* 71(3).

Ambrosio, J. (2004). No child left behind: the case of Roosevelt High School. *Phi Delta Kappan* 84. Retrieved fromhttp://www.questia.com/google.

Amrein, A. L., & Berliner, D. C. (2002). High-stakes testing, uncertainty, and student learning. *Education Policy Analysis Archives* 10(18). Retrieved August 22, 2003, from http://epaa.asu.edu/epaa/v10n18.

Anderson, S., & Rodway-Macri, J. (2009). District administrator perspectives on student learning in an era of standards and accountability: A collective frame analysis. *Canadian Journal of Education* 32(2), 192–221.

Angel, R. J., & Angel, J. L. (1993). *Painful inheritance: Health and the new generation of fatherless families*. Madison, WI: University of Wisconsin Press.

Armour-Thomas, E. (1989). *An outlier study of elementary and middle schools in New York City: Final report*. New York: New York City Board of Education.

Ash, K. (November 19, 2008). States slow to embrace online testing. *Education Week*.

Atalig, K. (November/December 2003). The research: Year-round education. *Knowledge Quest* 32(2), 48–49.

Bach, D. (February 16, 2005). Budget shortfall forces tough choices at Seattle public schools. *Seattle Post-Intelligencer*. Retrieved August 1, 2008, from http://seattlepi.nwsource.

Barron, R. (1993). The effects of year-round education on achievement, attendance and teacher attendance in bilingual school. Doctoral dissertation. *Dissertation Abstracts International* 54, 3935.

Bausell, C. V. (March 27, 2008). Tracking U.S. trends. *Education Week.*

Ben-Avie, M., Comer, J., & Joyner, E. (2004). *Six pathways to healthy child development and academic success: A field guide to Comer schools in action.* Thousand Oaks, CA: Corwin Press.

Bennett, R. (1998). *Reinventing assessment: Speculations on the future of large-scale educational testing.* Princeton, NJ: Educational Testing Service.

Bennett, R. E., Persky, H., Weiss, A. R., & Jenkins, F. (2007). Problem *solving in technology-rich environments: A report from the NAEP technology-based assessment project.* (NCES 2007-466). Washington, DC: National Center for Education Statistics, U.S. Department of Education. Retrieved on November 21, 2008, fromhttp://nces.ed.gov/nationsreportcard/pubs/studies/2007466.asp.

Berry, C. R., & Howell, W. G. (2008). Accountability lost. *Education Next* 8(1), 66–72. Retrieved from http://ebscohost.com.

Berryhill, J., Linney, J., & Fromewick, J. (2009). The effects of education accountability on teachers: Are policies too stress-provoking for their own good? *International Journal of Education Policy and Leadership* 4(5), 1–14. Retrieved from http://www.ebscohost.com.

Bilby, S., & Charles Stewart Mott Foundation (2002). Community-driven school reform: Parents making a difference in education. *Mott Mosaic* 1(2). Retrieved from http://www.ebscohost.com.

Blanc, S. (2003). Principals offer mixed perspectives on first year of takeover: Supports and challenges in the multiple provider model. *The Notebook*. Retrieved June 7, 2009, from http://www.thenotebook .org/editions/2003/summer/principals.htm.

Boaz, D. (2007). *Deregulating education*. Retrieved fromwww.cato.org.

Bodilly, S. J. (1998). *Lessons from new American schools' scale-up phase: Prospects for bringing designs to multiple schools.* Santa Monica, CA: RAND Corporation.

Boghossian, N. (July 21, 2005). LAUSD fails its special students. *Daily News of Los Angeles*, p. N1.

Bohte, J. (2001). School bureaucracy and student performance at the local level. *Public Administration Review* 61(1), 92–99.

Borja, R. R. (January 29, 2003). South Dakota drops online "adaptive" testing. *Education Week.*

Bound, J., Lovenheim, M., & Turner, S. (2009). *Why have college completion rates declined?: An analysis of changing student preparation and collegiate resources.* Retrieved from http://www.nber.org/papers/w15566.

Bourne, J. (2008). Centralization, devolution and diversity: Changing educational policy and practice in English schools. In G. Wan, G. (ed.), *The education of diverse student populations: A global perspective.* New York: Springer.

Boyd, D., Grossman, P., Ing, M., Lankford, H., & Wyckoff, J. (2009). *The influence of school administrators on teacher retention decisions.*

Boyd, D., Lankford, H., Loeb, S., & Wyckoff, J. (2005a). Explaining the short careers of high-achieving teachers in schools with low-performing students. *American Economic Review* 95(2), 166–171.

Boyd, D., Lankford, H., Loeb, S., & Wyckoff. (2005b). *The impact of assessment and accountability on teacher recruitment and retention: Are there unintended consequences?*

Boyd, D., Lankford, H., Loeb, S., & Wyckoff, J. (2006). How changes in entry requirements alter the teacher workforce and affect student achievement. *Education Finance and Policy* 1(2), 176–216.

Boyd, D., Lankford, H., Loeb, S., & Wyckoff, J. (2007). *Who leaves? Teacher attrition and student achievement.* Research report. Teacher Policy Research, Albany, New York.

Boyle, A. (2005). *Sophisticated tasks in e-assessment: What are they and what are their benefits?* 2005 International Computer Assisted Assessment Conference, Loughborough University, U.K. Retrieved on July 17, 2008, from http://www.caaconference.com/pastConferences/2005/proceedings/BoyleA2.pdf.

Bracey, G. (2002). The market in theory meets the market in practice: The case of Edison schools. *Education Policy Studies Laboratory at Arizona State University.* Retrieved November 2, 2005, from http://www.epicpolicy.org/files/EPSL-0202-107-EPRU.pdf.

Brady, R. (2003). *Can failing schools be fixed?* Washington, DC: Thomas B. Fordham Foundation.

Brekke, N. (1992). Year-round schools: An efficient and effective use of resources. *School Business Affairs* (27–37). In C. Kneese (1996), Review of research on student learning in year-round education. *Journal of Research and Development in Education* 29(2), 60–72.

Brooks, J. S., Hughes, R. M., & Brooks, M. C. (2008). Fear and trembling in the American high school: Educational reform and teacher alienation. *Educational Policy* 22(1), 45–62. Retrieved fromhttp://www.ebscohost.com.

Broun, A. R., Puriefoy, W. D., & Richard, E. (2006). *Public engagement in school reform: Building public responsibility for public education.* Public Education Network: Author.

Brown Center. (2003). *Charter schools: Achievement, accountability, and the role of expertise.* Washington, DC: Brookings Institution Press.

Bullard, R. D. (1990). *Dumping in Dixie: Race, class and environmental quality.* Boulder, CO: Westview Press.

Burch, P., & Spillane, J. (2004). *Leading from the middle: Mid-level district staff and instructional improvement.* Chicago: Cross-City Campaign for Urban School Reform.

Burkam, D. T., Ready, D. D., Lee, V. E., & LoGerfo, L. F. (2004). Social-class differences in summer learning between kindergarten and first grade: Model specification and estimation. *Sociology of Education* 77, 1–31.

Capper, C. A., & Frattura, E. M. (2009). *Meeting the needs of students of all abilities: How leaders go beyond inclusion.* Thousand Oaks, CA: Corwin Press.

Carnoy, M., & Loeb, S. (2002). Does external accountability affect student outcomes? A cross-state analysis. *Educational Evaluation and Policy Analysis* 24, 305–331.

Carroll, S. J., Reichardt, R. E., Guarino, C. M., & Mejia, A. (2000). *The distribution of teachers among California's school districts and schools.* (MR-1298.0-JIF). Santa Monica, CA: RAND Corporation.

Carter, R. L. (1999). *Year-round school: Not the solution for failing schools.* Educator as an evaluator – ED 60. University of Alabama in Huntsville.

Center for Comprehensive School Improvement and Reform. (2006). *7 actions that improve school district performance.* Washington, DC: Center for Comprehensive School Improvement and Reform.

Chicago Public Schools. (2007). *SES tutoring programs: An evaluation of Year 3 in the Chicago Public Schools.* Chicago: Author.

Christenson, S. L., & Adams, K. S. (2000). Trust and the family-school relationship: Examination of parent-teacher differences in elementary and secondary grades. *Journal of School Psychology* 38(5), 477–497.

Chute, E. (2007, June 29). Schools' racial balancing rejected. *Pittsburgh Post-Gazette*, p. A1. Retrieved August 1, 2008, from http://www.post-gazette.com/pg/07180/798069-84.stm.

CNN Newscast. (2008). *Minorities expected to be majority in 2050.* Turner Broadcasting System, Inc. Retrieved from http://articles.cnn.com/2008-08-13/us/census.minorities_1_hispanic-population-census-bureau-white-population?_s=PM:US.

Coburn, C. E., & Talbert, J. E. (2006). Conceptions of evidence-based practice in school districts: Mapping the terrain. *American Journal of Education* 112(4), 469–495.

Cole, A. (2010). School-community partnerships and community-based education: A case study of a novice program. *Penn GSE Perspectives on Urban Education* 7(1), 15–26. Retrieved from http://www.ebscohost.com.

Coleman, J. S., & Campbell, E. Q. (1966). *Equality of educational opportunity.* Washington, DC: Office of Education, U.S. Department of Health, Education, and Welfare.

Cooper, C. L., & Robertson, I., eds. (1986). *International review of industrial and organizational psychology*. Chichester, UK: Wiley.

Cooper, H., Valentine, J., & Charlton, K. (2003). The effects of modified school calendars on student achievement and community attitudes. *Review of Educational Research* 73(1), 1–52.

Coopers & Lybrand, L.L.P. (1994). *Resource allocation in the New York City public schools*. New York: New York City Public Schools. **[AQ: publisher?]**

Copland, M. (2003). Leadership of inquiry: Building and sustaining capacity for school improvement. *Educational Evaluation and Policy Analysis* 25(4), 375–395.

Corcoran, T. B., & Lawrence, N. (2003). *Changing district culture and capacity: The impact of the MISE partnership*. Philadelphia: Consortium for Policy Research in Education.

Costa, J. (1987). Comparative outcomes of the Clark County School District year-round and nine-month schools. Doctoral dissertation. *Dissertation Abstracts International*.

Crawford, P. (2011). *Report shows an increase in school failures to make AYP*. Retrieved from http://www.publicconsultinggroup.com/research/post/2011/04/29/New-Report-Shows-an-Increase-in-School-Failures-to-Make-AYP.aspx.

Crowson, R. L. (1992). *School-community relations, under reform*. Berkeley, CA: McCuthan Publishing.

Crowson, R. L., & Boyd, W. L. (1993). Coordinating services for children: Designing arks for storms and seas unknown. *American Journal of Education* 101(2).

Cuban, L. (1990). Reforming again and again. *Educational Researcher* 19, 3–13.

Cuban, L. (October 9, 1996). Techno-reformers and classroom teachers. *Education Week*.

Darling-Hammond, L. (2007). A bridge to school reform. National conference report. Wallace Foundation.

Darling-Hammond, L., & Ball, D. L. (1998). *Teaching for high standards: What policymakers need to know and be able to do*. CPRE Joint Report Series. Philadelphia: Consortium for Policy Research in Education.

Dawdidziak, J. (2010). *Back to common sense: Rethinking school change*. Lanham, MD: Rowman & Littlefield Education.

DeAngelis, K. J., & Presley, J. B. (2007). *Leaving schools or leaving the profession: Setting Illinois' record straight on teacher attrition*. (IERC 2007-1). Edwardsville, IL: Illinois Education Research Council.

Deeming, C. (2004). Decentralizing the NHS: A case study of resource allocation decisions within a health district. *Social Policy and Administration* 38(1), 57–72.

Delgado-Gaitan, C. (1996). *Protean literacy: Extending the discourse on empowerment*. London: Falmer Press.

Desimone, L. (1999). Linking parent involvement with student achievement: Do race and income matter? *Journal of Educational Research* 93(1),11–30.

Diziol, D., Walker, E., Rummel, N., & Koedinger, K. R. (2010). Using intelligent tutor technology to implement adaptive support for student collaboration. *Educational Psychology Review 22*(1), 89–102. Retrieved fromhttp://www.ebscohost.com.

Dougherty, K. J. (1996). Opportunity-to-learn standards: A sociological critique. *Sociology of Education* 69, 40–66.

Dubois, L. (Summer 2007). *No Child Left Behind: Who's accountable?* Retrieved from http://peabody.vanderbilt.edu/x7555.xml.

Dynarksi, M., Gleason, P., Rangarajan, A., & Wood, R. (1998). *Impact of schools restructuring initiatives*. Retrieved from http://www.mathematica-mpr.com/PDFs/restruct.pdf.

Edelman, M. (1985). *The symbolic uses of politics*. 2nd ed. Urbana, IL: University of Illinois Press.

Education Commission of the States. (March 2004). *State takeovers and reconstitutions*. Retrieved March 28, 2006, from http://ecs.org/clearinghouse/51/67/5167.htm.

Edwards, L., Thornton, P., & Holiday-Driver, N. (2010). Left behind but not forgotten: School counselors' ability to help improve reading achievement. *Alabama Counseling Association Journal* 35(2), 35–39. Retrieved from http://www.ebscohost.com.

El-Khawas, E. (2010). Teacher Education Accreditation Council (TEAC) in the USA. In D. D. Dill & M. Beerkens (eds.), *Public policy for academic quality*. New York: Springer.

Elmore, R. F. (1996). Getting to scale with good educational practice. *Harvard Educational Review* 66, 1–26.

Elmore, R. F., Ableman, C. H., & Fuhrman, S. H. (1996). The new accountability in state education reform: From process to performance. In H. Ladd (ed.), *Holding schools accountable: Performance-based reform in education* (65–98). Washington, DC: Brookings Institution Press.

Elmore, R., & Burney, D. (1997). *Investing in teacher learning: Staff development and instructional improvement in Community School District #2, New York City.* Philadelphia: Consortium for Policy Research in Education. Retrieved August 1, 2008, from http://www.nctaf.org/documents/archive_investing-in-teacher-learning.pdf.

Elmore, R., & Burney, D. (1998). *School variation and systemic instructional improvement in Community School District #2, New York.* Retrieved September 3, 2007, from http://www.lrdc.pitt.edu/hplc/publications/school%20variation.pdf.

Elsberry, J. (1992). An evaluation of the implementation of year-round education. Doctoral dissertation. *Dissertation Abstracts International* 53, 4146.

Epstein, J. L., Sanders, M. G., Simon, B. S., Salinas, K. C., Jansorn, N. R., & Van Voorhis, F. L. (2002). *School, family and community partnerships: Your handbook for action.* 2nd ed. Thousand Oaks, CA: Corwin Press.Retrieved March 28, 2006, from http://ecs.org/clearinghouse/51/67/5167.htm.

E-Testing at the state level—lessons learned. (June 16, 2008). *Presentation at the Council of Chief State School Officers Conference.*

Evergreen Freedom Foundation. (n.d.). Value added assessment. Retrieved from http://www.effwa.org/pdfs/Value-Added.pdf.

Everhart, N. (2003). The research: Year-round education. *Knowledge Quest* 32(2), 47.

Fardig, D. (1992). *Year-round education: Program evaluation report.* Orlando, FL: Orange County Public Schools. ERIC Document Reproduction Service, no. ED 357 047.

Fege, A. F., & Hagelshaw, A. (2000). Beware of "creeping corporatization." *Principal* 80(2), 52–56.

Ferguson, R. (1991). Paying for public education: New evidence on how and why money matters. *Harvard Journal of Legislation* 28, 465–498.

Feuerstein, A. (2002). Elections, voting, and democracy in local school district governance. *Educational Policy* 16(1), 15–36.

Firestone, W. A., & Martinez, M. C. (2007). Districts, teacher leaders, and distributed leadership: Changing instructional practice. *Leadership and Policy in Schools* 6(1), 3–35.

Fisher, C., Filby, N., Marliave, R., Cahen, L., Dishaw, M., Moore, J., & Berliner, D. (1978). *Teaching behaviors, academic learning time, and student achievement: Final report of Phase III B.* San Francisco: Far West Laboratory for Educational Research and Development.

Fishkin, J. S. (1991). *Democracy and deliberation: New directions for democratic reform.* New Haven, CT: Yale University Press.

Floyd, L. (March, 1998). Joining hands: A parental involvement program. *Urban Education* 33(1).

Fluellen, J. R. (2010). *Mindful learning 2020.* Occasional paper no. 8. Online submission. retrieved from http://www.ebscohost.com.

French, D., Atkinson, M., & Rugen, L. (2007). *Creating small schools: A handbook for raising equity and achievement.* Thousand Oaks, CA: Corwin Press.

Fullan, M. (2001). *The new meaning of educational change.* 3rd ed. New York: Teachers College Press.

Funkhouser, J. E., & Gonzales, M. R. (1997). *Family involvement in children's education: Successful local approaches.* Office of Educational Research and Improvement, U.S. Department of Education,available at http://www.urbanschools.org/pdf/Linkages/Partners.pdf?v_document_name=About%20Families%20and%20Schools%20as%20Partners .

Gallucci, C., Boatright, E., Lysne, D., & Swinnerton, J. (2006). *A partnership for improving education: The Center for Educational Leadership and the Highline school district.* Seattle, WA: Center for Educational Leadership.

Gardner, D. P., & National Commission on Excellence in Education (1983). *A nation at risk: The imperative for educational reform. An open letter to the American people. A report to the nation and the Secretary of Education.* Retrieved from http://www.ebscohost.com.

Garland, L. (2003). *Navigating treacherous waters: A state takeover hand-book.* Lanham, MD: Scarecrow.

Garn, G., & Cobb, C. (2008). *School choice and accountability.* Education Policy Research Unit, Arizona State University.

Gering, S. (2005). *Making a reform the work of the district: Lessons from Kansas City, Kansas.* Annenberg Institute for School Reform, *Voices in Urban Education.*

Gill, B. P., Timpane, M., Ross, K. E., & Brewer, D. J. (2001). *Rhetoric versus reality: What we know and what we need to know about vouchers and charter schools.* Santa Monica, CA: RAND Corporation.

Gill, B., Zimmer, R., Christman, J., & Blanc, S. (2007). *State takeover, school restructuring, private management, and student achievement in Philadelphia.* Santa Monica, CA: RAND Corporation.

Gelberg, D. (2007). The business agenda for school reform: A parallel universe. *Teacher Education Quarterly* 45–58.

Gijlers, H. H., Saab, N. N., Van Joolingen, W. R., De Jong, T. T., & Van Hout-Wolters, B. M. (2009). Interaction between tool and talk: How instruction and tools support consensus building in collaborative inquiry-learning environments. *Journal of Computer Assisted Learning* 25(3), 252–267. Retrieved fromhttp://www.ebscohost.com.

Glazerman, S. (2004). *Teacher compensation reform: Promising strategies and feasible methods to rigorously study them.* Washington, DC: Mathematica Policy Research.

Glazerman, S., Silva, T., Addy, N., Avellars, S., Max, J., McKie, A., Natzke, B., Puma, M., Wolf, P., & Greszler, R. (2006). *Mathematica policy research for the U.S. Department of Education.*

Glines, D. (1995). *Year-round education: History, philosophy, future.* San Diego, CA: National Association for Year-Round Education.

Goldhaber, D. (2006). *Everyone's doing it, but what does teacher testing tell us about teacher effectiveness?* CRPE working paper no. 2006_1. Center on Reinventing Public Education, University of Washington.

Goldhaber, D., Gross, B., & Player, D. (2007). *Are public schools really losing their "best"?: Assessing the career transitions of teachers and their implication for the quality of the teacher workforce.* Working paper 12. National Center for Analysis of Longitudinal Data in Education Research, Urban Institute, Washington, D.C.

Goldring, E. B. (1990). Elementary school principals as boundary spanners: Their engagement with parents. *Journal of Educational Administration* 28(1), 53–62.

Gordon, M. F., & Louis, K. S. (2009). Linking parent and community involvement with student achievement: Comparing principal and teacher perceptions of stakeholder influence. *American Journal of Education.*

Gouwens, J. A. (2009). *Education in crisis: A reference handbook.* Santa Barbara: ABC-CLIO.

Greenwald, R., Hedges, L. V., & Laine, R. D. (1996). The effect of school resources on student achievement. *Review of Educational Research* 66(3), 361–396.

Groff, J., & Mouza, C. (2008). A framework for addressing challenges to classroom technology use. *AACE Journal* 16(1), 21–46.

Gropman, A. L. (2008). Waning education standards threaten U.S. competitiveness. *National Defense.* Retrieved from http://nationaldefensemagazine.com.

Grossman, M. (2005). Wanted: school board candidates. *American School Board Journal* 192(11), 47, 53.

Guarino, C. M., Santibanez, L., & Daley, G. A. (2006). Teacher recruitment and retention: A review of the recent empirical literature. *Review of Educational Research* 76(2), 173–208.

Guay, F., Chanal, J., Ratelle, C. F., Marsh, H. W., Larose, S., & Boivin, M. (2010). Intrinsic, identified, and controlled types of motivation for school subjects in young elementary school children. *British Journal of Educational Psychology* 80(4), 711–735. Retrieved fromhttp://www.ebscohost.com.

Gutman, L. M., & McLoyd, V. C. (2000). Parents' management of their children's education within the home, at school, and in the community: An examination of African-American families living in poverty. *Urban Review* 32(1), 1–24.

Haney, W. M. (2000). The myth of the Texas miracle in education. *Education Policy Analysis Archives* 8(41). Retrieved August 22, 2006, from http://epaa.asu.edu/epaa/v8n41/.

Hansen, P., & Mulholland, J.A. (2005). Caring and elementary teaching: The concerns of male beginning teachers. *Journal of Teacher Education* 56, 119–131.

Hanushek, E. A. (1986). The economics of schooling, production and efficiency in public schools. *Journal of Economic Literature* 24(3), 1141–1178.

Hanushek, E. A., & Raymond, M. E. (2004). Does school accountability lead to improved performance? *Journal of Policy Analysis and Management* 24, 297–327.

Hanushek, E., Kain, J., & Rivkin, S. (2004). Why public schools lose teachers. *Journal of Human Resources* 39(2), 326–354.

Hanushek, E., & Raymond, M. (2005). Does school accountability lead to improved student performance? *Journal of Policy Analysis and Management* 24(2), 297–328.

Harp, L. (1996). Year-round schooling rejected. *Teacher Magazine* (online). Retrieved May 29, 2005, from http://www.edweek.org/tm/articles/1996/02/01/05year.h07.html.

Haser, S. G, & Nasser, I. (2003). Teacher job satisfaction in a year-round school. *Educational Leadership* 60(8), 65–67.

Haynes, V. D. (December 13, 2007). Special education to boost services; D.C. officials seek to comply with 2006 court order. *Washington Post*, p. B1.

Heinrich, C. J., Meyer, R. H., & Whitten, G. (March 2008). *Supplemental educational services under No Child Left Behind: Who signs up, and what do they gain?* Paper presented at the annual meeting of the American Educational Research Association, New York.

Heistad, D. (2006). *Analysis of 2005 supplemental educational services in Minneapolis Public Schools: An application of matched sample statistical design.* Minneapolis, MN: Minneapolis Public Schools, Research, Evaluation and Assessment Department.

Henkin, A. B. (1993). Social skills of superintendents: A leadership requisite in restructured schools. *Educational Research Quarterly* 16(4), 15–30.

Herman, J. (1991). Novel approaches to relieve overcrowding: The effects of concept 6 year-round schools. *Urban Education* 26(2), 195–213.

Hess, F. M. (1999). *Spinning wheels: The politics of urban school reform.* Washington, DC: Brookings Institution Press.

Hess, G. A. (2003). Reconstitution—three years later: Monitoring the effect of sanctions on Chicago high schools. *Education and Urban Society* 35, 300–327.

Hewitt, R. (2007). Human capital as the summum bonum of public education: Past and present. *Educational Forum* 71(2), 128–140.

Hewitt, T. W. (2008). Speculations on a nation at risk: Illusions and realities. *Phi Delta Kappan* 575–579.

Heyns, B. (1978). *Summer learning and the effects of schooling.* Orlando, FL: Academic Press.

Hill, P. (1995). *Reinventing public education.* Santa Monica, CA: Institute on Education and Training, RAND Corporation.

Hoff, D. J. (2007). Provision on tutoring raises renewal issues. *Education Week.*

Hofman, R. H., Dijkstra, N. J., & Hofman, W. H. A. (2009). School self-evaluation and student achievement. *School Effectiveness & School Improvement* 20(1), 47–68.

Holmes Partnership (2007). *Holmes Partnership trilogy: Tomorrow's teacher, tomorrow's schools, tomorrow's schools of education.* New York : Peter Lang Publishing.

Honig, M. I. (2003). Building policy from practice: Central office administrators' roles and capacity in collaborative education policy implementation. *Educational Administration Quarterly* 39(3), 292–338.

Honig, M. I. (2006). Street-level bureaucracy revisited: Frontline district central office administrators as boundary spanners in education policy implementation. *Educational Evaluation and Policy Analysis* 28(4), 357–383.

Honig, M. I., Copland, M. A., Rainey, L., Lorton, J. A., & Newton, M. (2010). *Central office transformation for district-wide teaching and learning development.* Center for the Study of Teaching and Policy, University of Washington.

House, N. G. (2000). Educating all of the city's children. In P. Senge, N. Cambron-McCabe, T. Lucas, B. Smith, J. Dutton, & A. Kleiner, *Schools that learn: A fifth discipline fieldbook for educators, parents, and everyone who cares about education* (303–309). New York: Doubleday.

Hoy, W. K. (2003). *An analysis of enabling and mindful school structures: Some theoretical, research, and practical considerations.* Working paper. Ohio State University.

Hoy, W. K., Blazovsky, R., & Newland, W. (1983). Bureaucracy and alienation: A comparative analysis. *Journal of Educational Administration* 21(2) 109–120.

Hoy, W. K., Sabo, D., & Barnes, K. (1996). Organizational health and faculty trust: A view from the middle level. *Research in Middle Level Quarterly* (Spring), 21–39.

Hoy, W. K., & Sweetland, S. (2000). School bureaucracies that work: Enabling, notcoercive. *Journal of School Leadership* 10, 525–541.

Hubbard, L., Mehan, H., and Stein, M. (2006). Reform as learning: School reform, organizational culture, and community politics in San Diego. New York: Taylor & Francis Group.

Huitt, W. (1987). Maslow's hierarchy of needs. In J. A. Simons, D. B. Irwin & B.A. Drinnien (eds.), *Psychology: The search for understanding.* New York: West Publishing.

Hunter, D. J. (1979). Coping with uncertainty: Decisions and resources within health authorities. *Sociology of Health and Illness* 1(1), 40–68.

Iatarola, P., & Fruchter, N. (2004). District Effectiveness: A Study of Investment Strategies in New York City Public Schools and Districts. *Educational Policy* 18(3), 491–512.

Ingersoll, R. (2001). Teacher turnover and teacher shortages: An organizational analysis. *American Educational Research Journal* 38(3), 499–534.

Inoue, Y. (2009). *Online education for lifelong learning.* London: Information Science Publishing.

Jackson, S. A., & Lunenburg, F. C. (2010). School performance indicators, accountability ratings, and student achievement. *American Secondary Education* 39(1), 27–44. Retrieved fromhttp://www.ebscohost.com.

Jackson, S., & Schuler, R. S. (1985). A meta-analysis and conceptual critique of research on role ambiguity and role conflict in work settings. *Organizational Behavior and Human Decision Processes* 36, 17–78.

Jeffery, J. V., & Polleck, J. N. (2010). Reciprocity through co-instructed site-based courses: perceived benefit and challenge overlap in an urban school-university partnership. *Teacher Education Quarterly* 37(3), 81–99. Retrieved from http://www.ebscohost.com .

Jimerson, L. (2005). Placism in NCLB: How rural children are left behind. *Journal of Equity and Excellence in Education* 38, 211–219.

Johnson, S. M., Berg, J. H., & Donaldson, M. L. (2005). *Who stays in teaching and why: A review of the literature on teacher retention.* Cambridge, MA: Harvard Graduate School of Education. Retrieved May 17, 2009, from http://assets.aarp.org/www.aarp.org_/articles/NRTA/Harvard_report.pdf.

Johnson, S. P. (2008). *The status of male teachers in public education today.* CEEP Education Policy Brief. Center for Evaluation and Education Policy, Bloomington, Indiana.

Katz, A. (April 10, 2003a). State takeover appears certain. *Oakland Tribune.* Retrieved August 1, 2008, from http://findarticles.com .

Katz, A. (December 26, 2003b). 13 schools in Oakland face the ax. *Oakland Tribune.* Retrieved August 1, 2008, from http://findarticles.com/p/articles/mi_qn4176/is_20031226/ai_n14560549.

Katz, M. (1971). *Class, bureaucracy and schools: The American illusion of educational change.* New York: Praeger.

Keedy, J., & Allen, J. (1998). Examining district norms from a rural school's site-based improvement perspective: Complementary or constructive? *Journal of School Leadership* 8(2), 187–210.

Kennedy, M. M. (1982). Evidence and decision. In M. M. Kennedy (ed.), *Working knowledge and other essays* (59–103). Cambridge, MA: Huron Institute.

Kiley, T., & Racusen, R. (2007). *America's high school drop out crisis needs new strategies, witness tell education and labor committee.* Proceedings of the press releases (p. 1). Retrieved from http://www.house.gov/apps/list/speech/edlabor_dem/rel042307.html.

Kim, J., & Sunderman, G. L. (2004). *Does NCLB provide good choices for students in low performing schools?* Cambridge, MA: Civil Rights Project at Harvard University.

Kirst, M. W. (1988). Recent state education reform in the United States: Looking backward and forward. *Educational Administration Quarterly* 24(3), 319–328.

Klein, C. L. (2006). *Virtual charter schools and home-schooling.* Youngstown, NY: Cambria Press.

Kleiner, M. M. (2000). Occupational licensing. *Journal of Economic Perspectives* 14(4), 189–202.

Knapp, M., Copland, M., Ford, B., Markholt, A., McLaughlin, M., & Talbert, J. (2003). *Leading for learning sourcebook: Concepts and examples.* Center for the Study of Teaching and Policy, University of Washington.

Kneese, C. (2000). Teaching in year round schools. *ERIC Clearinghouse on Teaching and Teacher Education* (online). Retrieved May 21, 2005, from http://www.kidsource.com/education/teach.year.round.html.

Kocek, J. (1996). *The effect of year round school on teacher attendance.* ERIC Document Reproduction Service, no. ED 398 181.

Koretz, D., Mitchell, K., Barron, S., & Keith, S. (1996). *Perceived effects of the Maryland School Performance Assessment Program.* Final report. Retrieved from http://research.cse.ucla.edu/Reports/TECH409.PDF.

Kowalski, T. J., Petersen, G. J., & Fusarelli, L. D. (2007). *Effective communication for school administrators: An imperative in an information age.* Lanham, MD: Rowman & Littlefield.

Kozol , J. (1991). *Savage inequalities.* New York: Crown Publishers.

Kridel, C. (2010). *Encyclopedia of curriculum studies.* Vol.1. Thousand Oaks, CA: Sage Publications.

Ladd, H. (2009). *Teachers' perceptions of their working conditions: How predictive of policy-relevant outcomes.* Working paper 33. National Center for Analysis of Longitudinal Data in Education Research, Washington, D.C.

Ladd, H. F. (1996). *Holding schools accountable.* Washington, DC: Brookings Institution.

Ladson-Billings, G. (2009). Education for everyday people: Obstacles and opportunities facing the Obama administration. *Harvard Educational Review* 79(2), 345–361.

Laitsch, D. (2006). *Assessment, high stakes, and alternative visions: Appropriate use of the right tools to leverage improvement.* Education Policy Research Unit.

Latham, G., & Pinder, C. (2005). Work motivation theory and research at the dawn of the twenty-first century. *Annual Review of Psychology* 56, 485–516.

Lawler, E. (1973). *Motivation in work organizations.* San Francisco: Jossey-Bass.

Lee, J. (2006*). Tracking achievement gaps and assessing the impact of NCLB on the gaps: An in-depth look into national and state reading and math outcome trends.* Cambridge, MA: Civil Rights Project at Harvard University.

Lee, J. (2007). *The testing gap: Scientific trials of test-driven school accountability systems for excellence and equity.* Charlotte, NC: Information Age.

Lee, J. (2008). Is test-driven external accountability effective? Synthesizing the evidence from cross-state causal-comparative and correlational studies. *Review of Educational Research* 78, 608–644.

Lee, J., & Wong, K. K. (2004). The impact of accountability on racial and socioeconomic equity: Considering both school resources and achievement outcomes. *American Educational Research Journal* 41, 797–832.

Lee, R. D., Jr., Johnson, R., & Joyce, P. (2004). *Public budgeting systems.* 7th ed. Sudbury, MA: Jones & Bartlett.

Lee, V., & Smith, J. B. (1996). Collective responsibility for learning and its effects on gains and achievement and engagement for early secondary students. *American Journal of Education* 104(2), 103–147.

Leithwood, K., Seashore Louis, K., Anderson, S., & Wahlstrom, K. (2004). *How leadership influences student learning.* Center for Applied Research and Educational Improvement, University of Minnesota and Ontario Institute for Studies in Education, University of Toronto.

LEP. (2010). Limited English Proficiency, a federal interagency website, LEP guidance and language access plans, available at: http://www.lep.gov/ .

Levin, H., & Kelly, C. (1994). Can education do it alone? *Economics of Education Review* 13(2), 97–108.

Levine, J. A., Murphy, D. T., & Wilson, S. D. (1998). *Getting men involved: Strategies for early childhood programs.* New York: Families and Work Institute.

Lewis, A. C. (1995). *Believing in ourselves: Progress and struggles in urban middle school reform.* New York: Edna McConnell Clark Foundation.

Loeb, S., Darling-Hammond, L., & Luczak, J. (2005). How teaching conditions predict teacher turnover in California Schools. *Peabody Journal of Education* 80(3), 44–70.

Lortie, D. C. (1977). *Schoolteacher: A sociological study.* Chicago: University of Chicago Press.

Lortie, D. C. (2002). *Schoolteacher.* Chicago: University of Chicago Press.

Lugg, C. A., & Boyd, W. L. (1993). Leadership for collaboration: Reducing risk and fostering resilience. *Phi Delta Kappan* 75(3), 253–258.

Madaus, G., Russell, M., & Higgins, J. (2009). *The paradoxes of high-stakes testing: How they affect students, their parents, teachers, principals, schools, and society.* Charlotte, NC: Information Age.

Malen, B., Croninger, R., Muncey, D., & Redmond-Jones, D. (2002). Reconstituting schools: "Testing" the "theory of action." *Educational Evaluation and Policy Analysis* 24, 113–132.

Malen, B., & Ogawa, R. T. (1988). Professional-patron influence on site-based governance councils: A confounding case study. *Educational Evaluation and Policy Analysis* 10(4), 251–270.

Malen, B., Ogawa, R., & Kranz, K. (1990). What do we know about school-based management? A case study of the literature a call for research. In W. Clune & J. Witte (eds.), *Choice and control in American education, Volume 2: Decentralization and school restructuring.* Philadelphia: Falmer Press.

Marenda, D. W. (1989). Partners in education: An old tradition renamed. *Educational Leadership* 47(2), 4–7.

Margolis, J., & Nagel, L. (2006). Education reform and the role of administrators in mediating teacher stress. *Teacher Education Quarterly* 33(4), 143–159. Retrieved from http://www.ebscohost.com.

Marks, D. (2009). Literacy, instruction, and technology: Meeting millennials on their own turf. *AACE Journal* 17(4), 363–377. Retrieved from http://www.ebscohost.com.

Marvel, J., Lyter, D. M., Peltola, P., Strizek, G. A., & Morton, B. A. (2006). *Teacher attrition and mobility: Results from the 2004–05 teacher follow-up survey.* (NCES 2007–307). Washington, DC: National Center for Education Statistics, U.S. Department of Education.

Marzano, R., & Kendall, J. (2008). *Designing and assessing educational objectives: Applying the new taxonomy.* Thousand Oaks, CA: Corwin Press.

Mathis, W. J. (2010). *The "Common Core" Standards Initiative: An effective reform tool?* Boulder, CO: Education and the Public Interest Center & Education Policy Research Unit.

McClure, L., Yonezawa, S., & Jones, M. (2010). Can school structures improve teacher-student relationships? The relationship between advisory programs, personalization and students' academic achievement. *Education Policy Analysis Archives* 18(17), 1–17.

McGhan, B. (1978). *Teachers' use of authority and its relationship to socioeconomic status, race, teacher characteristics, and educational outcomes.* Retrieved from http://www.ebscohost.com.

McGrath, D. J., & Kuriloff, P. J. (1999). "They're going to tear the doors off this place": Upper-middle-class parent school involvement and the educational opportunities of other people's children. *Educational Policy* 13(5).

McLaughlin, M., & Talbert, J. (2003). *Reforming districts: How districts support school reform.* Seattle: Center for the Study of Teaching and Policy, University of Washington.

McLaughlin, M. J., & Rhim, L. (2007). Accountability frameworks and children with disabilities: A test of assumptions about improving public education for all students. *International Journal of Disability, Development & Education* 54(1), 25–49. doi:10.1080/10349120601149698.

McNeil, L. M. (2005). Faking equality: High-stakes testing and the education of Latino youth. In A. Valenzuela (ed.), *Leaving children behind: How "Texas style" accountability fails Latino youth* (57–111). New York: State University of New York Press.

Meier, D., Kohn, A., Darling-Hammon, L., Sizer, T. R., & Wood, G. (2004). *Many children left behind.* Boston: Beacon Press.

Metz, M. H. (1990). Hidden assumptions preventing real reform: Some missing elements in the educational reform movement. In S. Bacharach (ed.), *Education reform: Making sense of it all* (141–154). Boston: Allyn & Bacon.

Miles, K. H. (2004). *Freeing school resources for learning: The "missing piece" in making accountability meaningful.* New American Schools District Issues Brief.

Miles, K. H., & Darling-Hammond, L. (1998). Rethinking the allocation of teaching resources: Some lessons from high-performing schools. *Educational Evaluation and Policy Analysis* 20, 9–29.

Miller, L., Roza, M., and Schwartz, C. (2005). *A cost allocation model for shared district resources: A means for comparing spending across schools. Developments in school finance 2003-2004.* Washington, DC: National Center for Education Statistics, U.S. Department of Education.

Mintrom, M. (2000). *Leveraging local innovations: The case of Michigan's charter schools.* East Lansing, MI: Michigan State University.

Mintrop, H., & Sunderman, G. L. (2009). Predictable failure of federal sanctions-driven accountability for school improvement and why we may retain it anyway. *Educational Researcher* 38(5), 353–364.

Miron, G., & Applegate, B. (2007). *Teacher attrition in charter schools.* Western Michigan University: Miron.

Moerschell, L. (2009). Resistance to technological change in academia. *Current Issues in Education* 11(6). Retrieved from http://www.ebscohost.com.

Monk, D., Pijanowski, J., & Hussein, S. (1997). How and where the education dollar is spent. *The Future of Children: Financing Schools* 7(3). Washington, DC: Princeton-Brookings.

Nakib, Y. (1995). Beyond district-level expenditures: Schooling resource allocation and use in Florida. In L. Picus & J. L. Wattenberger (eds.), *Where does the money go? Resource allocation in elementary and secondary schools* (85–105). Thousand Oaks, CA: Corwin Press.

National Center for Education Statistics. (2002). *Digest of education statistics, 2002.* Institute of Education Sciences, U.S. Department of Education.

National Center for Education Statistics. (2004). *The condition of education 2004, indicator 31: remedial course-taking.* Institute of Education Sciences, U.S. Department of Education.

National Center for Education Statistics. (2008). *State education reforms, Table 4.1: Number and types of open enrollment policies, by state, 2005.* Institute of Education Sciences, U.S. Department of Education. Retrieved from http://nces.ed.gov/programs/statereform/sssco_tab1.asp.

National Center for Education Statistics. (2009a). *The nation's report card: Mathematics 2009.* (NCES 2010–451). Institute of Education Sciences, U.S. Department of Education. Retrieved from http://nces.ed.gov/nationsreportcard/pdf/main2009/2010451.pdf.

National Center for Education Statistics. (2009b).*The nation's report card: Reading 2009.* (NCES 2010–458). Institute of Education Sciences, U.S. Department of Education.Retrieved from http://nces.ed.gov/nationsreportcard/pdf/main2009/2010458.pdf.

National Center for Education Statistics. (2010). *What is the average income for high school and college graduates?* Institute of Education Sciences, U.S. Department of Education. Retrieved from http://nces.ed.gov/fastfacts/display.asp?id=77.

National Commission on Excellence in Education. (1983). *A nation at risk: The imperative for educational reform.* ERIC Document Reproduction Service.

National Commission on Teaching and America's Future. (1996). *What matters most: Teaching for America's Future.* Retrieved from http://www.nctaf.org/documents/WhatMattersMost.pdf.

National Forum on Education Statistics, Core Finance Data Task Force. (2003). *Financial accounting for local and state school systems: 2003 Edition.* (NCES 2004–318). National Center for Education Statistics, U.S. Department of Education.

National Research Council (1999). Making money matter: Financing America's schools. In H. Ladd & J. Hansen (eds.), *Committee on Education Finance, Commission on Behavioral and Social Sciences and Education.* Washington, D.C.: National Academy Press.

National Task Force on Public Education (NTFPE). (2005). *Education Task Force: Report.* Retrieved from http://www.americanprogress.org/projects/education/report.html.

Nelson, B.G. (2002). *The importance of men teachers and reasons why there are so few.* Minneapolis, MN: Men Teach and Men in Child Care and Elementary Education Project.

New York State Education Department, Office of New York City School Improvement and Community Services. (2003). *2002–03 Registration Review Initiative: A summary of the Registration Review report findings.* New York: New York State Education Department.

North Central Regional Educational Laboratory. (n.d.). *Summary of goals 2000: Educate America act.* Retrieved from http://www.ncrel.org/sdrs/areas/issues/envrnmnt/stw/sw0goals.htm.

Norwood, P. M. (1997). Contextualizing parent education programs in urban schools: The impact on minority parents and students. *Urban Education* 32(3).

Nygaard, D. (1974). *Evaluations of year-round school programs.* Washington, DC: Educational Research Service. ERIC Document Reproduction Service, no. ED 087 092.

Odden, A. R. (2009). *Ten strategies for doubling student performance.* Thousand Oaks, CA: Corwin Press.

Odden, A., Archibald, S., Fermanich, M., & Gross, B. (2003). Defining school-level expenditure structures that reflect educational strategies. *Journal of Education Finance* 28(3), 323–356.

Opheim, C., Mohajer, K. H., & Read, R. W. (2001). Evaluating year round schools in Texas. *Education* 116(1), 115–120.

Oreopoulos, P. (December 2003). *Do dropouts drop out too soon? International evidence from changes in school-leaving laws.* NBER working paper no. W10155. Available at SSRN:http://ssrn.com/abstract=478664.

Ornstein, A. C., & Levine, D. U. (2008). *Foundations of education.* 10th ed. Boston: Houghton Mifflin.

Osburn, M. Z., Stegman, C., Suitt, L. D., & Ritter, G. (2004). Parents' perceptions of standardized testing: Its relationship and effect on student achievement. *Journal of Educational Research & Policy Studies* 4(1), 75–95. Retrieved from http://www.ebscohost.com.

US Department of Education. (2004). *No child left behind: Non-regulatory guidance,* available at www2.ed.gov/programs/titleiparta/parentinvguid.doc.

Partners in Education. (2000). *Partnerships 2000: A decade of growth and change.* Alexandria, VA: National Association of Partners in Education.

Payne, R. (2005). *A framework for understanding poverty.* Highlands, TX: Aha! Process.

Pelavin, S. 1979. *A study of year-round schools.* Vol. 1, *Final report.* Menlo Park, CA: Stanford Research Institute. ERIC Document Reproduction Service, no. ED 170 926.

Peterson, K. (January 26, 2006). *State of education: Who makes the grade?* Stateline.org. Retrieved from http://www.stateline.org/live/details/story.

Potter, A., Ross, S. M., Paek, J., McKay, D., Ashton, J., & Sanders, W. L. (2007). *Supplemental educational services in the state of Tennessee: 2005–06 (2004–2005 student achievement results).* Memphis, TN: Center for Research in Education Policy, University of Memphis.

Public Education Network. (2005). *Open to the public: Speaking out on "No Child Left Behind."* Retrieved from http://www.publiceducation.org/portals/nclb/hearings/national/Open_to_the_Public.asp.

Purcell-Gates, V., Duke, N. K., & Martineau, J. A. (2007). Learning to read and write genre-specific text: Roles of authentic experience and explicit teaching. *Reading Research Quarterly* 42(1), 8–45. Retrieved from http://www.ebscohost.com.

Puriefoy, W. (2005). The education of democratic citizens: Citizen mobilization and public education. In S. Furhman & M. Lazerson (eds.), *Public Schools: The institutions of American democracy* (235–51).

Quellmalz, E. S. et al. (2008). Exploring the role of technology-based simulations in science assessment: The Calipers Project. In J. Coffey, R. Douglas, & C. Stearns (eds.), *Assessing science learning: Perspectives from research and practice*. Arlington, VA: National Science Teachers Association Press.

Raymond, M. E., & Hanushek, E. A. (2003). High-stakes research: Accountability works after all. *Education Next* 3(3), 48–55.

Rickles, J. H., Barnhart, M. K., & Gualpa, A. S. (2008). *Supplemental educational services participation and impact on student achievement: The case of one urban district over five years*. Paper presented at the annual meeting of the American Educational Research Association, New York.

Ridgway, J., & McCusker, S. (2003). Using computers to assess new educational goals. *Assessment in Education* 10(3).

Rigden, D. W. (1991). *Business-school partnerships: A path to effective restructuring*. 2nd ed. New York: Council for Aid to Education.

Rioux, J. W., & Berla, N. (1993). *Innovations in parent and family involvement*. Princeton Junction, NJ: Eye on Education.

Rist, M. (1990). Business takes action in schools. *Education Digest* 56(11), 47–51.

Rivkin, S., Hanushek, E. A., (2005). Teachers, schools and academic achievement. *Econometrica* 73(2), 417–458.

Roberts, N. (1997). Public deliberation: An alternative approach to crafting policy and setting direction. *Public Administration Review* 57(2), 124–132.

Rothman, R. (2005). How can reforms last? *Voices in Urban Education*. Retrieved from http://www.annenberginstitute.org/VUE/wp-content/pdf/VUE9.pdf.

Rothstein, R. (2004). *Class and schools: Using social, economic, and educational reform to close the black-white achievement gap*. Washington, DC: Economic Policy Institute.

Rotherham, A. J., & Mead, S. (2004). *Back to the future: The history and politics of state teacher licensure and certification. A qualified teacher in every classroom? Appraising old answers and new ideas*. Cambridge, MA: Harvard Education Press.

Roza, M., Guin, K., & Davis, T. (2008). *What is the sum of the parts?* A report from the School Finance Redesign Project. Center on Reinventing Public Education, University of Washington.

Rubin, L. (1984). Formulating education policy in the aftermath of the reports. *Educational Leadership* 42(2), 7–10.

Sadker, D. M., Sadker, M., & Zittleman, K. (2008). *Teachers, schools and society*. New York: McGraw-Hill.

Saltman, K. J. (2005). *The Edison schools*. New York: Routledge.

Sanders, W. L., & Rivers, J. C. (November 1996). *Cumulative and residual effects of teachers on future student academic achievement*. Knoxville, TN: Value-Added Research and Assessment Center, University of Tennessee.

Sarason, S. (1996). *Revisiting the culture of school and the problem of change*. New York: Teachers College Press.

Sargent, P. (2001). *Real men or real teachers: Contradictions in the lives of men elementary school teachers*. Harriman, TN: Men's Studies Press.

Scafidi, B., Sjoquist, D. L., & Stinebrickner, T. R. (2005). *Race, poverty, and teacher mobility* Research paper series no. 06-51. Andrew Young School of Policy Studies, Georgia State University.

Schlechty, P. C. (1997). *Inventing better schools*. San Francisco, CA: Jossey-Bass.

Sennett, R. (2006). *Culture of new capitalism*. New Haven, CT: Yale University Press.

Sexual Harassment Support. (2009). *Sexual harassment in education*. Retrieved from http://www.sexualharassmentsupport.org/SHEd.html.

Shields, C. (1996). *Year-round education: Is it worth the hassle?* Paper presented at the University of British Columbia Robson Square Lecture Series, Vancouver, British Columbia.

Shor, R., & Friedman, A. (2009). Integration of nutrition-related components by early childhood education professionals into their individual work with children at risk. *Early Child Development and Care* 179(4), 477–486. Retrieved from http://www.ebscohost.com.

Silva, E. (2007). On the clock: Rethinking the way schools use time. *Education Sector Reports.* Retrieved from http://www.educationsector.org/publications/clock-rethinking-way-schools-use-time.

Sipple, J. W., Matheney, T. M., & Miskel, C. G. (1997). The creation and development of an interest group: Life at the intersection of big business and education reform. *Educational Administration Quarterly* 33, 440–473.

Skocpol, T. (1993). *Diminished democracy: From membership to management in American civic life.* Norman, OK: University of Oklahoma Press.

Smith, K. B., & Meier, K. J. (1994). Politics, bureaucrats, and schools. *Public Administration Review* 54(4), 551–558.

Smith, S., & Piele, P. K., eds. (1996). *Handbook on Educational Research.* 3rd ed. Eugene, OR: ERIC Press.

Smylie, M., & Wenzel, S. (2003). *The Chicago Annenberg Challenge: Successes, failures, and lessons for the future.* Chicago: Consortium on Chicago School Research.

Spillane, J., Reiser, B. J., & Reimer, T. (2002). Policy implementation and cognition: Reframing and refocusing implementation research. *Review of Educational Research* 72(3), 387–431.

Spring, J. (2009). *American education.* 14th ed. New York: McGraw-Hill.

Sullivan, A. (January 1, 2009). Patterns and predictors of English language learner representation in special education. *ProQuest.* Retrieved from http://www.ebscohost.com.

Thornton, M., & Bricheno, P. (2000). Primary school teachers' careers in England and Wales: The relationship between gender, role, position and promotion aspirations. *Pedagogy, Culture and Society* 8(2), 187–206.

Toch, T. (2006). *Margins of error: The education testing industry in the No Child Left Behind era.* Washington, DC: Education Sector.

Togneri, W., & Anderson, S. E. (2003). *Beyond islands of excellence: What districts can do to improve instruction and achievement in all schools.* Washington, DC: Learning First Alliance and the Association for Supervision and Curriculum Development.

Travers, E. (2003). *Characteristics of schools under diverse providers, 2002–2003.* Philadelphia: Research for Action.

Trinkl, F. H. (1973). Hierarchical resource allocation decisions. *Policy Sciences* 4(2), 211–221.

Tschannen-Moran, M. (2001). Collaboration and the need for trust. *Journal of Educational Administration* 39(4), 308–331.

Tyack, D. (1974). *The one best system: A history of American urban education.* Cambridge, MA: Harvard University Press.

Tyack, D., & Cuban, L. (1995). *Tinkering toward utopia: A century of public school reform.* Cambridge, MA: Harvard University Press.

UNESCO Institute for Statistics, Initials. (2007). Comparing education across the world. *Global Education Digest 2007.* Retrieved from http://www.uis.unesco.org/template/pdf/ged/2007/EN_web2.pdf

U.S. Department of Education. (1983). *A nation at risk: The imperative for educational reform.* Washington, DC: U.S. Department of Education, National Commission on Excellence in Education.

U.S. Department of Education. (2010). *A blueprint for reform: The reauthorization of the elementary and secondary education act.* Washington, DC: U.S. Department of Education.

Useem, E. (2005). *Learning from Philadelphia's school reform: What do the research findings show so far?* Philadelphia: Research for Action.

Viadero (September 30, 2003). Management guru says "student load" key to achievement. *Education Week.*

Villenas, S., & Dehyle, S. (1999). *Race is . . . race isn't.* Boulder, CO: Westview Press.

Walberg, H. J. (1984). Families as partners in educational productivity. *Phi Delta Kappan* 65, 397–400.

Warren, M. R. (2005). Communities and schools: A new view of urban education reform. *Harvard Educational Review* 75(2), 133–173.

Weber, K., ed. (2010). *Waiting for Superman: How we can save America's failing public schools.* New York: Public Affairs.

White, K. (2000). Mark your calendar. *Teacher Magazine* 11(4), 15–16.

Wildavsky, A., & Caiden, N. (2004). *The new politics of the budgetary process.* 5th ed. New York: Peterson Education.

Wohlstetter, P. (1995). Getting school-based management right: What works and what doesn't. *Phi Delta Kappan* 77(1), 22–26.

Wright, H. K., & Alenuma, S. (2007). Race, urban schools, and educational reform: The context, utility, pros, and cons of the magnet example. In J. L. Kincheloe & K. Hayes (eds.), *Teaching city kids: Understanding and appreciating them.* New York. Peter Lang Publishing.

Youngs, P. (2001). District and state policy influences on professional development and school capacity. *Educational Policy* 15(2), 278–301.

Zimmer, R., Gill, B., Razquin, P., Booker, K., & Lockwood, J. R. (2007*). State and local implementation of the No Child Left Behind Act.* Vol. 1, *Title I school choice, supplemental educational services, and student achievement.* Washington, DC: RAND Corporation.

Index

About the Author

Dr. Lynch is an assistant professor of education at Widener University. He spent seven years as a K–12 teacher, which gave him an intimate view of the impediments that hinder genuine education reform. He has focused the second stage of his career on researching topics related to educational policy, school leadership, and education reform, particularly in the urban learning environment. Dr. Lynch's scholarship is intended to make a redoubtable, theoretically, and empirically based argument that school reform and the closing of the well-chronicled achievement gap are possible. His research and commentaries have been featured in publications throughout the United States and have centered on issues ranging from school reform to politics. Throughout his career, he has been interested in developing collaborative enterprises that move the field of education forward. Dr. Lynch is also the author of *A Guide to Effective School Leadership Theories*, the forthcoming *Before Obama: A Reappraisal of Black Reconstruction Era Politicians,* and *The Call to Teach: An Introduction to Teaching and Learning.*

CPSIA information can be obtained at www.ICGtesting.com
Printed in the USA
BVOW070620281011

274628BV00001B/1/P